The Philosophy of Language

The Philosophy of Language

Historical Foundations and Contemporary Issues

by

ALBERT BORGMANN

MARTINUS NIJHOFF / THE HAGUE / 1974

ISBN 90 247 1589 X

PRINTED IN THE NETHERLANDS

To my parents

TABLE OF CONTENTS

INTRODUCTION

This book deals with the philosophy of language and with what is at issue in the philosophy of language. Due to its intensity and diversity, the philosophy of language has attained the position of first philosophy in this century. To show this is the task of Part Two. But the task can be accomplished only if it is first made clear how language came to be a problem in and for philosophy and how this development has influenced and has failed to influence our understanding of language. This is done in Part One.

What is at issue in the philosophy of language today is the question regarding the source of meaning. More precisely the question is whether we have access to such a source. Again Part One presents the necessary foil for Part Two in showing how meaning was thought to originate in Western history and how the rise of the philosophy of language and the eclipse of the origin of meaning occurred jointly. Today the question of meaning has come to a peculiarly elaborate and fruitful issue in the philosophy of language, and the fate of the philosophy of language is bound up with the future possibilities of meaning.

This is a brief study on a large topic. The systematic and historical scope may seem needlessly and detrimentally broad. But what is being argued here has its place within a long and wide compass, and there is a great deal of preparatory research that such a study can draw upon. The line of development can be drawn succinctly within the total area if scattered paradigms are singled out. This line must be exhibited and analyzed. Hence exposition and criticism alternate. The dual approach is also intended to make the topic accessible to a variety of readers since the topic is in the end a fundamental if not simple one.

PART ONE

HISTORICAL FOUNDATIONS OF THE PHILOSOPHY OF LANGUAGE

CHAPTER ONE

THE ORIGIN OF THE PHILOSOPHY
OF LANGUAGE

1. The accessibility of the original reflections on language. Heraclitus

The philosophy of language has its origin in the Presocratic era. We take Heraclitus as a representative of this period since his thought is most strongly directed towards the problem of language and world.

The term "Presocratic" is the expression of an embarrassment; we characterize these early thinkers by reference to what they are not: philosophers in the sense of Socrates, Plato, and Aristotle. We cannot help viewing the Presocratics through Greek metaphysics as it has been established by these three men. There is then no easy and obvious access to Presocratic philosophy.

Two other circumstances make access even more difficult. First, the teachings of the Presocratics are extant in fragments only. Second, the fragments are in a dead and primordial language. Ancient Greek is dead because although many scholars command it, no one today lives in and with Ancient Greek. It is primordial in that it first gave rise to philosophical discourse which deprives us of explanatory recourse to earlier language of a similar type.

This state of affairs is usually taken as an unfortunate accident of literary tradition. Consequently one sets out to remedy the situation to the extent that this is possible through such disciplines as philology, textual criticism, and doxography. This has resulted in the collection and examination of all fragments of the Presocratics, and the result is the indispensable basis of any treatment of Presocratic philosophy.

This remedial attitude commonly springs from a concern for completeness and consistency, and its undisputed basis is metaphysics in its derivative mode of common sense.[1] Presocratic philosophy then comes into view as an early and crude extension of metaphysics into

---

[1] The book by G. S. Kirk and J. E. Raven, *The Presocratic Philosophers* (Cambridge, 1966), is a paradigm of this approach.

the past. But what is to decide whether the perspective of what comes later at all permits an adequate view of what is earlier? The parallel of Greek art is relevant here: is early Greek sculpture adequately understood when it is measured against the grace and skill of the classical period? [2]

There is then an element of danger and blindness in bringing the whole weight of detailed and sophisticated erudition to bear on Presocratic philosophy. [3] Quite possibly Presocratic thought or at least Heraclitean thought is difficult in being simple, and its simplicity may not yield to sophistication alone. Indeed, Heraclitus warns:

> fr. 40 Learning of many things does not teach one to have insight. [4]

And positively speaking, he says:

> fr. 41 Wisdom is but *one* thing: to understand the thought which steers all things through all things.

Heraclitus stresses that this one thing is always in danger of being misunderstood, a danger that is not met through mere acquaintance with this one thing:

> fr. 1 Though the λόγος *is* as I have said, men always fail to comprehend it, both before they have heard it and once they have heard it. For although all things come to pass according to this λόγος, men are like people of no experience, even when they experience such words and works as I set forth when I distinguish each thing according to its nature and declare what it is; as for the rest of mankind, they are unaware of what they are doing after they awake, just as they forget what they did while asleep.

[2] Cf. Walter Kaufmann, "Before Socrates" in the anthology edited by Kaufmann: *Philosophic Classics*, 2nd ed. (Englewood Cliffs, 1968), I, 1–5, especially p. 3.

[3] On this point, Martin Heidegger and Karl Popper are in agreement. Cf. Heidegger's *Vorträge und Aufsätze*, 2nd ed. (Pfullingen, 1959), pp. 207–282 and Popper's "Back to the Presocratics" with an appendix "Historical Conjectures and Heraclitus on Change" in *Conjectures and Refutations* (New York, 1962), pp. 136–165. Cf. also Felix M. Cleve, "Understanding the Pre-Socratics: Philological or Philosophical Reconstruction?" *International Philosophical Quarterly*, III (1963), 445–464 and Charles E. Kahn, "A New Look at Heraclitus," *American Philosophical Quarterly*, I (1964), 189–203.

[4] The numbering of the fragments is that of *Die Fragmente der Vorsokratiker*, ed. Hermann Diels and Walther Kranz, 11th ed., 3 vols (Zürich, 1964). The translations are mine except where indicated. I have consulted the following English translations: Kathleen Freeman, *Ancilla to the Pre-Socratic Philosophers* (Oxford, 1948); G. S. Kirk and J. E. Raven, *The Presocratic Philosophers* (Cambridge, 1966); John Mansley Robinson, *An Introduction to Early Greek Philosophy* (Boston, 1968); Philip Wheelwright, *Heraclitus* (New York, 1964).

This λόγος is like nature in that nature (φύσις) is the basic and pervasive mode in which things "come forth" (φύουνσιν), a coming forth, however, that is hidden from ordinary inspection. Hence Heraclitus says:

> fr. 123 φύσις [nature] tends to hide itself.

Similarly in other fragments.[5] What is generally taken as an expression of Heraclitus' aristocratic contempt of the masses may also and perhaps primarily signify Heraclitus' realization that his fundamental insight remains closed off to man in his usual and daily concerns. Heraclitus does not pass sociological judgment, but characterizes a fundamental human trait. That trait will make it impossible for Heraclitus' teachings ever to be commonly available and understandable.

> fr. 108 Of all those whose λόγοι I have heard, no one has come to realize that wisdom is set apart from all else.

The fragmentary and forbidding nature of his teachings is then not so much a matter of the accidents of literary tradition as it is the very presence of his peculiar thought. The distinctions that we make between form and content, tradition and immediate presence, between the purposive and the accidental, are all based on later metaphysical events; and however far they may carry us, they could ultimately be inappropriate and even misleading.

There is no commonly acknowledged philosophy of language in Heraclitus' thought although the language of Heraclitus has been investigated repeatedly.[6] But it may well be the case that in Heraclitus we will find that origin of the philosophy of language where philosophy and language are still one so that the origin differs essentially from what it gives origin to. How can we approach this origin? Not in abandoning the achievements of the great metaphysicians, but in permitting the metaphysical views on philosophy and language to be challenged. A challenge is met when one exposes himself to it. So we must expose our views to Heraclitean thought, and we must allow this thought to call our attention beyond our initial views. The origin, even as Aristotle and Vico later conceive of it, is not the dead shell that is left behind, but the initial and pervasive force of a thing.

---

[5] Cf. fragments 2, 51, 72, 87, 93, 108.

[6] B. Snell, "Die Sprache Heraklits," *Hermes*, LXI (1962), 353–381; G. S. Kirk, "Heraclitus's Contribution to the Development of a Language for Philosophy," *Archiv für Begriffsgeschichte*, IX (1964), 73–77.

2. *Language and thought in Heraclitus*

We must now seek an approach to Heraclitus' thought which lets our common views come into play without being dependent on them. And so rather than beginning with one of the elusive teachings, celebrated for their obscurity, we turn to a simple and almost tangible device that Heraclitus uses repeatedly to make his point.

In fragment 48, Heraclitus says:

> fr. 48 The bow is called life, but its work is death.

Heraclitus plays here on the homonymy of the Greek words for *life* and *bow*; they have (except for the stress) the same form: *βιος. Apparently Heraclitus is struck by the fact that βιός (bow) does not give rise to βίος (life), but to the opposite: death. The bow contains and unites opposites within itself.

Elsewhere Heraclitus says:

> fr. 25 The greater the fate of death, the greater the reward.

Here Heraclitus establishes a proportion between death and reward. The proposition is supported by the Greek assonance of *fate of death* (μόροι) and *reward* (μοίραι).[7] The assonance is emphasized by chiasmus. The Greek word order of the fragment is roughly and partically: μόροι (death) the greater – the greater the μοίραι (reward). The symmetry of this arrangement heightens the significance that obtains between death and reward.

Finally let us remember fragment 1 where λόγος first seems to be used in the sense of a verbal statement that can be communicated, understood, and misunderstood (it is so understood in fragment 108 above also), and then in the sense of a force or pattern that determines the course of events. But clearly the sameness of the word λόγος is more than external; at the bottom of the differences in meaning and context one pervasive power seems to be intended. Yet the unity apparently is guaranteed by nothing but a word.

In all three instances, Heraclitus draws on dimensions of language that are immediate and almost palpable; but he does so in a way which is at least suspect to our thinking. The unravelling of our scruples will afford us with an opportunity of confronting our views with Heraclitus'

---

[7] Further plays on words in fragments 5, 15, 20, 26, 28, 72, 81, 114. Cf. Snell, "Die Sprache," pp. 369–371; W. J. Verdenius, "Der Logosbegriff bei Heraklit und Parmenides," *Phronesis*, XI (1966), 95–96; Kahn, "A New Look," pp. 192–193.

thought and language, and this confrontation will in turn give us some insight into the original possibilities of the philosophy of language.

A proper appraisal of these possibilities requires a tentative discussion of the problems of *homonymy* and *etymology*, where these terms are to be taken as focuses in a great complex of problems.

3. Homonymy and etymology

Homonymy is the simple and striking phenomenon in language that certain words are alike in form, but have entirely different meanings. Take for example "doe" – "dough".[8] It is clear that here the likeness of form is confined to the sound of the words, which are therefore called *homophones*. They are not spelled alike, i.e. they are not *homographs*. There are however homonyms which are both homophones and homographs, e.g. "char" *(chore)* and "char" *(trout)*. And there are a few homographs that are not homophones and are therefore generally not called homonyms, e.g. "slough" (pronounced like "food", meaning *mire*) and "slough" (pronounced like "tough", meaning *skin*).[9] In what follows here nothing will depend on these finer distinctions, and we will somewhat vaguely, but more conveniently speak of homonyms simply.

In the case of homonymy, we always distinguish between the homonyms, and as a rule, no great care is required since each homonym has its own referential environment. On occasion, however, a speaker may intentionally establish a connection between two disparate references merely through the sameness of form of the referring words. He then plays on the words as we say. We call such a play on words a *pun*, and we feel today that puns because of their irrational element must be confined to the realm of playfulness. We would not even begin to consider seriously an argument in which some inference from "dough" to "doe" played a decisive part. Puns are admitted on condition that nothing significant depend on them. Our refusal to attribute any significance to the sameness of form in homonymy manifests itself in our refusal to speak of *one* word as being homonymous. Homonymy is always taken as a relation of two or more words. If one *word* were said to have two entirely different meanings, we would insist on an explanation. That two words share their external shape we are willing to accept as an oddity.

---

[8] There is further "do" as in "do re me ...".
[9] One might mention "writer" (American pronunciation) and "writer" (British pronunciation) as homographs which are synonyms but not homophones (since they differ in at least two phonemes).

There are cases where a difference of meaning in the face of formal sameness is less easily detected than in the case "doe" – "dough". "Faith" for instance can mean *formally articulated creed* or *a man's fundamental attitude*. I may easily be led to draw conclusions from faith-as-creed to faith-as-attitude and vice versa. These conclusions are not as *a priori* unfounded and irrelevant as those based on strict homonymy. In the case of *faith*, there are different meanings, but they are significantly and systematically related to one another; and in such a case we speak of *ambiguity* rather than homonymy, and the systematic relatedness of the two meanings and the possibility of explaining that relatedness makes it seem reasonable to speak of *one* word with different meanings.[10] Ambiguity, as opposed to homonymy, is therefore used as a predicate of a word and not as a relation of two words. In case of systematic ambiguity, sameness of form is commonly accepted as a valid point of departure and reference in discussing a problem.[11]

Consider now the following example. Someone may bewail the progressive mechanization of our lives, and he may see in the computer an outstanding symptom of this dangerous development. He is further aware that the computer is in a way an electronic model of a mathematical or logical calculus. He also knows that the science of constructing and interpreting calculi is occasionally called *logistic*. A concrete example, where the man discerns the pernicious influence of logistic and computer, are the vast military apparatuses that embrace the globe. He sees in them intricate systems of coordinating, shipping, and supplying goods and machinery for the sole puropse of suppressing and destroying individual freedom. He believes that the science of military supply has become decisive in strategy, and he notes with some satisfaction that this science is called *logistics*.

It is easy to see how this man might try to render his arguments against technocracy and militarism and for freedom and peace more coherent and convincing by taking an alleged systematic ambiguity of logistic(s) as a basis and guideline.

However logistic and logistics do not have a common root and are strict (near-) homonyms.[12] *Logistic* (science of constructing and inter-

---

[10] The notion of systematic ambiguity is informally introduced here. It stands in opposition to arbitrary ambiguity an example of which is found in the multiple meaning of "bar" in *bar examination, bar stool, prison bars*.

[11] Paul Tillich in *Dynamics of Faith* (New York, 1957) makes extensive use of the systematic ambiguity of "faith".

[12] In German *(Logistik)* and in French *(logistique)*, they are strict homonyms. This, is at any rate the view advanced in Anglo-Saxon dictionaries. In the Romance dictionaries, *logis-*

preting calculi) is a cognate of *logic, logistics* (science of military supply which includes the *housing* of personnel) a cognate of *lodging*. This is a matter of etymology.[13] The etymological objection certainly would not of itself invalidate whatever is sound in the above arguments. Conversely, if the etymological kinship of two words is hidden or devious, we would not use it to confirm or start an argument however valid the parallel of both the significance and of the history of two words. One might for instance say that both logistics and lobbies tend to emancipate themselves from the role of servants of democracy and thus become dangerous to democracy. But one would hardly add: "This parallel is by no means accidental; 'lobby' and 'logistics' have a common etymological root."

Just as homonymies are confined to the minimal significance of playfulness, so etymological relationships are granted nothing more than an occasional and auxiliary pertinence. We insist on sharply defined meanings in words, and we tend to regard the historical and phonetic context of words as arbitrary and irrelevant. Aside from the evidence of the examples just given, one could further justify this attitude by pointing out that a proposition or an argument that is valid in one language ought to be valid in another language as well. However, if the validity of a piece of discourse were to depend on some homonymy or etymology, the basis of validity will be lost in most translations. Hence we refuse to concede validity to begin with. Before we accept this verdict as final, let us ask whether our attitude toward homonymy and etymology is in fact as negative today as it has appeared so far.

There is at least one realm of language today where homonymy is still appreciated as a persuasive force. This is the case in poetry, more particularly in rime, which can be defined as partial homonymy occurring in a regular manner. Rime is therefore subject to all objections that were raised against homonymy; and yet many great poems would not address us as powerfully without rime; and clearly rime has a function that goes beyond the innocuous and often comical playfulness of a pun. Without going into details let us tentatively explicate this by saying: The meaning of the poem avails itself of the music of language;

---

tique for instance, is given just one etymological origin and hence regarded as ambiguous. Cf. *Grand Larousse*, 3rd ed. (Paris, 1962), VI, 816.

[13] Regarding the interrelation of etymology, ambiguity, homonymy, cf. Willard Van Orman Quine, *Word and Object* (Cambridge, Mass., 1960), pp. 129–30.

and the sounds of language favor and elicit a certain modulation of the poem's meaning.[14]

Similarly etymology is a power with which every careful speaker reckons in his discourse. A word that denotes a thing is not only a label or sign of that thing, but also and always the record or more properly the presence of the experiences that a community of speakers has had with the thing named by the word. The paths of these experiences run parallel, cross one another, converge, bifurcate; etymology articulates these developments; the competent speaker and above all the poet is aware of the possibilities and dangers that these developments advance. Consider the networks of past experiences that are lit up in such words as *intercourse, confederate, pacify*. Consider the additional experiences that we today engrave on such words as *trip, escalator, orbit*.

Homonymy and etymology point to forces of language to which the poet seems to be pre-eminently responsive. The poet perceives how every word is alive in a network of eloquent relations of sound and meaning, in a network that provides possibilities of which the poet actualizes some in his poem, at the same time tying up new connections and creating new possibilities. What is true of words, similarly holds of phrases and syntactical patterns which are in part explored and explicated in the study of rhetorical figures.

Although apparently homonymy and etymology are still living forces in today's language, their influence is clearly waning. Rime has become secondary if not suspect in much of recent poetry; we are wary with puns as is apparent from the difficulties that we have in appreciating for instance the frequent puns in Shakespeare. There are exceptions. Undoubtedly much of Dylan Thomas' poetry owes its strong appeal to the use of rime and assonance.

Our awareness of the etymological extensions of words is very limited, presumably for three reasons: (1) We frequently do not command the languages into which the words of the vernacular extend historically (Old-French, Latin, Greek, the older Germanic dialects). (2) Our command of the contexts which sustain the semantic and morphological fullness and variety of words is limited, i.e. our knowledge of the great literature of the present and especially the past is scant. (3) There is a great mobility in language today in that ever new scientific and technological advances and the changing fashions require a rapid pro-

---

[14] Cf. the nursery rime: April/Come she will./May/She will stay./June/She'll change her tune./July/She will fly./August/Die she must./September/I'll remember. – The poetry of these verses has been spun out by Paul Simon.

duction, consumption, and suppression of words or at least uses of words. This mobility tends to disrupt the ties of words and syntactical patterns with their historical provenience.

We have seen that for an understanding of homonymy and etymology the distinction between form and meaning is essential. This distinction is a variant of what we later shall call the metaphysical distinction.[15] Even our limited discussion has shown its great analytic and explanatory power. But it has also shown that there are limits to the distinction. When applied to rime and etymology, the distinction reveals a number of indubitable facts but in the end accords these phenomena no more than some mysterious or arbitrary effect. There is obviously an incompatibility between the metaphysical distinction and the poetical dimensions of language. Does the failure lie with poetry or with metaphysics? Or is this perhaps an illicit disjunction?

4. The λόγος and language

We have seen in our earlier discussion that homonymy and etymology play important roles in Heraclitus' thinking. Let us look once more at fragment 48:

fr. 48 The bow (βιός) is called life (βίος), but its work is death.

The observation receives its poignancy from the Greek homonomy of *bow* and *life*. The two words are nearly alike in their form though in a certain sense opposed to one another in their meaning. The homonymy brings two semantically dissimilar words together so that not only the meanings are opposed to each other but also the relation of meanings (opposition) to the relation of the forms (likeness). The relations are left in opposition without an evaluative conjunction, "conjunction" taken in the grammatical sense. Heraclitus might have used "because" or "although". He could have said: "*Because* 'life' and 'bow' are alike in form, their meanings are opposed."[16] Or Heraclitus might have said: "*Although* 'life' and 'bow' are alike in form, they differ in meaning." Instead of an invalid argument, we now have a vacuous one.

---

15 Cf. section 10.

16 That kind of argument is sometimes called "from antiphrasis" or "from contraries", and it seems plainly invalid to us as it did already to the Roman grammarian Quintilian who asked: "Should we admit that some words are indeed derived from their opposite as for instance a grove [*lucus*] is dark with shade and not very light [*parum luceat*] ... ?" *Institutio oratoria*, Loeb edition tr. by H. E. Butler, 4 vols (Cambridge, Mass., 1936), I. vi, 34 (my translation). This argument has been condensed into *lucus a non lucendo*.

In fact, however, Heraclitus does not argue at all; he presents an opposition. The bow unites in itself two opposing forces: The bow, according to its *sound*, is akin to *life*; the bow, according to its *meaning*, is the bringer of *death*. To be present in the tension of opposites is not accidental to the bow. The bow is the unity of the opposing forces of wood and cord. To insist on a conjunctive "because" is to demand a definite order of grounds and consequences where Heraclitus sees the tension of opposing forces. To settle for a conjunctive "although" is to resign to the obvious and usual, an attitude which, as we saw, is in opposition to Heraclitus' central insight. Heraclitus emphasizes both the possibility of misunderstanding what is present in the bow and the importance of what the bow represents:

> fr. 51 They do not apprehend how being at variance with itself it agrees with itself: there is a harmony of one turning to the other as in the bow and the lyre.

What is it that agrees with itself? What is *agreeing* in Greek? It is ὁμολογεῖν, to be *homo*geneous with the λόγος.[17] To agree in the sense of fr. 51 is not to exhibit an accidental likeness or commonness with something else, but to be one with the λόγος.

The λόγος itself is such that it is at variance and in agreement with itself. How this is possible can be found out only if one turns to the λόγος itself rather than to some doctrine about the λόγος.[18] Hence Heraclitus admonishes his readers:

> fr. 50 Listening not to me but to the λόγος, wisdom is this: to agree (ὁμολογεῖν): one is all [the one lets all things be what they are].

The λόγος agrees with itself in constituting the one pervasive order of the universe. It is at variance with itself in being manifest in the variety of individual things which it orders.[19] But to agree is proper not only to the λόγος; we too are called upon to enter into agreement and consonance with the λόγος. To do so is wisdom, the simple thing that alone is important.[20] To enter into agreement is to enter into the divine. The divine is not some individual being but agreement as it

---

[17] Kirk in *Philosophers*, p. 193, wants to replace on philological grounds ὁμολογέει which is found in Diels and Wheelwright by ξυμφέρεται ("is brought together with itself").

[18] Cf. fragment 40 above.

[19] Cf. Heidegger, *What is Philosophy?* tr. Jean T. Wilde and William Kluback (New Haven, n.d. [German edition 1956]), pp. 46–49.

[20] Cf. fragments 41 and 108 above.

comes to pass.[21] It is apparent in what people commonly understand by divinity, but it is also partially distorted by this understanding. Hence Heraclitus says:

> fr. 32 The one which alone is wisdom is willing and unwilling to be called by the name of Zeus [the highest of the gods].

Zeus is the power and terror of lightning as it suddenly illuminates all and lets it be present.[22] He is the movement and brightness of fire as it consumes, transforms, and sustains things.[23] The violence and seeming confusion of these phenomena is like a war. And yet:

> fr. 53 War is the father of all and king of all, and some he shows as gods, others as men; some he makes slaves, others free.

War is the coming to pass of the agreement according to which the highest and the lowest beings are assigned their place.[24] The agreement is born of tensions and does not leave the tensions behind, but prevails as their unity like the bow and the lyre.

We have seen how it is possible to let oneself be drawn into Heraclitus' thinking by following variously the hints given by homonymy, etymology, mythology, empathy, and experience. In the process we often deal with language and with linguistic phenomena that are properly problems in the philosophy of language. Aside from homonymy, etymology, and related problems, the problem of the adequacy of names is touched upon by Heraclitus; in fragment 1 the basic distinction between a proposition (doctrine) and its verbal (words) and objective (works) representation has been utilized. But the regularities and ramifications of these problems are never pursued; rather they are given immediate and unique significance through reference to the central power called "λόγος", "φύσις", "Zeus", "lightning", "war", and still otherwise in other fragments. Language as a distinct phenomenon does not emerge and therefore neither does the philosophy of language.

Language in Heraclitus' philosophy is still one with the world order, with nature, with the divine, with lawfulness, with human reason. "Λόγος" stands for all these things.[25] The interconnections that con-

---

[21] Cf. fragments 5, 11, 67.
[22] See fragment 64.
[23] See fragments 30, 31.
[24] See fragment 55.
[25] See fragments 1, 2, 31, 45, 50, 57, 72, 108 among others. Cf. W. J. Verdenius, "Der Logosbegriff," *Phronesis*, XI (1966), 81–98 and XII (1967), 99–117; also Heribert Boeder, "Der frühgriechische Wortgebrauch von Logos und Aletheia," *Archiv für Begriffsgeschichte*, IV (1959), 82–112.

verge in "λόγος" are not explicated; rather they speak immediately in the sound, history, and connotations of this word. Heraclitus does not see his role in being an explicator, but rather in letting the word speak for itself and in so making others hear and speak the word. The problem of the unity and limits of language that dominates all later thought on language has not arisen here. All the subsequently diverging and tangential elements of language are here united in the word λόγος. The λόγος does not merely establish a connection between the problems of world order, nature, lawfulness, divinity, and reason on the one side and language on the other; it means or rather is of itself language, speech, word.[26]

The λόγος then is the eloquent and unified presence of language in Heraclitus' philosophy and, in its peculiar presence, the reason why there is no philosophy of language in Heraclitus' thought. Putting this differently one might say that the ideal philosophy of language is the cancellation of the philosophy of language.

5. The ambiguity of the λόγος

Let us in conclusion reflect on the possibility of such a limitary and ideal case. To begin with, "λόγος" in Heraclitus' thinking is a highly and systematically ambiguous term. Ambiguity, even when admitted as systematic and legitimate, is still generally considered to be a secondary and bothersome phenomenon. It is secondary in that we think of a word primarily as a certain sequence of sounds associated with just one meaning. Ambiguity is bothersome in that a multiplicity of meanings seems to invite confusion and error. Consider the case of Robert, who is John's father, Harold's son, Jane's husband, and Richard's colleague. The question "Who is Robert?" can validly be answered in a number of ways. We can consequently say: the name "Robert" is systematically ambiguous. However, it is obvious that in the present case ambiguity is neither secondary nor bothersome, but the reflection of the necessarily manifold manner in which Robert realizes his existence. There is no word that is strictly unambiguous, i.e. univocal, as long as the thing named or the function performed by a word unfolds

---

[26] Cf. Heidegger, *An Introduction to Metaphysics*, tr. Ralph Manheim (Garden City, 1961), pp. 98–164 and "Logos (Heraklit, Fragment 50)," in *Vorträge und Aufsätze*, 2nd ed. (Pfullingen, 1959), pp. 207–29. Cf. also Ernst Cassirer, *The Philosophy of Symbolic Forms. Volume One: Language*, tr. Ralph Manheim, 7th ed. (New Haven, Conn., 1968 [first published in German in 1923]), pp. 119–122.

its being to different views in different ways. And the multiplicity of views is in fact irrepressible.

Ambiguity is then at best a matter of degree. Ambiguity *can* be the reflection of the fullness and vivacity of a thing's presence. But this kind of presence of the thing requires a corresponding power of concentration on the part of the beholder. For us the λόγος threatens to disperse into unrelated meanings. To Heraclitus, it presumably was not only the object of an effort at concentrating, but also the source yielding energy for gathering. Λόγος in its basic etymological meaning is a collecting, a gathering, the presenting of a multiplicity as a unity. Heraclitus did not have to read these things into the λόγος, rather the λόγος was their presence.[27] We see here again how the λόγος is the presence and the solution of a problem in a unity which is prior to the distinction of problem and solution.

It is difficult for us to respond adequately to the speaking of the λόγος. The difficulty was already apparent to Heraclitus. He saw that the height and the radiance of the λόγος are diminished to the point of distortion in the everyday life of the many. The unity of tensions in the λόγος is sensitive and vulnerable in its encounter with human understanding. The unity can be shattered or obscured.

This possibility becomes apparent if we consider once more the varying significance that a pun can have. A pun, as we have seen above, draws two or more widely divergent meanings together by presenting these meanings in the external unity of one word. A pun has force if it succeeds in showing that to the initially trivial external unity there corresponds an unexpected and hidden unity of the meanings presented in the word. A profound and far-reaching insight is suddenly lit up in the pun. For a pun to be successful in this way, form, meaning, word, and reality must suddenly coalesce into one.

This is presumably how Heraclitus' puns must be understood. For us, however, such understanding is all but unattainable. We barely catch a glimpse of the alleged unity; and the claim of the pun is in such stark contrast to our soberly compartmentalized reality that the tension of pun and fact becomes intolerable and gives way to the comic relief that is found in good jokes. Puns are merely playful to us. In many cases the discrepancy of the pun's claim and the facts is so obvious right from the start that we cannot see anything in the pun but an inept and abortive attempt at making an important or witty point. Such puns even fail to be playful and are merely embarrassing or offensive.

---

[27] Cf. Snell, "Sprache," p. 365 and Verdenius, "Logosbegriff," p. 83.

Heraclitus speaks of the threat to, and the possible loss of, the unity of the λόγος in terms that seem morally evaluative to us. But obviously they are not moral in the sense that they mean to pass judgment on a particular action or attitude through recourse to a moral law. What is at issue is the fate of the law that governs all there is, the physical, mental, aesthetic, and the moral.

If the unity of the λόγος is shattered or obscured, then a kind of confusion and possibility of error results that we call ambiguity. Ambiguity is itself highly ambiguous. It can designate the live and full presence of a thing on the one hand and the confusion and haziness that have befallen a thing on the other.[28] It is only proper then to search for measures that might serve to dispel the confusion. If for some reason Robert has become a questionable character in my opinion and I cannot dissociate myself from him, I must take pains to distinguish between his accomplishments and failures as a friend, a colleague, a father, a husband, a son, a citizen before I presume to pass judgment on him.

The philosophy of language was born when ambiguity qua richness *and* confusion became explicitly apparent in its ambiguity and steps were taken to come to grips with ambiguity. Heraclitus' thought does not present a philosophy of language yet, but it gives birth to the philosophy of language, and in representing the coincidence of the problems and possible solutions of a philosophy of language, it remains a challenge to the philosophy of language.

6. The dispersion of the λόγος. The Sophists

The λόγος of early Greek culture and philosophy dispersed into a great number of aspects and levels of reality. Why this happened is difficult to understand. How it happened is apparent from political, social, and religious developments. Regarding the philosophy of language, the dispersal of the λόγος is clearly visible in the work of the men who were called Sophists.

Sophistry is understandable only in its attitude towards the problem of language and reality. The Sophists started from the premise that the λόγος as the all encompassing order was no longer in force and that the departed λόγος had left behind a mass of unrelated, freely manageable

---

[28] One might want to use a separate term for the positive meaning of "ambiguity", e.g. *plurisignification* or *polysemy*. But such usage, if consistent, deprives "ambiguity" of ambiguity, and such deprivation may amount to a distortion.

fragments which the individual could use to his own liking. The Sophists may have been the authors as much as the observers of this state; they were at any rate, clearly aware of the decay of the Presocratic λόγος. But in another sense they adhered very closely to the (implicit) Heraclitean view of language in that they did not make a basic distinction between language and reality. Language, for them, was that side of reality where reality was essentially accessible and manageable. One comes to grips with reality, one appropriates it and changes it most efficiently through language, that is through the use of language in speech. One has misunderstood what the world is all about if he toils with the recalcitrant and brute things themselves. One has insight into reality when he proceeds to manage things through speaking cleverly and efficaciously to others. Rhetoric is the practice and teaching of such speaking.

This basic position of the Sophists took quite different forms. One is represented by Protagoras (480–410 B.C.) who held that:

> fr. 1 Of all things the measure is man: of the things that are [he is the measure or reason] that they are, of the things that are not [he is the measure or reason] that they are not.

The significance of the fragment in our context is that apart from man and prior to his dealings, there is no pervasive order, indeed nothing that truly exists. It is impossible then for man to do anything wrong since there never can be an independent standard against which his deeds could be measured. Man deals most successfully with reality through speech and argument, and language is relevant solely as the more or less successful formation and appropriation of reality. Language in ever giving rise to reality is impossible apart from reality; reality is impossible prior to language.

While Protagoras' position implies that no use of language can ever be wrong, Gorgias (483–375 B.C.) argues that no use of language can ever be right:

> fr. 3 In his book *On Not-Being or On Nature*, Gorgias set out to prove three successive points: first, that nothing exists; second that even if it does, it is incomprehensible by men; and third, that even if it is comprehensible, it is certainly not expressible and cannot be communicated to another.[29]

---

[29] The translation is Robinson's in *Introduction*, p. 295.

The proof for the third point which is primarily relevant here contends that a certain type of entity (e.g. visible things) is accessible to a certain human faculty (vision) and in no other way. Words too are physical entities of a particular type, perceivable through a certain sense (hearing), and just as opaque and self-sufficient as for instance rocks. This does not make it impossible to utter and hear words. But on this view, there is no room for any argument to the effect that a given sentence is right in the sense that it characterizes or communicates a state of affairs. However, the sense of futility and resignation that seems to prevail in what Gorgias says is in sharp and ironical contrast to what Gorgias does. His arguments are neither novel, nor profound. They merely display Gorgias' virtuosity in doing things with words. The arguments press this type of language use to the extreme. Nothing is impossible for the proficient speaker; he can disprove the possibility of being, thinking, and speaking, and in doing so he emerges in his solitary omnipotence.

Although the Sophists made no fundamental distinction between language and reality, they were presumably well aware of the peculiarities of linguistic structures and techniques. The results of their research have been lost. But they may have survived in the work of later grammarians and philosophers, among them Plato.[30]

---

[30] Cf. Peter M. Gentinetta, *Zur Sprachbetrachtung bei den Sophisten und in der stoisch-hellenistischen Zeit* (Winterthur, 1961), pp. 22–45.

CHAPTER TWO

THE FOUNDATION OF THE PHILOSOPHY OF
LANGUAGE

*7. The transition from the harmony with language to the investigation
of language. Plato*

Plato (427–347 B.C.) was the first to recognize and investigate language
as a philosophical problem; he did so primarily in the dialogue *Cratylus*.[1]
The problem is approached in terms of the origin of language where
origin means both beginning and essence. More specifically, the question regards the correctness of names. "Name" is taken by Plato in the
sense of any word that denotes an entity. We find here for the first
time an explicit statement regarding the henceforth decisive triad:
language (names), reality (things), and their interrelation (correctness).

Plato considers two explanations of the interrelation. Although he
has reservations about either, the explanations have become as influential as the statement of the problem. Plato asks whether the correctness of names stems from nature (φύσει) or convention (θέσει).
These alternatives reflect the Heraclitean and Sophistic positions.

The mere fact that a disjunction between nature and convention is
admitted shows that nature no longer has the unitary and comprehensive force that it had in the Presocratic era, where men could have
agreed on a convention only if it in turn and to begin with agreed with
the pervasive order, with φύσις or λόγος. Yet some connection with the
earlier thought remains intact. Correctness of the names by nature
means an interrelation of words and things such that it is apparent and
secured in itself, independently of the whims of man. Do the words
indicate of themselves why they denote a certain thing? This is argued
at length in the *Cratylus* by means of a technique that is usually but
somewhat inaccurately called etymology. Etymologies, as indicated

---

[1] I will use the Stephanus pagination in the references. I have used the Loeb edition, tr. by
H. N. Fowler (Cambridge, Mass., 1963).

before, are always peculiar to some one language. In particular the kind of etymology that Socrates, the main speaker in the dialogue, practices in the *Cratylus* cannot be translated from Greek into English. But the following is roughly an English counterpart.

(1) Question: Why is the strawberry called "strawberry"? Answer: Because it is *buried* in *straw* when it is shipped.

(2) Question: Why is the flea called "flea"? Answer: Because it *flees* when you try to catch it.[2]

We are inclined to call such explanations *playful etymologies* or *nonsense etymologies*. (1) is playful or nonsensical with regard to the component *berry*. The component "straw" is legitimately associated with *straw* from the historical point of view though not in the proper manner. The *New English Dictionary* suggests that "straw" either means *stalk* and refers to the runners of the plant or it means *particles of straw or chaff*, "describing the appearance of the achenes scattered over the surface of the strawberry." The first meaning is now largely obsolete, the second somewhat remote; hence one is tempted to give "straw" a more definite and tangible meaning.

While (1) is, as far as I know, a hypothetical case, there are instances where a secondary explanation or secondary motivation of a word or component is a fairly obvious fact. Thus "hamburger" was first dissociated from the city of Hamburg and thus became semantically opaque. But then the first component was taken to mean *ham* or *meat*. Evidence for this is the substitution of *fish* or *chicken* for *ham* in "fishburger" and "chickenburger".[3] Or a "wiz [wizard] at math" is taken to be someone who can *whiz* through mathematical problems which is then reflected in the spelling "whiz".[4]

Such secondary motivations are also called *folk etymologies*. Evidently there are different types of such etymologies; many are presumably hidden and private; only a few become apparent through analogical formations or changes of spelling.[5]

The playful etymology of (1) then borders on folk etymology. (2) is a

---

[2] According to the comic strip *B. C.* by Hart of July 19, 1969, Wiley's Dictionary contains the following entry: "prō·test′ v. an amateurish demonstration designed to test the pro's."

[3] I owe this example to E. Bagby Atwood.

[4] This is Dwight Bolinger's example in *Aspects of Language* (New York, 1968), p. 105.

[5] Cf. Bolinger, *Aspects*, pp. 100–121 and Ferdinand de Saussure, *Course in General Linguistics*, tr. Wade Baskin (New York, 1966), pp. 122–139, 173–176 for further ramifications of this phenomenon. – In the investigation of folk etymologies, one should always beware of *the fallacy of imputed ingenuity*; "he is a whiz at math" may reflect a straightforward spelling mistake.

playful etymology only insofar as it sounds, and may be intended to sound, silly. In fact, however, the association suggested is historically correct.

Obviously playful etymologies and folk etymologies in the strict sense lack historical validity, and therefore Socrates' etymologies are usually dismissed as crude and mistaken; or it is argued that Plato himself meant to mock and discredit etymologizing.[6] There are indeed indications in the dialogue that Socrates traces the connections and ancestries of words in a playful, rather than a scientific way.[7] But play has its own dignity. Just as in playing the world reveals dimensions that are not open otherwise, so playing with words discloses peculiar aspects of language.[8] Plato follows here the Heraclitean tradition where, as we have seen, plays on words have their own significance.[9]

Play, if it has not degenerated into stupidity or chaos, has its rules. The purpose of Plato's playful etymologies is to reveal the network of sounds and meanings that sustains every word and that vibrates and responds in its entirety when a word is thoughtfully or playfully spoken. This network as it prevails at a given time (synchronically) emerges only partially through the work of scientific etymology whose perspective always extends from a given point (word or root) into the past or the future (diachronically).[10] That Plato is not interested in tracing genealogies, but in explicating all directions of the present connections of sound and meaning within which a word is located is clear from Socrates' insistence on finding as many and as varied connections as possible; in cases where Socrates has recognized an obvious philological derivation, he goes on to bring out additional connections which are philologically unverifiable.[11] Assuming that every language has its characteristic network, a word taken over from another language would remain a relatively foreign body without roots and extensions in the texture of the language that it has entered. Hence Socrates argues

---

[6] Cf. Fowler's introduction to the *Cratylus*, p. 4; David Crystal, *Linguistics, Language, and Religion* (New York, 1965), p. 15; Cassirer, *Language*, p. 123. Further references in Georgios Anagnostopoulos, "Plato's *Cratylus*: The Two Theories of the Correctness of Names," *Review of Metaphysics*, XXV (1972), p. 691, n. 2. The following view is closer to that of Josef Derbolav, *Der Dialog "Kratylos" im Rahmen der platonischen Sprach- und Erkenntnisphilosophie* (Saarbrücken, 1953), pp. 30–32.

[7] See *Cratylus*, 398D, 399E–400A, 400B, 401E, 410E, 411A, 420E, 421D.

[8] Cf. Johan Huizinga, *Homo ludens. A Study of the Playelement in Culture*, tr. R. F. C. Hull (New York, 1950) and Eugen Fink, *Spiel als Weltsymbol* (Stuttgart, 1960).

[9] So does play itself if Heraclitus' fragment 52 is authentic and not to be taken ironically.

[10] For the origin of this terminology, cf. section 49.

[11] See *Cratylus*, 402E–403A, 405A–E, 413E, 417A–B and C, 419D.

conversely from the absence of connections to the foreign origin of a word.[12]

Socrates plays his game at great length; the expanse of the etymologizing appears meaningful only when these linguistic reflections are appreciated as the succession of the various moves and phases of play. However, such playing no longer evokes the presence of the all-encompassing λόγος. Therefore play repeatedly comes to be regarded as research, i.e. as a searching for reliable and terminal regularities. When the playful etymologies are considered as explanations, they are obviously either circular or infinitely regressive since according to this procedure the correctness of a word for a thing is justified by showing that this word is derived from others of like or similar form which stand for entities like, or similar to, that thing. Naturally, the problem that has been settled for this word arises again for its antecedents.

8. The origin of language from nature or convention

One way of avoiding the circle or halting the regress is to show that there are certain root words from which all others are derived; the root words in turn are validated in a different way.[13] The contention that the correctness of words springs from nature requires a validation of the root words which is somehow natural. This basic validation proceeds in analogy to the derivative one in that it reduces the rootwords to "elements" (letters or sounds) which in turn, however, reflect certain events or properties in a self-evident way, e.g. /i/ designates the subtle, /d/ and /t/ rest, /l/ gliding, /a/ greatness, etc. [14] Socrates emphasizes that these elements do not directly imitate natural noises *(onomatopoeia)*, but capture the essential nature of a thing *(sound symbolism)*.[15] But even this refinement fails to save the nature theory of language since it is always possible to find counter examples for any alleged sound symbol.

A variant of the sound symbolism theory contends that there was a superior or divine lawgiver or namemaker who fashioned the names fittingly, taking the ideal name as a standard.[16] The argument is re-

---

[12] *Ibid.*, 410A, 424A.

[13] *Ibid.*, 410A–421D; the virtues are derived from the root words *flowing, rushing, going,* the vices from their opposites *stopping, holding, binding.* Cf. Derbolav, *Der Dialog,* pp. 33–34.

[14] 426B–427E.

[15] 423A–424C. On the distinction between onomatopoeia and sound symbolism, cf. Wolfgang Kayser, *Das sprachliche Kunstwerk,* 8th ed. (Bern, 1962), pp. 101–104.

[16] 386D–390B, 391D–393D.

jected as evasive, at least to the extent that it invokes a divine origin of names.[17]

The thesis that the correctness of words is based on convention is associated with the teachings of the Sophists. However, convention, for them, had the extreme and particular meaning of doing in each instance what was deemed favorable by the individual without regard to any independent criterion. The use of words was therefore beyond the reach of any evaluation and simply the most powerful way of doing things. In this context the question as to the correctness of words could not be raised meaningfully.[18]

Plato refutes this position tentatively by showing that we distinguish in all our dealings with things between adequate and inadequate procedures. What may have some plausibility in the special and intricate case of speaking, becomes evident as unfounded when seen in the general context of human actions: they are all guided by the standard of the intrinsic nature of the particular action.[19]

But this does not generally refute convention as the basis of correctness. Convention works as long as it is consistent.[20] In the *Theaetetus*, Plato suggests more particularly that convention gets language underway; it is not a force within language and therefore not subject to the rules of language.[21] Nor is convention an event within ordinary reality which is encountered and accessible in language. Convention is the naming of the primary, absolutely simple elements which, due to their simplicity, have no porperties except one, the property of being nothing but themselves. Hence there is no predication or knowledge regarding them, no explanation, no truth or falsehood. They can only be perceived. But once they have been named, the names can be combined in various ways, and these combinations may or may not correspond to the nature of those complex things which are the items of our ordinary world. Now only is there knowledge, explanation, and truth. "For the combination of names is the essence of the λόγος."[22] And λόγος means here: explanation, discourse, language.

---

[17] 425D–426B, 436A–D.
[18] 385E–386A, 436B–C.
[19] 386E–390E. For a more elaborate discussion of this point see Anagnostopoulos, "Plato's *Cratylus*," pp. 702–708.
[20] 385A–E, 436B–E.
[21] *Theaetetus*, 201D–202C. I have used the Loeb edition, tr. H. N. Fowler (Cambridge, Mass., 1961).
[22] 202B.

9. The interrelation of word and thing

But this program fails to deal effectively with the persistent problems
that arise regarding the interrelation of word and thing. Two of these
problems are readily apparent.

First, the word must essentially differ from the thing, otherwise it is
a needless duplication of the thing.[23] Second, the word must be essentially connected with the thing, it must reveal or re-present the thing.[24]
In Heraclitus, the word was the unquestioned and eloquent presence
of the thing. In Plato, there is only a vestige of this experience where
Socrates takes pains to point out that his investigations of the etymology of divine names is concerned only with the inadequate (oblique)
names that the mortals give to the gods and so observes the rules of
piety. He thereby implies that the true (direct) names of the gods
would be their direct presence; and the vain curiosity regarding these
names would be equal to the impiety of trying to wrest from the gods
the mystery of their divinity.[25] Only the ideal word ("name") lets the
thing be truly present.[26] But the ideal word is not the one we use day
to day.

There are however problems in the interrelation of word and thing
that are less easily stated. First, there is an elusiveness in the interrelation inasmuch as a word can also be looked at as a thing, and a
thing (a sound, an engraving, a picture) can turn out to be a word.
Moreover, the word and thing aspects of an entity can conflict. In the
Sophist, Plato considers sentences such as: "Being and one are the
same." The things, denoted by "being" and "one" may indeed be the
same. But to express this state of affairs, I must use words which, in their
plurality, contradict the asserted unity.[27] Similar problems arise with
words such as *rest, motion, other, not-being*.[28] Second, there is the problem that the interrelation word-thing is not always one-one, but frequently many-one.[29] There is then the ambiguity mentioned in sections
3 and 5. There are in fact ambiguities which for Plato seem to reach the
point of contradictions in cases where we use contrary words for one
entity; e.g. we call a man tall (relative to a child) and short (relative to

---

[23] *Cratylus*, 432D. Cf. section 33 below.
[24] 433B.
[25] 400D–401A.
[26] 386D–390B, 391D–393D.
[27] *Sophist*, 244B–245E. The Loeb edition is tr. by H. N. Fowler (Cambridge, Mass., 1961).
[28] 237A–257A.
[29] 251A–E.

a tree).[30] Third, there is the problem of an interrelation which is recognized as non-existent so that a proposition asserting the interrelation would be false. But if the proposition is negated and then becomes true, it seems that the resulting proposition asserts both the existence and non-existence of the interrelation.[31]

Plato still takes a word to be the revelation (the making open or apparent) of a thing and an instruction regarding the thing's nature.[32] But the interrelation of word and thing has become unreliable and needs to be secured. To know the name of a thing is not always to know the thing itself.[33] Hence the revelation of reality that the poets give in words is dubious and must be rejected.[34]

But for Plato the ever shifting and elusive phenomena of immediate reality are no more reliable than words. The absence of a firm ontic basis is the reason why the theory of the foundation of language advanced in the *Theaetetus* remains an isolated proposal in spite of its important insights. If reality had been indubitably articulate, Sophistry would have been impossible. But just as the Sophists had not criticized but rather adopted that part of Heraclitus' teachings which pointed up the unity of language and reality, so Plato testifies to the cogency of Heraclitus' insight in dismissing both language and reality as unreliable.

This joint dismissal is clearly stated in the *Seventh Letter* where Plato enumerates four dimensions of a thing: its name, its definition, the thing in its tangible presence, and the knowledge of the thing. All four are declared weak and inaccurate.[35]

In this connection, Plato consistently and emphatically describes the predicament of philosophy in the face of the infirmity of language. In the *Phaedo*, Plato points out how the inclination towards tangible things makes it impossible for man to become a philosopher; in the *Seventh Letter* he argues that definite commitment to language, partic-

---

[30] Cf. *Phaedo.* 102A–103A. Loeb edition tr. by H. N. Fowler (Cambridge, Mass., 1938). For ways to deal with this problem cf. Quine, *Word and Object*, pp. 126–127.

[31] *Sophist*, 237A. – To us these three difficulties appear to be confusions rather than genuine problems. In sorting out the confusions, we would in one way or another invoke the metaphysical distinction which is Plato's achievement and which, as we shall see, enabled him largely to dispel the confusions. The point is that the confusions *are* real problems as long as the metaphysical distinction is not a matter of course.

[32] *Cratylus*, 433B, 435D–E; in the *Sophist*, 262C–D, the sentence is regarded as a revelation in this sense.

[33] *Cratylus*, 438D–439B.

[34] *Republic*, 392C–398B, 595A–607A; Loeb edition in 2 vols, tr. Paul Shorey (Cambridge, Mass., 1953).

[35] *Seventh Letter*, 342A–344D; Loeb edition tr. by R. G. Bury (Cambridge, Mass., 1952).

ularly to written language, is inimical to philosophy.[36] Since the poets seem to bear eloquent witness *for* the power and adequacy of language, the condemantion of the poets is not a curious incidental feature of the *Republic*, but evidence of a profound dissent regarding the nature of language and reality.

The separation of language and reality is a necessary first step toward overcoming the ambiguity of the λόγος. But the separation can neither be tolerated as ultimate, because then words and language would no longer refer to reality, nor can it be relativized and given a basis by recourse either solely to language (since then there would be no truth and falsehood as the Sophists insisted) or solely to reality (since then there would not be any possibility of rising above reality in language; we could not speak *about* reality).

10. Language and the metaphysical distinction

This fundamental difficulty is overcome through the positing (or perhaps the discovery) of a third ontological realm, the realm of forms, essences, or ideas (τύποι, εἴδη, or ἰδέαι) which are both language-free and beyond immediate reality.[37] A consistent and consequential distinction is made here between familiar and tangible reality on the one hand and a realm of general and purely intelligible entities on the other. The natural or physical is opposed to the scientific or metaphysical.[38] This constitutes the metaphysical distinction.

The ideas are the prototypes of the fleeting and frail items of the everyday world which now, in relation to the exemplary and immutable reality of the ideas, becomes apparent as a secondary and derivative reality. Just as our commerce with reality attains (and to some degree always has attained) stability and success through reference to the ideas, so the vagaries of ordinary language can be dealt with through recourse to the ideas. The doctrine of ideas emerges everywhere as the

---

[36] *Phaedo*, 66B–69C; *Seventh Letter*, 341C–E; *Second Letter* (same edition), 314B–C.

[37] *Cratylus*, 432E–433A among countless others. Anagnostopoulos in "Plato's *Cratylus*," pp. 711–14 argues that "invoking the theory of Forms makes little sense in the present context" (p. 711). We must reply that (1) it is implausible that admittedly "Plato uses language which has always been associated with the theory of Forms" (pp. 711–12), but that he here uses it to a different purpose for he would then be using the locutions of his central theory for a more peripheral topic; (2) the ontological status of the "necessary and sufficient conditions" which are the supposed referents of the language of Forms is left unclear and the metaphysical distinction would have to be invoked after all if it were to be clarified.

[38] This is of course not the etymology of the word "metaphysics" which moreover was unknown to both Plato and Aristotle.

answer to the perplexing problems or as the grain of truth that can be salvaged from a traditional view.

Thus the nature theory of language is acceptable to the extent that the ultimate elements of language (letters or sounds) are copies, not of the incidental and variable acoustic shape that a phenomenon may have (as onomatopoeia would have it), but of the unchangeable essence (idea) of the thing.[39] The related view according to which a superior or divine namemaker had fashioned the words is valid if it is understood that the particular, incidental word, made by the namemaker, does not of itself evoke and re-present the thing; rather the individual word ("name") does this through participating in the ideal, never fully materialized name which achieves in an ideal and perfect way what a particular name never accomplishes but deficiently and fallibly, i.e. to let the thing be present.[40]

Where the interrelation is dubious, reference to the idea provides insight into the adequacy or inadequacy of the interrelation. This holds true not only for simple interrelations (word-thing) but also for higher order interrelations (word-word, i.e. interrelation-interrelation in a sentence).[41] If for instance Socrates says: "Theaetetus, with whom I am now talking, flies," Socrates obviously joins two words which stand for phenomena the ideas of which (*man* and *flying* as opposed to *bird* and *flying* or *man* and *sitting*) are incompatible.[42]

In addition to the proper joining of ideas within the sentence, the sentence itself must measure up to the idea of a sentence; i.e. it must be a syntactic unit composed of noun ("name" in the narrow sense) and a verb.[43] This is the first extant definition of these two types of words where a verb is roughly defined as indicating action and a noun as indicating the agent.[44]

---

[39] 423A–424C.

[40] 386D–390B, 391D–393D. – The namemaker is guided by the one ideal name "whether he be here or in a foreign land" (390A; cf. 389D). Here is the point where through the metaphysical distinction a universal grammar becomes possible. Cf. sections 20, 26, 52, and 53.

[41] 431B.

[42] *Sophist*, 259E, 262E–263D. – For Plato the conjunction *man – flying* was presumably a priori false. For a more detailed discussion of the relation of compatibility and truth see K. Lorenz and J. Mittelstrass, "Theaitetos fliegt. Zur Theorie wahrer und falscher Sätze bei Platon," *Archiv für Geschichte der Philosophie*, XLVIII (1966), 142–145.

[43] *Sophist*, 262A–D. This is an explication that goes in part beyond Plato. Plato did not speak of the *idea of a sentence*. But it seems a legitimate extension, especially in view of the subsequent tradition.

[44] 262A–D. Cf. R. H. Robins, *Ancient and Medieval Grammatical Theory in Europe* (London, 1951), p. 17. Plato uses the Greek equivalents of noun and verb in the (earlier) *Cratylus* (425A), in the *Republic* (601A), and in the *Theaetetus* (206D) without definitions and not necessarily in the technical sense.

The metaphysical distinction first gives rise to the philosophy of language, and it is henceforth a motive power in all philosophizing on language; it is everywhere a decisive force however hidden or suppressed it may be. But that it does not deal with all the problems of language which were uncovered by Plato is already apparent from the ambiguity of the explanatory reference to the realm of ideas, which is sometimes to an ideal ontic entity (e.g. the idea of *man*) and at other times to an ideal linguistic entity (e.g. the idea of *name*). The consequence is that at least some of the problems that obtain regarding the relation of thing and word are not solved by the doctrine of ideas, but simply transferred to the realm of ideas.[45]

More importantly, the problem of correlation is not only one *within* the doctrine of ideas, but the one that is basic *to* the doctrine of ideas. What the doctrine of ideas presupposes but can never furnish is an account of the essential nature (the idea) of the relation of idea to phenomena and an account of what essentially constitutes the idiosyncrasy of phenomena generally and in particular the uniqueness of a given phenomenon over against the realm of ideas.

It testifies to Plato's greatness that in the *Parmenides* for instance he bared these difficulties with an incisiveness that has not been surpassed since.[46] Moreover and more especially, he points to two phenomena which are decisive for the life of language, but not explicable according to the doctrine of ideas. The first concerns the correctness of words which is said to rest largely on custom.[47] Custom is not fixed by the eternal and immutable order or ideas, but grows and unfolds in the course of history. The other regards the validity of sentences which always requires an "about-which" (subject) of discourse.[48] Again, the intent of my speaking is not prescribed from eternity by ideas; it rather springs from the uniqueness of the situation and the speakers in which the discourse comes to pass.

---

[45] Success and failure are closely linked in Plato's program as we find it primarily in the *Cratylus*. Kuno Lorenz and Jürgen Mittelstrass come to a more positive conclusion in "On Rational Philosophy of Language: The Programme in Plato's *Cratylus* Reconsidered," *Mind*, LXXVI (1967), 1–20. The view here argued is closer to Josef Derbolav's in "Das Problem des Metasprachlichen in Platons 'Kratylos'," *Lebendiger Realismus*, ed. K. Hartmann and H. Wagner (Bonn, 1962), pp. 181–210. Anagnostopoulos in "Plato's *Cratylus*," pp. 716–17, denies that the theory of ideas is brought into play at all; but this is unacceptable as argued in note 37 above.

[46] *Parmenides*, 130A–135B; Loeb edition tr. by H. N. Fowler (Cambridge, Mass., 1963).

[47] *Cratylus*, 435A–B.

[48] *Sophist*, 262E.

II. The distinction between grammar and logic. Aristotle

The philosophy of language which first emerged in Plato's thought receives its articulation in the research of Aristotle (384–322 B.C.). All the resulting articulated divisions are in a sense philosophies of language. But they assume new names and procedures, and the new diversity and precision in the philosophy of language makes one comprehensive philosophy of language impossible.

Language comes most sharply and narrowly into focus where Aristotle determines its place in the ontological order of things, i.e. where he answers the question: What kind of thing is language, what other things is it related to, and how is it related to these things? Aristotle distinguishes four separable layers of reality. The most basic are the things or dealings in our world (πράγματα). These issue in copies or likenesses, namely in the affections of the soul. These affections in turn give rise to external signs (σημεῖα), namely sounds (φωναί). These sounds again are symbolized in letters (γράμματα).[49] We find here the roots of the modern disciplines *pragmatics*, *semantics*, and *phonetics*.[50] Moreover, it becomes apparent that the letters (γράμματα) represent the most typical and definitive precipitate of language, and it is for that reason that the investigation of language is henceforth predominantly grammar. In the written form, language exhibits the fixity and accessibility that scientific research requires.[51]

Beyond explicating the origin of grammar, Aristotle also concretely advances the state of this art by making more comprehensive and systematic distinctions than Plato. He distinguishes between letters, syllables, and words, defining "word" as the smallest meaningful unit of language.[52] He further distinguishes between nouns, verbs, and conjunctions, between phrases, propositions, and sentences. And in each

---

[49] *On Interpretation*, 16a4–8. I have used the Loeb edition, tr. Harold P. Cook (Cambridge, Mass., 1962). The references are to the Bekker pagination.

[50] The modern definition of these disciplines has first been outlined by Charles W. Morris, *Foundations of the Theory of Signs*. International Encyclopedia of Unified Science (Chicago, 1938–1962), vol. I, part 2.

[51] The Greek word γραμματική which is the origin of our word grammar originally designated the elementary instruction in reading and writing in ancient Greece. *Grammar* in its initial form is thus the practical and intuitive anticipation of later scientific grammar. Cf. Robins, *Grammatical Theory*, pp. 12 and 37 and Paul Abelson, *The Seven Liberal Arts*, 2nd ed. (New York, 1939), pp. 1–2.

[52] Actually he gives that same definition for "noun" and "verb" rather than for the general term "word". See *Poetics*, 1456b20–1457a31; Loeb edition tr. by W. Hamilton Fyfe (Cambridge, Mass., 1965). Cf. *Interpretation*, 16b26–40.

case, elaborate subdistinctions are made.[53] The resulting terms and insights have become nearly trivial for us. But this in itself is an indication of how thoroughly we have appropriated this view of language. At the bottom of the innumerable and sophisticated grammars that have been formulated since is the simple and consequential (metaphysical) distinction between the external ("grammatical") shape of language and its ("semantic") reference to the ("pragmatic") objects and events of our world.

Once the external shape of language was so precisely delimited, it became apparent that the recurring types of external patterns did not at all points consistently coincide with types of reference. In Heraclitus' thought, the λόγος was at once the tangible reality of words and the disclosure of the meaning of the world. Now that the former dimension was made the specific subject of the science of γράμματα, i.e. the subject of grammar, there originated a particular science of the λόγος (now taken in a narrower sense), namely logic, which was not concerned with the basic order of the world (which was Heraclitus' concern in his teachings of the λόγος), but investigated the basic modes of comprehending and expressing anything that can be encountered in or beyond the world. The λόγος which for Heraclitus was *the disclosure and unity of reality* is for Aristotle *a piece of language that refers to reality*, "a vocal sound that stands for something" (φωνὴ σημαντική).[54]

The distinction between grammar and logic is not a radical one in Aristotle's investigations.[55] For the most part they coincide; for instance the various externally, i.e. grammatically ascertainable positions of words such as *every* and *not* in sentences correspond to various basic forms of comprehension and signification, i.e. they indicate logical properties of a sentence. There are however logical distinctions that are not reflected in language as is the case with complex questions where the external form is insufficient as a basis for an understanding that could provide an answer to the question because the question is the external (grammatical) coincidence of two logically distinct ques-

---

[53] *Poetics*, 1456b20–1457a30 (the authenticity of this chapter has been doubted). Cf. also Miriam Therese Larkin, *Language in the Philosophy of Aristotle* (The Hague, 1971), pp. 27–33.

[54] *Interpretation*, 16b26–17a8. Aristotle's treatment of the λόγος, i.e. his logic, is narrower and more precise than Heraclitus' concern with the λόγος, but still broad and informal compared with modern logic. In this section, *logic* and *logical* are used in the comparatively wide sense. – While "λόγος" is a technical term for Aristotle, the etymological ancestor of "logic" did not have the technical meaning for Aristotle that "logic" has for us.

[55] The crucial point is that grammar and logic begin to diverge in Aristotle's research. Larkin in *Language in the Philosophy of Aristotle*, pp. 35–40, poses the question "Language: Grammar or Logic?" The question is complex and unanswerable.

tions.[56] Nor is it apparent from the external shape of two sentences having the same subject, but different predicates whether these propositions can be combined into one proposition with a complex predicate.[57] Similarly in the case of two sentences with the same (external) subject where the subject is ambiguous. Conversely, there are differences in the grammatical appearance that involve no logical differences, e.g. some differences in word order.

The criterion for coincidence or divergence of grammatical and logical features is the (univocal, ambiguous, or redundant) relation of the sentence to reality. The distinction between grammar and logic requires then a prior distinction of true and false sentences. And in turn, a sentence can be true or false only if it is intended to point out a fact. Not all sentences have this intention. Aristotle distinguishes therefore between sentences in general and sentences "that point out" (λόγοι ἀποφαντικοί, commonly translated as "propositions").[58] Only sentences that point out can be true or false.

We are here at the source of the emphasis on propositions in all subsequent logic and grammar. This emphasis first sets off sharply all other forms of speech and then devaluates them. First it properly establishes the fact that non-propositional forms of language are not true or false in the propositional sense, then it concludes that they are not true or false in any sense and hence either nonsensical or arbitrary. Aristotle mentions "man" as an item of language that is neither true nor false.[59] This of course is so if "man" is taken as a fragment of a proposition. However, there clearly are situations where one-word exclamations are exclusively true in the sense that any grammatically more complex expression would be awkward, ambiguous, or inefffective. Aristotle further contends that a prayer can neither be true nor false.[60] Again a prayer can be true in the sense that it actualizes the humility and sincerity that are called for when a mortal addresses the

---

[56] *Topics*, 160a35–160b13; Loeb edition tr. by E. S. Forster (Cambridge, Mass., 1966); *Interpretation*, 20b22–31.

[57] *Interpretation*, 20b31–21a34. One of Aristotle's example: (1) *that man is a cobbler* and (2) *that man is good* cannot be combined into (3) *that man is a good cobbler*; cf. on the other hand (4) *this is a man* and (5) *this is white*. Aristotle's explanation: "Predicates, if accidental to the subject or one to the other, do not coalesce into one" (21a8–10). Quine (*Word and Object*, pp. 103, 132, 138) would say that "good" in (2) is predicative, but syncategorematic (a qualifier of "cobbler") in (3). But Quine's distinction does not suffice (and is not intended) to deal with Aristotle's problem as (6) *this building is red* and (7) *this building is a barn* show. Cf. also J. J. Katz, "Semantic Theory and the Meaning of 'Good'," *Journal of Philosophy*, LXI (1964), 739–766.

[58] *Interpretation*, 17a1–5.

[59] *Ibid.*, 16a11–19, 17a17–20, 20a34–37.

[60] *Ibid.*, 17a1–5. Cf. Larkin, *Language in the Philosophy of Aristotle*, pp. 26–27.

gods; or it may be false because of the greed and vanity it reflects. Certainly, we make use here of a systematic ambiguity of the terms *true* and *false*. But systematic ambiguity is adequately dealt with only if the systematic bond and basis are recognized and none of the component meanings suppressed.

12. Language as instrument. Rhetoric and poetics

Language is no longer of itself the presence of the world; it rather is (1) a segment of the world, fixed and accessible in writing and as such the subject of grammar, (2) a means of pointing out and representing anything within the world and as such the subject of logic. Grammar treats of the shape of the instrument called language; logic deals with the possible functions of this instrument.

The general and instrumental view of language gives rise to additional disciplines in the philosophy of language which deal with the major ways in which language is in fact used, namely formal speech and poetry with their concomitant disciplines of rhetoric and poetics.

Both poetry and speech make use of language as a tool.[61] However, poetics and rhetoric do not present actual uses of language, but are in turn instrumental in a narrower way: they explicate systematically and generally the possibilities of using language in poetry and speech, thus exhibiting the instrumentarium of the poet and the speaker. It becomes evident here that once the λόγος has dispersed into language and reality, reality ever recedes from language and vice versa depending on where the emphasis is placed. In poetics and rhetoric the emphasis shifts frequently. Where Aristotle speaks of the subjects and aims of poetry and speech, language moves into relative obscurity. Where linguistic problems are investigated, comparatively little depends on poetry and speech as the contexts of these problems.

Hence the most explicit treatment of language is carried out under the same title in the *Poetics* and in *The Art of Rhetoric: style or diction* (λέξις). Grammatically speaking, style is the proper arrangement of meters and of the elements of language as they are isolated and described by grammar.[62] Logically, style is "presentation through words" and the knowledge of "how [not what] one must speak."[63]

In pursuing the various ways in which style actualizes grammar and

---

[61] *Poetics*, 1447a1–28, 1456a33–1456b19; *Rhetoric*, 1355b1–7, 25–35.
[62] *Poetics*, 1449b20–31, 1456b20–22.
[63] *Ibid.*, 1450b15–20; *Rhetoric*, 1358a36–1359a29.

logic, Aristotle explicates in a most sensitive manner what has since become the basic vocabulary of all stylistics: plot, high style (distinctive as opposed to ordinary parlance), metaphor, simile, antithesis and parallelism, clause, period, synonymy, homonymy, euphony, assonance, rime, pun, rhythm.[64] But since he insists that language rests on convention and since he has so sharply distinguished between language and reality, these terms cannot be grounded either in the natural unfolding of reality or in the pervasive order of the world, i.e. neither in φύσις nor in the λόγος.[65] Nor can the terms be derived from grammar or logic except in the trivial sense noted above. In stylistics, an entire dimension of language is isolated and eventually becomes irreducible. Aristotle lays the foundation for this development. Consider his treatment of metaphor. In a metaphor, one thing is made forcefully present through recourse to another. Aristotle investigates the finest differences and techniques of this sort of presentation.[66] But how language can bring about the coincidence of two different things without dissolving or losing either, and how on the contrary it creates a singularly unified and articulate reality, this question is neither posed nor answered by Aristotle.[67]

13. Language as the theme and the basis of Aristotle's investigations

In conclusion, we must show how the disappearance of the explicit philsosophy of language into grammar, logic, and stylistics is far less definitive and the division into these disciplines less rigid than it appears in a modern account. In Aristotle's philosophizing, the Greek language provided and preserved a living context of relations and ancestries that did not survive the translations. Qua context, language is for Aristotle more than the theme of investigation; it remains in an apparent and forceful way the basis of investigation.

We observed above that Aristotle does not explicitly relate metaphor to that ground and unity of the world that the Presocratics called φύσις or λόγος. But the relation still prevails obliquely. Aristotle insists repeatedly that the use of metaphor cannot be derived from something

---

[64] *Poetics*, 1449b20–1452a21, 1457a31–1459a16; *Rhetoric*, 1403b3–1414a29. A good many of these terms Aristotle may have taken over from the tradition.
[65] Regarding the convention thesis see *Interpretation*, 16a19–21, 27–29. Especially the second passage shows that the problem is more involved than may appear in the above presentation. Cf. section 13.
[66] *Poetics*, 1457a31–1459a16; *Rhetoric*, 1410b6–1413b2. Aristotle uses "metaphor" in a wider sense also. Cf. Larkin, *Language in the Philosophy of Aristotle*, pp. 72–75.
[67] Cf. section 23 below.

else.[68] The right use of metaphor is an indication of εὐφυία, i.e. of a felicitous disposition issuing from and following φύσις. The proficient use of metaphor is the sighting of the ὅμοιον, the pervasive likeness to which we respond in ὁμολογεῖν, i.e. in agreeing.[69] Metaphors must ἁρμόττειν, i.e. exhibit the pervasive harmony of the universe.[70] This they do if they proceed ἀνάλογον, i.e. according to the λόγος.[71]

The Greek word for style or diction itself is λέξις, a derivative of λέγειν: to assemble, to gather, to speak. Thus λέξις is parallel to λόγος, likewise a noun derived from λέγειν. In λέξις then we must realize not merely a particular way of saying things, but the speaking and the presence of the collected unity of the λόγος.

The Greek word for plot is μῦθος, which does not designate primarily a configuration of facts and events, but is the speech in which some reality becomes actual, above all the decisive deeds and fates of the gods, the myths.

An example for the interconnectedness of the grammatical terms is the word for case or inflection: πτῶσις. It means falling or tumbling, in particular the ways in which a die falls. Just as the die in being handled and thrown reveals its various aspects in its falls, so also noun and verb in their uses, i.e. in their cases and inflections.[72]

Finally an example from logic. The Aristotelian categories are usually taken as the highest, irreducible genera. Actually, κατηγορία is derived from ἀγορεύειν (to say publicly) by way of κατηγορεῖν: to say something of someone, to charge, to accuse. The κατηγορίαι then are the fundamental ways of saying something of someone or something. The categories are forms of language.

All these key words certainly also had a more restricted and technical meaning than the preceding discussions would lead one to believe. But it is significant for Aristotle that he initiates an era of scientific precision and yet had access to the suggestive thinking of the earlier period. With all the technical rigor of his linguistic research, he is still aware of the unsearchable power that language has as poetry: "For poetry is something that is full of the god."[73]

---

[68] *Poetics*, 1459a3–7; *Rhetoric*, 1405a2–9.
[69] *Poetics*, 1459a3–7. Cf. Heraclitus' fragments 50 and 51 in section 4 above.
[70] *Rhetoric*, 1405a9–11. Cf. Heraclitus' fragments 8 and 51.
[71] *Rhetoric*, 1405a9–11.
[72] This semantic derivation is not entirely certain. Cf. Robins, *Grammatical Theory*, p. 33. Cf. also Heidegger, *Introduction*, pp. 49–50.
[73] *Rhetoric*, 1408b17–18.

14. Language as a segment of reality. The Stoics and the classical grammarians

Presocratic philosophy is followed by Sophistry and can be adequately understood only in light of that event. Similarly it is necessary that we briefly take note of the work of the Stoics and classical grammarians so that the full sweep of the movement that begins with Plato and Aristotle comes into view.

The Stoics advanced logic by elaborating Aristotelian research and by adding substantially new parts.[74] Similarly, in their philosophy of language they distinguished in more subtle ways between the levels of reality that extend between reality and the spoken word. They distinguished between the thing (πρᾶγμα) or the designatum (σημαινόμενον) and the (verbal) sign (σημεῖον) as the extremes which are mediated by a meaning (λεκτόν) that is not identical with either the thing or the particular sign. The meaning which is approximately the same for all persons is again distinguished from the individual representation (φαντασία) that is never exactly the same for any two persons.[75]

As the threefold division of thing, meaning, and sign was more incisive, so the resulting spheres were more sharply isolated and hence more susceptible to autonomous investigation. This is especially true of the signs. The notion of the sign in the Stoic sense characterizes more successfully the dimension that was intended by the earlier notion of letters (γράμματα). Consequently, grammar attained its first culmination among the Stoics. They delimited for the first time a theory of the phonetic elements that compose individual words; they isolated five parts of speech and in characterizing them distinguished between the primary grammatical categories that constitute the parts of speech (verb, noun, etc.) and the secondary categories that modify the parts of speech and are, in some instances, shared by different parts of speech (number, person, etc.).[76]

The Stoics still insisted at least in some instances that to certain

---

[74] Ascription of Stoic teachings to individual philosophers is difficult because of the fragmentary and summary source material. The founder of the school at any rate was Zeno of Citium (336–264 B.C.), the main proponent of logical and linguistic research is Chrysippus (281–201 B.C.). The Stoic tradition was continuous into the first century A.D. Cf. Karl Barwick, *Probleme der stoischen Sprachlehre und Rhetorik*. Abhandlungen der sächsischen Akademie der Wissenschaften zu Leipzig, Philologisch-historische Klasse, vol. 49, no. 3 (Berlin 1957).

[75] See William Kneale and Martha Kneale, *The Development of Logic* (Oxford, 1962), pp. 138–158.

[76] See Robins, *Grammatical Theory*, pp. 25–36 and Gentinetta, *Sprachbetrachtung*, pp. 93–118.

classes (e.g. nouns) or forms (e.g. the dative case) there belonged a meaning inherent to those classes or forms. This insistence on inherent meanings continued to obscure pervasive morphological regularities. It was the achievement of the classical grammarians to sever these semantic connections further and to apprehend and present the outward form of Greek and then Latin in a way which remained unchallenged for more than thirteen centuries (i.e. up to our century) and provided the model for the description of all other languages during that period. The first of these men was the Greek grammarian Dionysius Thrax of Alexandria (first century B.C.); the men whose work was most consequential for the subsequent developments were the Latin grammarians Donatus (around 400 A.D.) and Priscian (around 500 A.D.).[77]

But in proportion as we get a firmer and fuller grasp on the outward form of language, one question moves quite into the dark and becomes ever more difficult to pose and answer, the question namely: How is it that the formal system described by grammar is so pervasively and flexibly meaningful? Or in other words: How can language present reality? It seems that the Stoics did in fact pose the question and that they answered it according to the φύσει view developed in the *Cratylus*.[78] But what was a metaphysical exploration in Plato has here become a scholastic and ontic position. Two segments of reality are given, the things and the signs; the question regards their connection only. The question how language can be the articulation and presence of all reality is irretrievably lost. Language in this profounder sense recedes, and so does reality when attention turns to language ontically conceived as noted before.[79] Things within the latter framework may no longer appear in their own right as things (πράγματα), but as mere variables of the system of signs, i.e. as designata (σημαινόμενα). Grammar is thus the execution of a program that had been conceived aphoristically and ironically by Gorgias.[80]

---

[77] Robins, *Grammatical Theory*, pp. 36–68.
[78] Cf. Barwick, *Probleme*, pp. 58–79 and section 8 above.
[79] Cf. section 12 above.
[80] Cf. section 6 above.

CHAPTER THREE

THE EXPLORATION OF THE RANGE OF LANGUAGE

15. The study of language in the Middle Ages

The dispersion of the philosophy of language into logic, grammar, rhetoric, and poetics which became apparent in Aristotle's thought did not entirely obliterate the common root of these disciplines. Research in these fields, to be sure, diverged more and more. But the educational organization which evolved in the system of the seven liberal arts provided at least a pedagogical unity. The liberal arts arose as a group of distinct subjects of research and education already in ancient Greece. They were taken over and further articulated by the Romans and eventually furnished the basis of Medieval education.[1] A division of the seven arts was made here into two groups, the *trivium*, comprising grammar, rhetoric, and logic, and the *quadrivium*, consisting of arithmetic, geometry, astronomy, and music.

The *trivium* was also called the science of language *(sermocinalis scientia)*, and its branches taught one to speak congruously or correctly (grammar), ornately or elegantly (rhetoric), and truly (logic).[2] However, this rationale for the divisions within the science of language was not so much the articulation of a living and apparent unity as an a posteriori justification of a traditional aggregate of disciplines. For quite different explanations were given for the same unity; it was for instance argued elsewhere that language either affects or signifies. If it affects, it is directed either towards our powers of comprehension (and is then the subject of logic) or towards our power of acting (and is

[1] See Abelson, *Liberal Arts*; Heinrich Roos, *Die Modi significandi des Martinus de Dacia. Forschungen zur Geschichte der Sprachlogik im Mittelalter*. Beiträge zur Geschichte der Philosophie und Theologie des Mittelalters, vol. 37, no. 2 (Münster, 1952), pp. 72–84.

[2] See C. Thurot, *Extraits de divers manuscrits Latins* (Paris, 1869), p. 470 and Ernest A. Moody, *Truth and Consequence in Medieval Logic* (Amsterdam, 1953), p. 1.

then the subject of rhetoric). If language signifies, it is the subject of grammar.[3]

Of the three branches, rhetoric was most immediately practical and so most dependent on application. However, the monastic and scholastic life did not provide an opportunity for formal legal or political speeches. Rhetoric therefore did not undergo significant changes excepting the manuals for letter writing *(artes dictaminis)* which answered a real need.[4]

Logic continued in the Middle Ages to separate itself more sharply from the content or matter of language, i.e. from the uniqueness and seeming arbitrariness of reality as it is reflected in language. This led on the one hand to a more refined and consistent presentation of the formal features of language. The two disciplines of Medieval logic which carry out this formal or syntactic analysis are represented by the treatises on syncategorematic terms and the treatises on consequences.

The greater formal rigor in these fields led, on the other hand, to more sharply formulated questions regarding the connection between language and reality. If language is in important ways a formal system, what are the elements in language that refer directly to reality and what is the basis of the referential power of these elements or terms? Or in different words: Which properties enable a term to refer to a thing? These problems are dealt with in the treatises on the properties of terms.

16. Terms and things. John Buridan

Obviously the status of the formal features of language is the more precise and secure, the more definitely tangible and indubitable the material correlate is. It is therefore quite consistent to delimit reality as being constituted merely by the physical objects of the world with their concrete properties. There is then no such reality as the universal concept *house*; what is real are the individual houses out there. Similarly with the real white things as opposed to *whiteness*. *House* and *whiteness* are merely names, latin *nomina*; hence this ontological position is called Nominalism. According to the opposing view, Realism, universal concepts have intelligible (though of course not material) reality.

We shall discuss some of the problems that arose on the basis as

[3] Thurot, *Extraits*, p. 470.
[4] See Abelson, *Liberal Arts*, pp. 52–71.

sketched above by following John Buridan (about 1300–1358), a Nominalist, whose work represents the perfection and completion of a development that had begun with Peter Abelard who in turn drew from Aristotle's *On Interpretation* and commentaries thereon, from Stoic material and Priscian's grammar, among other sources. Abelard's thought was given the nominalistic rigor by William of Ockham, the teacher of Buridan.[5]

The first property of a term is signification.[6] A word such as *man* signifies something to us, it delimits a certain type of entity. Signification is the referential power of a word, and any significant categorematic word has this power. It derives from the concept, which is the immediate and universally given mental counterpart of something and which is therefore called a natural sign. The natural sign is then matched with a certain physical entity (a string of letters or sounds) by convention. A term is thus an artificial (conventional) sign.[7] The referential power is actualized in sentences.[8] Following Aristotle, Buridan makes the sentence the locus of truth because it is through predication that words not only delimit a certain type of entity but stand for one or more of the tokens of the type in question. The property of *standing for an entity* is called *supposition*.[9] The presence or absence of supposition presupposes signification and in turn determines the truth or falsehood of a sentence. The truth of a sentence is established if of each of its categorematic terms ("house", "dog", or whatever) I can say "this is a dog" (or "a house", or whatever), pointing to the entity for which "dog" or "house" or whatever stands. If a term is quantified by such words as *some, every, no,* and the like, there is a conversion procedure

---

[5] The subsequent discussion is based on John Buridan, *Sophisms on Meaning and Truth*, tr. Theodore Kermit Scott (New York, 1966). Scott has also provided an extensive and helpful introduction.

[6] *Sophisms*, pp. 63–82. – A "term" is a categorematic word.

[7] Buridan interposes the concept between word and thing in order to deal with significant terms which yet stand for nothing (e.g. *chimera* which is a complex concept, composed of real, but incompatible constituents) and with other problems of extension and intension. Cf. *Sophisms*, pp. 70–78. Alan R. Perreiha has argued, in "Buridan and the Definite Description," *Journal of the History of Philosophy*, X (1972), 153–60, that Buridan operates with an equivalent of Russell's notion of definite descriptions (cf. section 35 below) and thus solves problems such as posed by *chimera*. This might have been consistent with Buridan's Nominalism and would have obviated his recourse to the notion of concept at least in this case. But it is at odds with Buridan's actual practice. Perreiha inconsistently adduces Buridan's mention of (natural vs. artificial) concepts as evidence for Buridan's grasp of the notion of definite descriptions (p. 158).

[8] *Sophisms*, pp. 83–96.

[9] *Ibid.*, pp. 97–108.

for every case such that the quantifiers are eliminated and the test by
ostension (demonstration) is applicable. E.g. the sentence

(1) Some men are politicians.

is converted into the disjunctive series:

(2) This man is a politician or that man is a politician or ...

enumerating all men in question by pointing out, by proper names, or
in some other way.[10] The scope of individuals for which supposition is
to be tested can be restricted or amplified by qualifiers of space and
time. It is obvious that the referents of "some men" differ in these
three examples:

(3) Some men are politicians.

(4) Some men were politicians.

(5) Some men in the United States are politicians.

These problems are treated under the heading of ampliation and restriction.[11]

A categorematic term not only signifies a type of entity and can then
stand for some tokens of this type; it lights up moreover a context of
related types of entities unless it has the sharply defined deictic function that belongs to proper names, demonstrative and egocentric pronouns. Such terms are called absolute, the other categorematic terms
(e.g. common nouns) connotative.[12] In certain sentences, connotation
must be removed (the intertypical context must be cut off) or specified
if these sentences are to be intelligible. I can for instance say of a white
piece of wood that will be charred: "The white will be black." In at
least one sense, this sentence is contradictory because the white is
white and will never be black.[13] To avoid misunderstanding, I remove
the context (connotation) of white things from the subject by replacing
the connotative term by an absolute one, e.g. "the white" by "this
thing".

Connotation is also the word that Buridan uses to designate the
scope of discourse of verbs such as *know, understand, be acquainted*, etc
(i.e. of *verbs of propositional attitude*): more precisely, he speaks of

---

[10] These distinctions are quite common in Medieval Nominalism, but far less innocent than
they appear. Cf. Peter Thomas Geach, *Reference and Generality* (Ithaca, New York, 1962),
pp. 47–107. The points made in section 17 do not require a close discussion of these difficulties.

[11] *Sophisms*, pp. 144–179.

[12] *Ibid.*, pp. 109–143.

[13] In another sense, the sentence is quite acceptable. Frequently, Buridan's points are
misdirected when English is taken as the object language because of semantic differences
between English and Latin. This point should have deserved some elaboration in Scott's
Introduction.

objects of knowledge, understanding, or acquaintance as connoting the reasons for being known, understood, or made acquaintance with. That failure to specify the connotation that attaches to an object of a verb of propositional attitude can give rise to confusion is clear from this example.[14] Assume that Robert's father is approaching us in the dark. I happen to know that Robert's father would meet us here, but Robert does not know this; all he knows is that there is *someone* who is approaching us. I might then say to Robert:

(6) You know the one approaching.

He could well reply that he does not. Who is right? It depends on the connotation of "the one approaching" or, equivalently, on the scope of discourse of "you know". "The one approaching" in (6) has at least two connotations.

(I) "The one approaching" is known on the basis of the cognitive possibilities of the situation in which (6) is uttered.

These possibilities are by hypothesis restricted.

(II) "The one approaching" is known through cognitive situations and processes which are prior to the situation in which (6) is uttered.

Since "the one approaching" is by hypothesis Robert's father, we know that there are such prior situations and processes for Robert.

Now Robert is correct in denying (6) if

(a) in (6) Robert is said to know "the one approaching" with the connotation (I) and (II), and

(b) (6) is taken to claim that Robert knows "the one approaching" with connotation (II) *by way of connotation (I)*; or more precisely, (6) expresses the claim that Robert is in a position to identify "the one approaching" with connotation (II) on the basis of his knowledge of "the one approaching" with connotation (I).[15]

It is obviously condition (b) which is not met; hence Robert is correct in denying the truth of (6) in the sense of (a) and (b).

On the other hand, (6) is true if it is taken in the sense of (a) only though Robert would have to plead ignorance if asked if (6) were true in sense (a).

Finally (6) is true if

---

[14] This is essentially Buridan's example. See *Sophisms*, pp. 124, 126, 133–134.
[15] Here *know* is roughly equivalent to *recognize*.

(c) Robert is said in (6) to know the one approaching with connotation (I).[16]

It would seem to us that this is an overly restricted connotation and,
alternatively, a trivial sense and scope of *know*.

But it is precisely this connotation which Buridan favors because
this restriction enables him to maintain the simple and rigorous nominalistic correlation of word and thing. Obviously the expressions
"Robert's father" or "your father" and "the one approaching" stand
for the same thing; hence we would expect them to be interchangeable
salva veritate. Substitution of "your father" for "the one approaching"
yields:

(7) You know your father.

How does (7) compare with (6)? There are two possibilities. First one
might not at all recognize (7) as a substitute of (6), i.e. one might not
recognize a direct relation as obtaining between (7) and the event of a
person approaching speaker and hearer in the dark. In that case (7)
would be false in senses (a) through (c) (with appropriate substitutions
in conditions (a)–(c) and connotations (I) and (II)); but (7) would be
true in this sense:

(d) In (7) Robert is said to know his father with connotation (II)
(with appropriate substitutions in (II)).

Second, if (7) is uttered simultaneously with a gesture of pointing to
the one approaching, then the cognitive situation of (7) is so enriched
that connotation (I) involves connotation (II) and (7) is true in all the
senses (a) through (d) (substitutions provided).

Supposition, we said, is a term's property of standing for something.
But this is again an ambiguous locution in that a term such as "man"
may stand for radically different things. Cf. "Man is a rational animal"
with "Man is a three-letter-word." In the former instance, "man"
stands for all human beings; in the latter, "man" stands for itself as an
orthographic, printed entity.[17] The former supposition is called personal (also formal or significant), the latter material.

This difference of supposition is really a difference of intention or aim.
In uttering or writing "man" I can intend or aim at entirely different

---

[16] Here *know* is roughly equivalent to *perceive*.

[17] In a common notation not used here for technical reasons a sequence of letters is
to be significant (is to refer to something) whenever it appears in ordinary print or (for
occasional emphasis) in italics. Whenever the sequence of letters appears in single quotes,
that sequence is to be taken as merely a mark to which we may or may not assign meaning.
This notational convention, though quite effective, is itself based on a complex philosophy
of signs and symbols. Nelson Goodman has shed some light on this problem in *Languages of
Art. An Approach to a Theory of Symbols* (Indianapolis, 1968), pp. 127–173.

entities. Buridan wrestled with similar intentional ambiguities in what he (and the tradition) called *insolubles,* i.e. sentences that we would call paradoxes.[18] They were not thought to be strictly unsolvable by Buridan. He was confident that he had procedures, establishing conclusively the truth or falsehood of these sentences. The relative recalcitrance of the problems and the subtlety of the solutions made the insolubles particularly instructive pieces of language. An insoluble is for instance:

(8) If every proposition is affirmative, then none is negative.

According to the treatises on the consequences (Buridan's own in particular), this proposition is a conditional, composed of two propositions, the antecedent and the consequent. The truth of a conditional depends on the respective truth of the component propositions. More precisely, it was held that a conditional is always true except when the antecedent is true and the consequent false.[19]

Now it appears that (8) is true merely by virtue of its form, i.e. solely by virtue of its syncategorematic terms and their arrangement. The truth of the antecedent seems formally to entail the truth of the consequent, and the falsehood of the antecedent the falsehood of the consequent. But let us assume now that the antecedent ("every proposition is affirmative") is true; assuming further that every proposition is either true or false, the truth of the consequent ("no proposition is negative") follows indeed from the truth of the antecedent; and yet the consequent is false because there is in fact at least one negative proposition, namely the consequent. Thus we have a true antecedent and a false consequent and hence a false conditional.[20] Intuitively, however, it still seems quite true to say: "If every proposition is affirmative, then none is negative."

[18] I.e. if we follow Quine's distinction where a paradox is a conceptual puzzle which can be solved within the framework of our present thought whereas an antinomy requires a (partial) transformation of that framework if it is to be accommodated. See Quine, "The Ways of Paradox," in *The Ways of Paradox and Other Essays* (New York, 1966), pp. 3–20.

[19] This corresponds to what is called *material implication* in modern logic, and it is fraught with corresponding difficulties. Cf. the selections in Gary Iseminger, ed., *Logic and Philosophy* (New York, 1968), pp. 60–108 and particularly pp. 195–244.

[20] One might argue that if the consequent is false then so is the antecedent, and the conditional is true. To save the insoluble one has to use some devious argument to the effect, e.g., that the antecedent when uttered can in fact be assumed to be true since the falsifying consequence is as yet nonexistent.

17. The antagonism of language and reality

Buridan carries the philosophy of language to a point where language not only is no longer the unified and comprehensive disclosure of the world (as the Heraclitean λόγος), but where there is an antagonism between reality and language such that a certain state of affairs can be the case (is "possible" in Buridan's terminology, i.e. possibly true in fact), but this cannot be expressed in all logically permissible ways (it may not be "true" in Buridan's terminology, i.e. true in language). It could for instance be that there are no negative propositions in the world. But if I were to state this by saying

(9) No proposition is negative.

then there would be at least one negative proposition, namely (9) and what I said is wrong. We have here a state of affairs that is the case on condition that it not be stated in the language of (9). Buridan deals with this problem by preserving in cases of conflict truth of fact, disregarding what bearing truth in language may have on truth of fact; i.e. in (8) above, he disregards the falsehood of the consequent that springs from language since the consequent is possible (can in fact be true), and he thus preserves the truth of the conditional in agreement with intuitive comprehension.[21]

These difficulties are analogous to those arising from confusion of supposition. For (8) seems true when our intention is directed towards the significance of (8), but appears to be falsified when our intention regards both the significance and the form in which the significance of (8) is expressed. Buridan, as we saw, solves the problem without being able to give a satisfactory explanation for the solution. If we concur with Buridan that the solution is nonetheless correct and generally applicable, we have to admit that Buridan relies on powers of language that do not enter into his philosophy of language. More generally we must say that the high degree of precision and explicitness in his philo-

---

[21] Scott says in his Introduction, p. 52: "A proposition is possible just because what it asserts could be the case, not because it could be true ... Possibility is a property of propositions, not of 'states of affairs,' but it is not the property of possible truth." This quotation, when contrasted with what has been said above, brings out nicely the difficulty of drawing a sharp line between language and reality. To be sure, *possibility* as Buridan uses the word is a property of propositions. But it is a property that is also and necessarily a property of a state of affairs (it is also and ultimately ontic possibility; Scott circumscribes this by saying "what it asserts [some state of affairs] could be the case [is possible]"). There is something awkward about attributing ontic possibility to a proposition; but this is inevitable if the paradox of (9) is to be understood. Instead of *ontic possibility* one could speak of *semantic possibility*; but *semantic* would in turn require an explication in terms of language (logic and syntax) and reality (the ontic).

sophy corresponds to a like degree of covering up dimensions of language.

Buridan solves paradoxes at the expense of further paradoxes. The significance of his work lies in the fact that he did not simply shift the burden of proof to paradoxes of the same order. Rather he revealed and solved some definite problems of language and by implication pointed to entirely different problems a solution for which is presupposed in his own problem solving although the implied problems are not recognized by him.

These fundamental problems center around the paradoxical phenomenon that the sharp division which Buridan draws between language and reality is always and already undercut by language and yet undercut in such a manner that the division is preserved.

In the solution of the insoluble (9), the decisive distinction between language and reality or the true and the possible is made by means and within the scope of language. Buridan *tells* us of the distinction, and he can do so successfully only if he is able to tell us in language and without falsifaction that certain states of affairs enter into certain types of language only on penalty of being falsified.

Similarly, the ontology which according to Buridan is at the bottom of significant and true instances of language rests on language and owes its stability and accessibility to language. At first sight, Buridan seems precisely to evade such dependence by reducing supposition (the matching of word and object) to ostension. The sentence

(10) The desk is grey.

is true if among others the condition is met that "desk" stands for a desk; and this is so if pointing to the appropriate object I can truly say: "This is a desk." Nothing but agreement based on convention seems to be invoked in this test.[22] One might object first that neither on this page nor in Buridan's book has there been a pointing hand nor a pointed-to desk. Instead bits of language have been produced. One could in turn refute this objection by an argument from a hierarchical order of signs such that at any particular occasion the tangible and primal act of establishing a sign which is the fundament of the hierarchy can be performed. But any ostension requires the fulfillment of con-

---

[22] Characteristically, Buridan does not use the notion of *concept* as a natural sign for an explanation of supposition; it is a relatively foreign body in his philosophy of language. At first sight, to be sure, it seems that the difficulties presented in the sequel could be solved by recourse to *concept* in Buridan's sense. However, the explanation of concept formation would then have to rely on analogous implicit and decisive support by language if Realism is to be eschewed.

ditions which can be satisfied only by means of language. First the situation must be characterized as ostensive, otherwise the recipient of the ostension may take my behavior to be an act of greeting, warning, or in any of other innumerable ways. Second the object of the ostension must be delimited beforehand. If I point my finger to the desk, the recipient could otherwise conclude that I am showing him my finger or that I am indicating a certain direction or pointing to a particular material, color, shape, or to a part of the desk, or the desk and the chair, etc. It would obviously be self-defeating to try and remove the ostensive ambiguities by means of ostension.[23]

Whenever Buridan uses notions that resolve paradoxes but do not in turn lead to paradoxes, these notions are relatively independent of or opposed to his ontology, and their explanatory power is proportional to a lack of precision. This is the case with signification, connotation, concept as a natural sign, and intention, a term that is occasionally invoked as a basis for the explication of homonymous expressions.

Since we can talk about these difficulties and elucidate them with some measure of success, we seem entitled to the conclusion, anticipated above, that language undercuts the distinction of language and reality in taking the distinction over into language (presenting it in language), yet without at the same time dissolving the distinction. But as the discussion of connotation of objects of knowledge has shown, language depends in turn for its efficiency on the significance of a situation and on its relation to that significance. Sentence (7) is significant depending on whether and how the significance of the situation is understood and on how the situational significance bestows significance on language.

Such meaning bestowal is a strictly original event which cannot be replaced by any kind or amount of speaking. If I launch into a series of sentences explaining and specifying the correlation of words and things, the last of these sentences (or the one of the highest explanatory order) either is certified by the significance of the situation and then lights up all other past and future discourse, or such certification is not forthcoming, and language is then not truly under way.

This root problem can be approached in the grand manner of Heraclitus and Vico, but also in Buridan's painstaking and minute

---

[23] On the problem of ostensive definitions generally cf. Quine, *Word and Object*, pp. 35–40 and Ludwig Wittgenstein, *Philosophical Investigations*, 3rd. ed. (New York, 1968), sections 28–35. Regarding the basic significance of this problem for Nominalism, see Richard Rorty, "Pragmatism, Categories, and Language," *Philosophical Review*, LXX (1961), 197–223.

analyses of the collisions of language qua thing with language qua meaning. There is, to be sure, the constant danger that one may get lost in fine distinctions without ever getting to the root problem.

18. Speculative grammar. Thomas of Erfurt

Latin was the scholarly language of the Middle Ages; it had ceased to be a vernacular, i.e. a living language for everyday life. Hence there was a need for aspiring scholars to acquire a command of Latin, and there were two tools to this end: grammar and the writings of the Classical authors. Grammar came to be used as a term for both subjects and thus included what was formerly called poetics and what later developed into the history and theory of literature. Grammar in this sense had therefore two related functions: first to make scholarly discourse accessible, second to acquaint students with the wisdom of the Ancients.[24] The works of the classical grammarians Donatus and Priscian were largely adequate for this purpose. There was little need for further development, and in fact there has been little change in grammar generally till half a century ago.

The success of these grammars was based, as we have seen in section 14, on the consistency in describing Latin from a morphological point of view. One who wants to master Latin has to acquire (aside from the vocabulary) a command of a certain multiplicity of forms and syntactic constructions. An inventory of forms is the most economical way of dealing with this material. Explicit consideration of meanings would have created needless confusion since it would have led to recalcitrant questions such as why there were different forms to convey the same meaning and how one form could serve different functions without ambiguity.

Philosophically, this was nonetheless an unsatisfactory treatment of language. Certainly, one of the fundamental facts of language is that it conveys meaning, be it cognitive, emotive, or whatever. A morphological grammar does not deny this; on the contrary, it is based on the implicit assumption that the significative power of language is so strong that as soon as the forms of language are assembled even into the most rudimentary and artificial pieces of actual language (normally the sentences of exercises), this significative power immediately and automatically infuses form with meaning. A morphological description

---

[24] Cf. Roos, *Modi significandi*, pp. 84–99; G. L. Bursill-Hall, *Speculative Grammars of the Middle Ages* (The Hague, 1971), pp. 13–36.

of language always proceeds in anticipation or through recollection of meaning in actual discourse.

Towards the end of the Middle Ages, there was a growing realization that the various grammatical forms can be understood fully only if they are exhibited as modes of signifying.[25] In addition to the morphological or empirical grammars there was a need for a philosophical or speculative grammar. These endeavors were carried out in initial opposition to the pursuit of grammar as a preliminary and subordinate stage of the study of literature, and it was again eclipsed by this concept of grammar in the Renaissance.[26]

We want to take as a basis for more detailed discussion the work of Thomas of Erfurt, formerly attributed to Duns Scotus, which bears the usual title *On the Modes of Signifying, A Speculative Grammar* (first half of the 14th century) and is the best known among these grammars.[27]

The fact that the author is comparatively unknown and was not definitely identified till 1922 is indicative.[28] In their instrumentaria, the speculative grammars were quite conventional. They took Priscian's grammar as a guideline and sought to explain the mode of signifying of all the major grammatical forms in terms of Scholastic (Realistic) epistemology and ontology. Substantively, their achievement was limited; nevertheless, the problem that they raised was of the first importance, and even within the narrow bounds of the conventions which they adopted unquestioningly, they attained some remarkable insights that were regained only recently.

[25] The emergence of this realization is an intricate development traced by Jan Pinborg, *Die Entwicklung der Sprachtheorie im Mittelalter*. Beiträge zur Geschichte der Philosophie und Theologie des Mittelalters, vol. 42, no. 2 (Münster, 1967), pp. 21–56. Cf. also Roos, *Modi significandi*, pp. 99–120.

[26] See Robins, *Grammatical Theory*, pp. 80–81 and Martin Grabmann, "Die Entwicklung der mittelalterlichen Sprachlogik," *Philosophisches Jahrbuch*, XXXV (1922), 129–130. Another significant factor in the demise of speculative grammar was the second rise of nominalism. See Pinborg, "Die Erfurter Tradition im sprachlichen Denken des Mittelalters," *Universalismus und Partikularismus im Mittelalter*, ed. Paul Wilpert (Berlin, 1968), pp. 181–184 and *Entwicklung*, p. 135.

[27] Joannes Duns Scotus, *Grammaticae Speculativae Nova Editio*, ed. Marianus Fernandez Garcia (Quaracchi, 1902). There is an English edition, *On the Modes of Signifying. A Speculative Grammar*, tr. Charles Glenn Wallis (Ann Arbor, 1938). Wallis says rightly (p. iii): "This is only the draft of a translation ..." On the reputation of this grammar, cf. Pinborg, "Erfurter Tradition," p. 174.

[28] The identification was made by Grabmann, "Sprachlogik," pp. 132–135, 199–202. Cf. Pinborg, "Erfurter Tradition," p. 175.

19. The interconnections of being, understanding, and signifying

Thomas of Erfurt takes two approaches towards exhibiting the foundations and ramifications of the significative power of language. The first approach is more general and consists in the presentation of an intricate system of interrelations between language and reality.[29] More particularly, this system tries to point out the partial identities and differences between the significative power of language and the cognitive and ontological realms.

The basis of this system is the distinction of three spheres or modes of reality: the modes of being, understanding, and signifying. The mode of being is proper to things inasmuch as they are distinct from, and thus the object of, understanding and signifying. Precisely in order to preserve the autonomy of things in their existence, Thomas leaves the mode of being relatively isolated in the system of interconnections. In Thomas' words: "... he who speaks of the mode of being speaks of things inasmuch as they are given simply or from the point of view of their existence."[30]

The modes of understanding and signifying, on the other hand, which are the modes of operation of the intellect and of words respectively, exhibit a multiplicity of dimensions.

First each of the modes is divided according to the operative distinction of activity and passivity. In the operation of the intellect, there is some (active) understanding and some corresponding (passive) thing that is understood. Similarly in the significative operation of the word.

Each of the four resulting dimensions is then divided according to the ontological distinction of matter and form which can tentatively be taken in the straightforward way illustrated by a statue where we can have the same matter (marble) with different forms (David and Apollo) or the same form (Apollo) with different matters (a bronze statue and a marble statue).

We now have a tree of distinctions with the trunk *mode* on the first level, branching on the second level into *understanding, signifying,* and *being,* the first two branches being divided on the third level into *active*

---

[29] *Grammatica,* sections 1–19. References are to the section numbers which are found both in Garcia's text and in Wallis' translation. A detailed exposition of Thomas' grammar along with the grammars of Siger of Courtrai and others is given by Bursill-Hall in *Speculative Grammars.*

[30] *Ibid.,* sect. 12: "... qui dicit modum essendi dicit proprietatem rei absolute sive sub ratione existentiae." The translation is mine.

and *passive,* and finally each of these four branches bifurcating on the fourth level into *formal* and *material.*

(1)

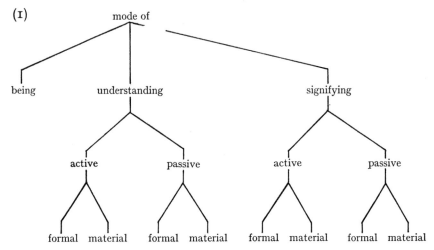

These divisions lead to a tree of one, three, four, and eight branches on levels one through four respectively as diagram (1) suggests. But actually, some of the branches coalesce, thus reducing the number of branches and transforming the tree into something like a net as is apparent in diagram (2).[31] Thomas presents the structure of this net-

(2)

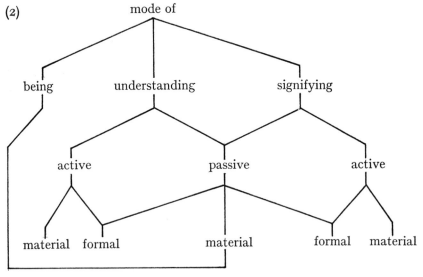

---

[31] P. A. Verburg has given an equivalent quasi-algebraic formulation of these modal interrelations (which Thomas of Erfurt shares with Radulphus Brito) as follows. A stands for

work in a series of questions and answers regarding the agreement (convergence) or difference (divergence) of the various elements.

On the third level, the passive modes or dimensions of understanding and signifying (what is understood and signified) coincide (the branches converge). On the fourth level, the matter of what is signified and understood is just one: the tangible, irreducible dimension of a thing that never enters into an act of signifying or understanding (there is never any material marble in my understanding or saying "Michelangelo's David"). Thus the material dimension of what is understood or signified coincides with the mode of being.

It is nonetheless the *thing* which I understand or signify; and it is the form of the thing understood or signified that is present in my understanding or signifying. Hence, on the fourth level, the formal mode of the passive understanding and signifying (i.e. of the very thing that is understood and signified) coincides with the formal modes of (active) understanding and signifying. But since understanding and signifying are distinct modes, there remain two different forms. This difference is anticipated on the third level: the active modes of understanding and signifying are distinct. Each has its matter: in signifying it is the word (as an acoustic entity or as an inscription), in understanding the thought (scholastically it is the passive or possible intellect; in modern terms one might think of a neural event or a brain state). And each has its form: the thing qua understood or qua signified.

To put the same matter differently, the forms of signifying and understanding coincide with the form of the thing; but they do not simply coincide with one another, since e.g. the word "marble statue" essentially (and that means: qua form) differs from the thought "marble statue". They are alike only insofar as the thing *(marble statue)* is intelligibly (i.e. qua form) present both in the word and in the thought "marble statue".

But not only are the forms of the active modes also the form of the passive mode (of the thing); they are also both immediately (though

the mode of being; B stands for the passive mode of understanding; C stands for the passive mode signifying; b stands for the active mode of understanding; c stands for the active mode of signifying. Then the following holds.

   A = B = C materially
   A ≠ (B = b) ≠ (C = c) formally
   A ≠ b ≠ c materially and formally

Quoted by Pinborg, *Entwicklung*, p. 120. – These interrelations are the result of a complex controversy and history. See Pinborg, *Entwicklung*, pp. 109–23. The following remarks explicate this result systematically. Cf. also Bursill-Hall, *Speculative Grammars*, pp. 48–55, 348, 352–53 where further distinctions of these modes are represented diagrammatically.

not exclusively) the form of the material thing as diagram (2) shows. This is a reflection of the (familiar Realistic) claim that the form *marble statue* has its primary existence in the thing, not in the word or the thought. The form qua form of active signifying (i.e. of the word) is only mediately the form of active understanding (i.e. of the thought). Word, thought, and thing are materially separate entities and connected only through their common intention (i.e. their form).[32]

This is a bold and to some extent illuminating representation of the interplay of identities and differences of language and reality, an interplay that is a challenge for every philosophy of language. It presents an articulate and uncommon formulation of, though not an answer to, the questions that are currently dealt with under the headings of reference and intensionality, and of language and thought.

Obviously the scheme is fraught with serious difficulties on every level. These can only be mentioned here. First, it is not at all clear on what grounds the modes of being, understanding, and signifying can be distinguished as three coordinate realms since each mode is inseparably bound up with the others.[33] Being is nothing unless it is intelligible and signifiable; understanding is nothing unless it *is* (is real) and is signifiable, signifying is nothing unless it *is* (is real) and is intelligible.[34] Second, the active-passive distinction overlaps with the form-matter distinction. Third, "form" and "matter" are used ambiguously; "form" means both *the intelligible structure of the thing* and *a particular aspect of the thing*; "matter" means correspondingly *the unstructured and unintelligible substratum of a thing* and *the substantial "what" of a thing which can be viewed from different standpoints*.[35] Fourth, it is not clear whether the scheme represents an ontological order or a genetic process. In the Scholastic tradition, the diagram can be read not only from top to bottom, but also roughly from left to right. On that view, some being is rendered intelligible through abstraction by the active or agent intellect (understanding), and the abstracted form is given existence in

---

[32] Actually word and thought have two forms each; otherwise word, thought, and thing would not be recognizable as three separate entities. This duplicity is apparent in Buridan's distinction between personal (or formal or significant) and material supposition. In section 52 below, the difference is rendered in terms of semantic as opposed to linguistic ontologies.

[33] It is therefore impossible to find an appropriate generic term for the three modes and for their conceptual issues. Hence the vague terminology in the explication above.

[34] This first difficulty could be solved scholastically along the lines of the doctrine of the transcendentals. Cf. section 24 below.

[35] These ambiguities are systematic and designate one stage in the development of *form* from the Platonic sense *(true reality)* to the predominant modern meaning *(formality)*. For the historical details see Pinborg, *Entwicklung*, pp. 115–17.

the passive intellect (understanding). The thing, once it is understood, is then signified through the activity of the word.

There is no simple way of dealing with these questions. Ontological systems can attain some consistency and precision if they leave thought and language unquestioned. Similarly, linguistic theories can afford to be clear and cogent if the ontological status of the controlling concepts remains unchallenged. But there is no rigorous and schematic way in which the interrelation of language and reality can be delineated. Whatever distinctions and identifications regarding language and reality are established, either language or reality blur the distinctions and thus weaken the identities.

20. The depth and extent of the signifying power of language

The second way in which Thomas of Erfurt investigates the significative power and complexity of language is more specifically grammatical. The achievement of the investigation lies in Thomas' discovery of levels of grammar. Whereas morphological or empirical grammar clings to language as it is given directly in its various forms, Thomas in his speculative grammar realizes that the function of language can be properly grasped only if we turn to higher levels or structures of language which in some way issue in what is given directly, but cannot be simply read off from this final issue. On the other hand, without this theoretical dimension, the empirically most immediate level of language must appear significatively opaque or distorted.

The investigation falls into two parts: the first is a discussion of individual forms and is called etymology by Thomas; the second is syntax.[36] As indicated before, Thomas follows the traditional division of language into parts of speech. Every such part is seen as the intersection of substantive ("essential") and formal ("accidental") modes of signifying. Thomas explicates this Stoic division in terms of the Scholastic distinction between substance (an entity insofar as it is distinct and autonomous) and accidents (traits that inhere in a substance and do not exist independently).[37] The application of the Scholastic di-

---

[36] The first part comprises sections 20–183, the second 184–230. – Thomas' word for syntax is *diasynthetica*.

[37] Presumably to avoid confusion between the ontological term *substantia* and the grammatical term *substantivum*, Thomas calls the two modes of signifying *essentialis* and *accidentalis*. In section 4, Thomas seems to make a distinction which is antecedent to the one mentioned and distinguishes between signification which makes a vocal sound into a basic semantic unit (*dictio*), and the consignification which makes that unit into a part of speech,

chotomy is based on the observation that a word apart from its varying (i.e. "accidental") inflections and the ways it is compounded with other words signifies in a typical and constant (i.e. "substantial") mode that it shares with other words. Nouns, for instance, all signify "in the mode of entities and determinate apprehension" according to Thomas; that is they all signify something that has some sort of being and is captured in some definite apprehension.[38] From this most general substantive mode Thomas descends by way of division to more specific ones, e.g. common and proper nouns, and so down to the most specific ones.

The formal or accidental modes are expressed in the inflections or compositions of words and consist in the case of the noun in gender, number, case, etc.[39] While some of these can be identified quite easily with a particular mode of signifying (e.g. *feminine gender* signifies *of female sex, plural* signifies *more than one)*, there are in all instances numerous counter-examples.[40]

In some areas, Thomas succeeds in going beyond conventional explanations; he shows for instance that all cases can express either the origin and foundation *(principium)* or the goal *(terminus)* of the state of affairs expressed in a sentence whereas traditional grammars usually define the nominative case as the one expressing the origin or foundation of the sentence's state of affairs, the oblique cases supposedly indicating various goals or ends of the subject.[41] He thus makes a distinction which is parallel to the modern one between logical and grammatical subject. However, the specific characterizations of each case are plainly circular or, putting it more charitably, they appeal to presumably irreducible linguistic experiences. The genitive for instance is defined thus: "The genitive is the mode of signifying qua origin and foundation or goal respectively with the added property of functioning according to the locution *'whose' some other thing is* ... ."[42]

i.e. an essential mode of signifying. But here as elsewhere, Thomas is rather loose in his distinctions. Cf. note 45 below.

[38] For the comparative flexibility and precision of this definition see Martin Heidegger, *Die Kategorien- und Bedeutungslehre des Duns Scotus* (Tübingen, 1916), pp. 170–173. A reprint of this treatise is now available in *Frühe Schriften* (Frankfurt am Main, 1972), pp. 131–354.

[39] The accidental modes are further divided into those whose modification is restricted to the modified word (absolute ones) and those that establish through their modification a syntactic relationship between the modified word and some other word (relative ones).

[40] Thomas deals with just one counter example and not very successfully at that.

[41] Exceptions are the vocative (goal only) and nominative (origin only). Because of the latter exception, Thomas ends up with two origins in passive constructions, a consequence that he does not consider.

[42] *Grammatica*, section 88 (my translation). This is a fairly interpretive translation of a phrase that is highly idiomatic. Wallis, after some unsuccessful attempts (section 85), simply

The different classes of noun declensions in Latin exhibit a definite formal regularity; but here Thomas does not seek to explicate concomitant modes of signifying although this is to some extent possible.[43] And he is similarly cautious in other instances of morphological regularities.[44]

Thomas treats of syntax under the titles of construction, congruity, and perfection.[45] These terms stand for what Thomas calls the transformations of the modes of signifying.[46] Among other things, the analyses of the modes of signifying were to show that these modes represent elements (Thomas calls them *constructibles*) which according to their nature can be joined in certain ways. The union of two constructibles is called a construction. The constructibles, however, are not united coordinately; rather one constructible is always dependent relative to the other which terminates (complements) the first. The principal constructible of every construction is the finite verb, and it is dependent, requiring as a terminating constructible a noun.[47] The verb can in turn terminate an adverb and the noun depend on another noun. Thomas considers only extremely simple constructions; and in particular he does not deal with the question whether one constructible can terminate or depend on more than one constructible. From his discussion and examples it seems that he visualizes the structure of a sentence as having its center in the finite verb which is dependent on a noun in one direction and thus constitutes with this noun the primary construction and which terminates some constructible in the other direction and thus constitutes a secondary construction with that constructible; this concatenation procedure can presumably continue in-

gives the Latin expressions *(ut cuius est alterum* in this instance). Heidegger, *Kategorienlehre,* p. 197, is more felicitous.

[43] E.g. nouns derived from past participles and ending in -*or* frequently designate agents. Cf. *Grammatica,* section 95.

[44] *Ibid.,* sections 135, 137–143.

[45] Thomas emphasizes in sections 225 and 229 that in the order of construction, congruity, and perfection each subsequent transformation presupposes and essentially enriches the preceding one. There are however numerous remarks about construction that preempt the functions of congruity (sections 4, 22, 187, 229) and perfection (sections 187, 188); and there are remarks about congruity (sections 219, 229) that leave no function for perfection. For the sake of simplicity and intelligibility I will present Thomas' view as though the three types of transformations were consistently separated.

[46] Latin *passiones*: the processes that the modes of signifying "undergo" and the results of these processes.

[47] See sections 190–196. Thomas obscures this important observation through his ill conceived attempt at characterizing transitive and intransitive constructions through the position of the determining noun relative to the verb (preceding noun: intransitive; subsequent noun: transitive). The problem of a satisfactory distinction between transitive and intransitive constructions seems to have been generally recalcitrant; cf. Pinborg, *Entwicklung,* pp. 53, 127–30.

definitely in both directions by way of tertiary and subsequent constructions.

Construction is the union of constructibles. It is the task of congruity to secure the *due* union of constructibles.[48] Apparently the laws of construction are so broad as to permit undue or deviant unions. Congruity is to eliminate these and to fix the remaining ones. However, undue unions are of two kinds, meaningless unions such as "quickly man" and improper unions such as "categorical cap."[49] The former are called discrepancies and must be eliminated, the latter are called repugnances and are the concern of the logician (of the semanticist as we would say); grammatically they are admissible. All congruous constructibles are then fixed through the specification of endings.

Construction unites constructibles; congruity secures (filters and fixes) these unions. However construction is a potentially infinite process which is not terminated by congruity but merely checked and labeled. It is the task of perfection to determine at what stage the generative and explicative processes of construction and congruity are to be stopped. Perfection is guided by the purpose "of expressing a composite concept of the mind and of generating perfect sense in the mind of the hearer."[50]

The three transformations are obviously not temporally and empirically successive stages in the process of speaking. Presumably the intent of my speech (perfection), the concatenating of words (construction), and the external characterization of the concatenations by means of endings (congruity) are empirically more or less simultaneous. However it is just such a departure from the empirically given that enables me to see how a string of sounds can have a definite physiognomy such that it is eloquent and informative as a whole. The sequence of sounds that is given to the listener is like the successive assembling of brushstrokes, each actualizing certain possibilities and excluding others, each

[48] These terms have a convenient ambiguity in Thomas' usage, designating grammatical manipulations *and* their results.

[49] We would call the former syntactically deviant, the latter semantically deviant. However, in a highly inflected language such as Latin with a correspondingly free word order, I can syntactically unite almost any two words if I am free to determine the endings. The area of syntactical deviance is therefore much smaller, and given Thomas' weak syntactical theory it is not at all possible to delimit this area concisely. It is probably for that reason that Thomas deals under the title of *discrepancy* with a problem that we would expect to be covered by *construction*.

[50] *Grammatica*, section 227 (my translation). – What Thomas explicates in the analysis of the transformations is in Johannes Lohmann's terminology the *status perconstructus* which according to Lohmann is the end and goal of the history of language. See his *Philosophie und Sprachwissenschaft* (Berlin, 1965), pp. 133–135.

entering into definite relationships with all prior ones until with the last stroke I see a certain face or figure that means something to me. In such a sketch, the sequential genesis is inevitable but ultimately immaterial, and I easily abstract from it, concentrating on the emerging configuration which in the end is totally present and explicit, covering up the sequential dimension.[51] In hearing a sentence, I similarly respond to the entire configuration which however is never given explicitly and as a simultaneous whole. Accordingly, the individual parts of speech are significant as the surface of an intricate structure of significations which all coalesce and are hidden in one temporally extended phonetic compound. The further we move away from the accidental terminations of these structures in immediately observable features, the closer we come to the substance of the structure, i.e. to those dimensions that are necessary and universal for the identity of the structure in question. This is merely implied in Thomas' grammar. In other speculative grammars, however, the conclusion is in fact drawn that all grammars are essentially one and the same and differ only in accidental (low level) traits.[52]

In the light of modern research, we are inclined to affirm Thomas' outline of syntax in principle, and we can, on the other hand, clearly determine the shortcomings of his outline: his transformations are too weak to generate any considerable fragment of the possible Latin sentences.[53] They are too weak for two reasons: First, Thomas was not sufficiently resolute in his departure from the empirical data; his theoretical terms (noun, verb, etc.) are just one step removed from the terminal empirical elements; and so he cannot explicate structures that encompass several terminal elements. Second, theoretical terms of a higher order would have led to interconnections of the terminal elements that would not have been merely serial but hierarchic.[54] And even such

---

[51] Such simultaneous and interwoven presence of all parts is the ideal mode of actuality not only of a sentence but possibly of an entire literary work of art. Such is, e.g., Thomas Mann's claim for his *Magic Mountain*; see his "The Making of the *Magic Mountain* [1953]," in *The Magic Mountain*, tr. H. T. Lowe-Porter (New York, 1965), pp. 724–725.

[52] See Pinborg, *Entwicklung*, pp. 24–30 and Thurot, *Extraits*, pp. 122–128. The problem of universal grammar becomes important again in sections 26, 52, and 53. Cf. also section 10 above, particularly note 40.

[53] A very brief comparison of Thomas' grammar and Noam Chomsky's approach is given by Robert G. Godfrey, "Late Medieval Linguistic Meta-Theory and Chomsky's Syntactic Structures," *Word*, XXI (1965), 251–256. Cf. sections 51 and 53 below. See also Bursill-Hall, *Speculative Grammars*, pp. 327–41.

[54] There is an order (hierarchy) of dependences in the string that is the result of *construction*. One could formalize this by means of arrows with subscripts. However, the hierarchy is merely postulated and not proper to this (primitive) formal system. Cf. also note 41 and the above remarks on whether two words can depend on or terminate a single third word. Further cf. Bursill-Hall, *Speculative Grammars*, pp. 337–38.

a generative procedure would have required as a complement rules that would have permitted variations in the terminal order as it emerged from the generative procedure, i.e. rules of transformation.

We tend to be much more doubtful about the first and principal part of Thomas' grammar which tries to show two things: First, that the vocabulary of a language falls into basic modes of signifying; second, that these modes of signifying are so structured as to fit together in certain definable larger units which we call sentences.[55] Even granting adequacy to the guidelines of conventional morphological grammar, it is apparent that Thomas fails the first task in at least two ways: he admits the impossibility of assigning a mode of signifying to certain grammatical regularities (e.g. the classes of declensions and conjugations); and to some features, signifying power is assigned in a circular or merely appellative way (e.g. the cases). Where he succeeds in assigning modes of signifying to grammatical forms (nouns, pronouns, verbs, etc.), the results seem at least debatable.[56] Thomas fails the second task in that the transformations, contrary to Thomas' claims, are in no essential way derived from the signifying power of their elements.

In spite of these shortcomings, it is clear that Thomas' conception of grammar is broader than what is covered by current research in generative and transformational grammar to which in other regards it bears such surprising resemblance. Against this broader concept, a decisive limitation of the present endeavors comes into relief quite sharply as we shall see later on.[57] We have touched on this problem at the conclusion of the discussion of part one of Thomas' grammar. It became apparent there that an adequate account of what it means to speak must carry linguistics over into epistemology and ontology. More particularly, the connection between linguistics and ontology turned out to have two aspects. One is the constitutive and regards the question what constituents must be distinguished in an actually and fully present instances of language. The other aspect is the significative one and concerns the problem of how reality comes to be present in actual instance of language. Both aspects are dealt with again and in different ways in part two of the speculative grammar. The analysis of levels of

---

[55] In the early Wittgenstein's terminology, this appears as an attempt at delimiting the logical space of the sentences through the modes of signifying. See sections 32 and 33 below.

[56] The project of the so called *inhaltsbezogene Grammatik* of Leo Weisgerber and his school is a much more thorough and sophisticated attempt in this direction. But it faces the same difficulties as Thomas did. See Weisgerber's *Die vier Stufen in der Erforschung der Sprache* (Düsseldorf, 1963).

[57] See sections 51–53.

language is a type of constitutive analysis. The term *perfection* designates the representing power of language. It will become clear that present grammatical research has worked very successfully in the constitutive realm. But precisely through those successes, proper access to the radical problem of signification has been all but closed off.

21. Theology and language. Thomas of Aquino

It is debatable whether Thomas of Aquino (1225–1274) is primarily a philosopher or a theologian. Undoubtedly, he is not a philosopher of language. Still it is possible to systematize the references to language in his works into a philosophy of language.[58] Although Thomas of Aquino's writings antedate those of John Buridan and Thomas of Erfurt, it is apparent from such a systematization that already in Aquinas' time many of the later views were either current or under discussion, and Thomas uses these for his metaphysical and theological purposes.

What is of interest in Aquinas' philosophy are not these incidental and technical remarks, but those sections of his thinking where the problem of language becomes of systematic concern.[59] Obviously the central object of Thomas' reflection is God, be he the god of the philosophers or the God of Abraham, Isaac, and Jacob. When the question as to the reality and nature of God is posed, language turns out to be the privileged dimension or medium in which God is present to man. More concretely, God speaks to man through nature and revelation, man speaks to God in prayer and of God in philosophy and theology. Since God, on Thomas' account, is the ground of reality or is being itself, Thomas is led to speak about the problem of language and reality in a way which is logically and linguistically far less explicit, but in some ways more radical than the investigations of Buridan and Thomas of Erfurt, and it is therefore discussed in conclusion of the Medieval period.

The most explicit and extended treatment of language is found in question 13 in the first part of the *Summa Theologiae* where Thomas deals with the names of God.[60] The initial article of this question

---

[58] This has been done by Franz Manthey, *Die Sprachphilosophie des hl. Thomas von Aquin* (Paderborn, 1937).

[59] Thomas' philosophy is of course just one possible systematic context for this problem which has received much attention in the last 25 years. A good survey of the various contributions in the field is provided by Ronald E. Santoni, ed., *Religious Language and the Problem of Religious Knowledge* (Bloomington, 1968).

[60] I have used the Latin-English edition of the *Summa Theologiae*, vol. 3, tr. Herbert McCabe (New York, 1964). I will use the standard abbreviation where "Part One, question 13, article 1" is rendered as 1a, 13.1.

regards the difficulty of referring to a transcendent being by means of a language that is appropriate to finite entities. The answer to the problem is evasive in the sense that it defines the range of language as coextensive with thinking and notes that some sort of inferential knowledge of God is possible. In the second article the problem is redirected to language when Thomas asks "whether any word is used with respect to God in a primary way." [61] He rejects the answers that take a predicate such as *good* to be a concealed negative *(not evil)* or causative *(the cause of all goodness)* and insists, with reference to the intention of the ordinary speaker, that when we say *good* of God we use a word that usually refers to created things and hence is inappropriate in the sense of being unusual when referring to God; but it is most appropriate in the sense that in connection with God it designates goodness itself which is the foundation of all good things that we know directly. The interpenetration of adequacy and inadequacy, found in positive predicates, holds similarly for propositions as is argued in article 12. Propositions are inadequate in that they unfold one thing into subject and predicate which runs counter to the oneness of God. On the other hand, it is the singular peculiarity of a proposition to achieve and present the unity of subject and predicate; since no entity equals God in his undivided unity, a proposition attains its highest actuality when it speaks of God.

This is the central point of Aquinas' reflection on language, which is presented in a number of alternative ways in the remaining articles. Thus the words applied to God are metaphorical in the mode of their expression (the *way* in which we express ourselves in calling God a lion is mediate or secondary), but literal in their intent (*what* we mean by lion is directly true of God).[62] And again because of the relative inappropriateness of our words in discourse about God, they express meanings that are distinct relative to us (and are so heteronymous), but point to the one undifferentiated reality of God (and are in that sense synonymous).

22. Analogy

In talking about God, we use words that apply to creatures as well and, as we have seen, in a certain way primarily so. Are these words, refer-

---

[61] *Loc. cit.* (translations are mine).

[62] Article 3. The same point is made in article 6 where the relative primacy of the metaphorical usage is emphasized.

ring to radically different beings, used univocally (without any ambiguity) or equivocally (homonymously)? The first usage would deny the fundamental difference between the world and God, the second would render discourse meaningless. Thomas proposes a third usage where a word spans a difference in its reference, a difference however that is structured and held together in a definite way. This is analogical usage.[63]

Analogy is a relation that is expressed by a word, e.g. "healthy". Let us call such a word *analogical*. The analogical word constitutes the relation of analogy between two further words, e.g. "diet" and "man"; let us call these words the *analogues*, and let us speak of one analogue being *analogous* to the other with respect to the analogical word.

If one of the analogues (e.g. "animal") is the primary subject of an analogical word (e.g. "healthy") and the other analogue (e.g. "urine") is its subject in a derivative or secondary sense (e.g. urine is healthy not in itself, but as a symptom of health), then we speak of *attributive analogy*.[64] Speaking more generally, attributive analogy obtains wherever the analogy is grounded in a direct ontological relation between the analogues, for instance in the cause-effect or the substance-accident relation.

But if a word contains within itself the power of predicating something significant of two essentially different entities, we say that it constitutes *proportional* (i.e. *relational*) *analogy*; for the interaction of the one analogy with the two analogues can be expressed in a relation (proportion) of one or more terms where the variables range over the analogues or some entities that are related to the analogues as components or bases of the analogues.

Vision for instance is a proportionally analogical word since it applies to the intellect as well as to the sense of sight.[65] It expresses the

[63] Article 5; cf. article 10. – *Analogy* in Thomas is a central ontological and linguistic problem. It has therefore received a vast amount of scholarly attention. Much of the material is dealt with by Marcia L. Colish in *The Mirror of Language: A Study in the Medieval Theory of Knowledge* (New Haven, 1968), pp. 161–223, especially pp. 209–222.

[64] Thomas does not have an explicit terminology and is moreover not very consistent in his distinctions for reasons that will be discussed later. The present account follows *On Truth*, tr. Robert W. Mulligan, James V. McGlynn, Robert W. Schmidt, 3 vols (Chicago, 1952–1954), 2.11 corpus; the Latin text in *Opera Omnia*, ed. Vernon J. Bourke, 25 vols (New York, 1948–1950), vol. 9. – A different acount of analogy in *Summa*, Ia 13.5 corpus.

[65] This may be for us or in English a philosophical thesis rather than an explication of the ordinary meaning of "vision". But that would not of itself invalidate the thesis but merely move the problem into another arena, possibly one that is as important as that of ordinary language analysis. Cf. what Edmund Husserl has to say about *seeing* in *Ideas. General Introduction to Pure Phenomenology*, tr. W. R. Boyce Gibson (New York, 1967), pp. 75–76, 350–354 and Martin Heidegger on *sight* and *seeing* in *Being and Time*, tr. John Macquarrie and Edward Robinson (New York, 1962), pp. 182–188.

way in which the power of grasping and appropriating which some *x* possesses is located in some entity *y*, where *x* is either "the intellect"or "(bodily) vision" and *y* is "the mind" in the case of the intellect and "the eye" for bodily vision.

A word that is proportionally analogical may also have an ordinary univocal use; "vision" for instance is ordinarily used univocally in reference to the eye. Relative to this ordinary use, the analogical use is called *metaphorical*. Words which are proportionally analogical without reference to an ordinary use (such as *being* and *good*) are said to constitute *proportional analogy proper*.[66]

The function of analogy is to secure talk about God which is both meaningful (nonequivocal) and cognizant of divine transcendence (nonunivocal). But "analogy" is rather the title of a problem than the solution of it. For even after analogy with its two varieties has been introduced, the problem of how significance and adequacy are jointly possible in discourse about God persists. This appears from Thomas' indecision as to the appropriate kind of analogy. In the treatise *On Truth*, Thomas expressly rejects attributive analogy because it presupposes an ontological tie between God and creation which would deny God's transcendence. But in the *Summa Theologiae*, Thomas declares the foundation of analogy to lie in the fact that "whatever is said of God *and* creatures is said according to a certain ordination that the creature has to God as its principle and cause in which all the perfections of things pre-exist in a pre-eminent way."[67] But this ordination would seem to be expressed most adequately through attributive analogy.

This type of analogy also secures connotative meaning for the name "God". The most adequate name of God is "He who is" precisely because it is freest of finite implications and designates existence itself.[68] But for this reason it is also furthest removed from what we understand directly and completely. However, through attributive analogy, the name "God" (whether we accept the etymology mentioned by Thomas or not) draws meaning from what we take to be effects of God: his providence and care. "God" can acquire such meaning only if

---

[66] It is possible to distinguish further types of analogy. A primarily technical and terminological survey of Thomas' analogy is given by James F. Ross, "Analogy as a Rule of Meaning for Religious Language," *International Philosophical Quarterly*, I (1961), 468–502. – *Analogy* is of course a form of systematic ambiguity. Cf. sections 5 and 6 above and section 24 below.

[67] *Summa Theologiae*, 1a, 13.5, corpus of the article.

[68] Article 11.

we understand providence and care in the immediate sense which is instantiated by men.[69]

An entirely different problem arises in the case of proportional analogy. Here the analogy is not grounded in an ontological relation which in turn is primarily fastened to one of the analogues; rather it is the power of language which mediates between the finite and the infinite. But if there is this third power, God's transcendence and omnipotence is challenged from a direction which is entirely different and rather more mysterious than the danger of assimilating God to finite creation. We come to the same problem when we investigate the kind of discourse that is said to be directed from God to man.

23. Metaphor

When God addresses man, there is again a plurality of senses as Thomas explains elsewhere in the *Summa*.[70] The plurisignification is effected by metaphorical or symbolical use of language; it bestows intelligibility and universality on revelation by presenting the recondite in a tangible and familiar way that is open to all; it renders revelation idiosyncratic so as to shield it from abuse. The plurality is secured against external confusion by the unity of the vehicle (the representing image) of the metaphor; the inner consistency, underlying the plurality, is guaranteed by, and to be explained by reference to, the author of revelation, God, who comprehends at once what for us is unfolded into a multiplicity.

This view is given a more detailed exposition through a two-stage theory of meaning. A metaphorical expression is said to have at the first stage the literal meaning which is the designatum of the expression, i.e. the thing referred to by the expression.[71] If we were to say "the arm of God wrought miracles", the literal meaning of "arm" would be *bodily limb*. Further, the expression has by way of the designatum at a second stage a spiritual meaning.[72] "The arm of God" means *God's power*.

The literal meaning, then, serves as a barrier for the disbeliever

---

[69] Article 8.

[70] 1a, 1.9 and 10. The Latin and English text in *Summa Theologiae*, vol. 1, tr. Thomas Gilby (New York, 1964).

[71] The literal meaning can have one of three modes: "historical" (descriptive), "etymological" (explanatory), "analogical" (see below).

[72] This again is threefold: "allegorical", "moral" (prescriptive), "analogical" (pointing beyond itself without an allegorical vehicle).

because he cannot go beyond it. For the believer, it provides in its immediacy a secure avenue to the spiritual meaning. For the theologians, it prescribes a scope of possible interpretation and a point of reference. This account has its merits as a systematic rendition of what was current in Thomas' days and as a pedagogical directive. Philosophically it is unsatisfactory because it does not explain the origin of, and the passage to, the second stage. Thomas invokes God as the author of spiritual meaning and faith as the guide to it.

Obviously, the two-stage theory of meaning depends on the discreteness and cohesion of at least the first stage. In calling the meaning of this stage "literal", Thomas suggests that the expression in question has just the definite and autonomous meaning that is required. But in admitting a plurality of literal senses, among them the analogical, Thomas undercuts his theory. The analogical meaning, presumably literal, extends already to the divine and is so spiritual. An expression as an isolated verbal entity does not convey just one meaning. The occurrence of that expression in some piece of language is therefore not *of itself* a sufficient indication of the presence of just one definite meaning. It is difficult to realize this because usually one of the competing meanings is tacitly given a priority, and this primary meaning is taken as being always present, e.g. "arm" means primarily *bodily limb*.[73] If the omnipresence of this meaning is inviolable, competing meanings are degraded to modifications of the primary meaning. The claim is that the primary meaning is self-sufficient while secondary meanings require for their intelligibility the (perhaps subliminal) presence of the primary meaning. So if "arm" means (in the secondary mode) *power, work, loving embrace,* then I can understand all this only if I also understand that "arm" means primarily *bodily limb*. But not vice versa.

However, the claim that there can be an autonomous primary meaning is unfounded. "Arm" in the literal meaning has significance and cohesion because it can be power, work, love, and the like. The literal *arm* would disintegrate into meaninglessness were it not for its transliteral significance. Any understanding of and concern with something like an arm is possible only through the presence of what Thomas calls spiritual meaning.

But spiritual meaning is elusive and ambiguous. Institution of the literal meaning promises to provide a meaning that, to be sure, is

---

[73] I am using Thomas' rough definition.

narrower and more prosaic than the spiritual, but also determinate and reliable enough so that we can curb abuse of the word and get on with our everyday problems. To have provided fixed meanings (ideas) which emancipate us from the vagaries of language and reality is the achievement of Plato. Thomas' use of the literal meaning reflects Plato's theory of ideas and anticipates scientific accounts of reality which seemingly render the literal meaning precise and thus provide points of reference which lie beyond the idiosyncrasies of language and improve on the crude and frequently inconsistent items of the everyday world.

These fixed and workable meanings, however, are not self-sufficient. But Thomas seems to make them so; and the passage to the spiritual meaning does then no longer appear as an advance to the basic and decisive dimension, but as the addition of some possible embellishment to the basic literal meaning. Thomas might have argued that whenever we speak of *arm*, we speak more or less directly, but necessarily in any case, of something like power, work, love.[74] And we do so, not in mentally adding to *arm*, but in understanding *arm* itself fully. In the language of revelation, this understanding may reach its highest intensity, an intensity that cannot be sustained in everyday language, but may nonetheless radiate transformatively into that language. In the discussion of the names of God, Thomas had at least entertained the possibility that a word attain its fullest force in a metaphor which would therefore not be a derivative usage. In the metaphor "God is a lion," the vehicle "lion" does not mean the zoological species *Felis leo*, but it means *power and majesty*. Yet a metaphor differs from a simile in that tenor ("God" in the present case) and vehicle of a metaphor are not like one another in a specifiable respect as would be the case in "God is like a lion" (where the common trait is implied) or in "God is strong and imperial like a lion" (where it is expressed).[75] The import of a genuine metaphor cannot be adequately presented in other words.[76] Conversely, the reality that is opened up in it cannot be present but in the metaphor.

[74] Scientific discourse of *arm* (in anatomy, physiology, etc.) has the unique trait of suspending directness (in the sense above) to the degree of seeming elimination of all directness. But at one point, the subliminal and sustaining directness must come into the open.

[75] The presence of "like" does of course not consistently distinguish similes from metaphors. – The *vehicle-tenor* terminology is due to I. A. Richards, *The Philosophy of Rhetoric* (New York, 1965 [first published in 1936]), pp. 95–101.

[76] Such metaphors are variously called "metaphors that cannot die" (Alston, *Philosophy*, pp. 103–106), "irreducible metaphors" (Paul Edwards in Santoni, *Religious Language*, pp. 146–155), or "depth metaphors" (Wheelwright, *Heraclitus*, pp. 94–99). As Wheelwright shows *(loc. cit.)*, depth metaphors are akin to what Quine calls antinomies. Cf. note 18 above.

We have found before that the meaning of a word is not a sharply delimited entity but the horizon of the experiences which are deposited in the word and the focus of the relational network that these experiences have woven. Overlappings of the networks give rise to ambiguities and synonymies. In a pun, a wide field of interconnecting networks is lit up at once from two distant points through the likeness in sound of two words; and if the pun is successful, the entire area between the two points comes to life and to light.[77]

And now in a metaphor, a new region for networks and a new horizon for experiences is opened up. Such a creative event takes its point of departure from the established meanings of tenor and vehicle, but then transforms both these meanings and gives rise to new dimensions of language without giving rise to a single new word; for the new areas that a metaphor makes available cannot (not yet, in the case of an eventually dead metaphor; never, in the case of a great metaphor) be centered around the focus of a word and embraced by the horizon of that word.[78]

24. Language and rational theology

Analogy and metaphor are recognized by Thomas as linguistic phenomena. But it has become apparent that, properly investigated, they lead to problems that go to the roots of meaning and reality and thus beyond language. An understanding of the root problems of meaning and reality is already an understanding of God. This understanding of God is not directly revealed by God, but derives from the nature of reality. Thomas, in opposition to theologians such as Anselm of Canterbury and Bonaventure and as a student of Albert the Great, defended a clear demarcation between the natural and the revealed knowledge of God. Now as we have seen, it is in pursuit of problems of language that natural knowledge of God announces itself. There lies then a natural theology in the study of language, and the place of Thomas' remarks in the Summa testify to this. But Thomas is, on the other hand, very cautious. Whereas he readily accepts the universal rational theology that comes from a study of being, language is to remain a mere medium where the uniqueness of the Christian God announces itself. Thomas' metaphysical groundwork does not allow for a *positive* elucidation of historicity in language (if such elucidation is at all possible). Hence

---

[77] Cf. sections 3 and 7.
[78] Cf. Goodman, *Languages*, p. 72.

Thomas' treatment of analogy is ultimately lacking in consistency, and with regard to the status of metaphor, he takes the consistent but simple position according to which there are two separate levels of meanings, the literal and the spiritual where the latter derives its power and validity from without language, i.e. from the authority of revelation.

This cautious view still allows reality to emerge *through* though not *from* language. The most singular instance is creation where the world comes into being through God's speaking. In the human realm, things are done with words in the sacraments where God comes to be present in some way through the speaking of the appropriate words.

The simultaneous coming forth of language, reality, and the divine towards which analogy points, is only preserved in the etymology of the word "analogy"; it designates a relation ἀνὰ λόγον, according to the λόγος. But there is also a systematic treatment of the unfolding of the λόγος when Thomas speaks of the way in which being unfolds itself in the transcendentals of *the one, the true,* and *the good.*[79] Whatever has being, possesses oneness, truth, and goodness to the extent of the power of its being. Truth has its final issue in the proposition. Thus language springs from the same root as, and is co-original with, the coherence and the value of reality. But again, this unfolding of being is not a strictly principal event, but one that is relative to the finitude of man and does not include or touch the transcendent God.

[79] *On Truth,* 1.1 corpus.

CHAPTER FOUR

LANGUAGE AND THE RISE OF THE MODERN ERA

25. Language and the foundation of science and reality. Descartes

The beginning of modern philosophy is signaled by Descartes' (1596–1650) fundamental questioning of all knowledge. The instrument of examination was the methodological doubt which unmasked all traditional knowledge as ultimately unfounded and left no certainty except itself: the process of doubting. Such reflection was not novel in itself and had been undertaken in much the same way by Augustine some 1300 years before. The significance of Descartes' doubt lay in the new concept of knowledge which was the positive aspect and the end of this doubt. For something to be admitted as knowledge, it had to justify itself not in being impressive, useful, edifying, or hoary, but in furnishing incontrovertible credentials as to its origin. Incontrovertible, that meant for Descartes: universally valid for a precisely defined domain of entities; in short, only scientific knowledge would from now on count as knowledge proper.

The genius and the failure of Descartes' thinking are apparent in his realization that the scientific domains are characterized by an unprecedented internal consistency and a rigorous and progressive interrelatedness, but are at the same time without an ultimate, scientifically explicit foundation.[1] Hence, the methodological doubt which had made room for the new scientific enterprise was also to provide a scientifically satisfactory *foundation* for the sciences. Descartes' arguments to this end failed historically in that the Cartesian foundation of the sciences was never accepted and developed in the way in which the sciences were. It failed historically because it had failed philosophically. The methodological doubt which so effectively destructs our world, seem-

---

[1] René Descartes, *Discourse on Method*, tr. Laurence J. Lafleur, 2nd ed. (Indianapolis, 1956), p. 6.

ingly based on mere belief, cannot at all serve as an unshakable basis and origin for the reconstruction of an unassailable world. Pure, radical doubting does not reveal an irreducible and substantive ego, as Descartes believed. The ego in turn does not of itself and necessarily point to God. And so the reinstitution of the world (which we knew and believed in to begin with) on the basis of God's wisdom and goodness is without justification.

Language is only incidentally a topic of Descartes' investigations. But the scarce remarks on language that we do find complement the general outline of Descartes' philosophy, and additionally and more importantly, they point out how the problem of language is connected with the significance and limitations of Descartes' thought.

One would expect that an investigation of language would play an important part in those considerations of Descartes' *Meditations* (1641) where the unreliability of sense impressions is argued. For if sense impressions are irretrievably unreliable, then language with its common nouns and verbs illicitly leads us to believe that there are entities which exist as invariably and commonly as the words that we use in referring to them. If, on the other hand, we can ascend from sense perception to reliable knowledge, one would like to find out with what accuracy language reflects this knowledge and why. Descartes brings up this very problem only to conclude: "I prefer to pass over this matter . . ."[2]

It is apparent from remarks in the earlier *Discourse on Method* (1637) that language for Descartes was not a peculiar or fundamental disclosure of reality, but merely a means of communicating or representing something real. Fiction and historiography are therefore not to be judged as works of language but with regard to the (scientifically understood) fidelity of their reports.[3] This evaluation continues and renders more precise Plato's separation of reality from language, substituting scientific truth for the realm of ideas as a standard for and beyond language and everyday reality. In the case of eloquence and poetry where it is more apparent that language and the reality which it presents can perhaps not ultimately be separated, Descartes indeed refrains from splitting the two dimensions apart and from evaluating them by means of scientific truth. But neither does he grant these unified powers the status of a fundamental and binding disclosure of the world. On the contrary, he considers them innocuous and unveri-

---

[2] *Meditations on First Philosophy*, tr. L. J. Lafleur, 2nd ed. (Indianapolis, 1960), p. 31.
[3] *Discourse*, pp. 4–5.

fiable pleasantries.[4] Descartes' views are in no way novel here; but within the framework of his philosophy they attain a consistency that they did not have in the tradition.

26. The problem of the uniqueness and autonomy of language

In another connection, Descartes develops a more original view of language. As remarked earlier, the scientific investigation of the world reveals domains of great internal consistency which are increasingly interrelated through coordination and subordination so that the differences among the various realms and orders of the everyday world diminish and seem to disappear. Here again Descartes' attitude is ambivalent. On the one hand he recognized and supported the progressive simplification and unification of the world. On the other hand, he sought to establish a boundary which scientific investigation would be in principle unable to transgress. It is clear from what has been said why he wanted to draw the limit within man. As Descartes tells us expressly, he tried in his physiological investigations to integrate man as fully as possible into the network of natural laws and causes.[5] But man was for Descartes not merely an extended (natural) thing, but also a thinking (rational) thing. And it was in and through man as the thinking thing that Descartes thought to have discovered the point of unassailable certainty from which he felt he was entitled to ascend to the supreme being whence, finally, it seemed possible to rebuild all of reality and its laws with indubitable certainty.

Language was to serve as evidence that there is a dimension in man that can never be reduced to the facts and laws of nature. To demonstrate this, Descartes takes his point of departure from two distinctive features of human speech.[6] The first trait becomes apparent when language is viewed with regard to its origin in the speaker. Language has the unique function of communicating thoughts. Language-like utterances on the part of machines or animals are not expressions of freely and autonomously produced reflections, but necessary responses to specific stimuli. The second trait emerges when we consider how the speaker is related to the world. While animals excel in response to certain definite tasks where they may well surpass man, only man is free of limiting predispositions and can respond to any situation what-

---

[4] Loc, cit.
[5] Ibid., p. 30.
[6] Ibid., pp. 36–38.

ever. This second feature is not clearly and exclusively pointed out on the basis of language, but it can be easily applied to and exemplified in language: human vocal responses are not confined to certain types of stimuli and messages, but can reflect and deal with any state of affairs.

There is then apparently a dimension of universality and infinity in human language that is not found in comparable phenomena. But the question remains whether Descartes' definition suffices to establish the uniqueness of human language and thus to secure the independence and authority of reason relative to nature. Again there is neither historical nor philosophical evidence to support a positive answer. Already Descartes' contemporary, La Mettrie, misunderstood Descartes to mean that men, animals, and machines are basically of the same structure, and language was, in this mistaken interpretation, a pervasive and thus indicative feature. Although La Mettrie clearly failed to recognize what Descartes had *intended*, he rightly saw that what Descartes had *demonstrated* did not at all vitiate La Mettrie's own thesis.[7]

One might surmise that Descartes would have succeeded only had he shown that in language the whole of reality is opened up to man while the language-like features in animal behavior only serve to fit animals into a definite and greatly limited segment of the total world. Clearly Descartes' observations tend in this direction, but never raise the problem of the connection of language and reality comprehensively. As long as this problem is not at least explicated, there can be no objection to the subsumption of language under reality. Descartes tried to prevent the conflation of language and physical reality by closely associating language with reason. But just as language had failed as evidence for the autonomy of reason over against nature, so Cartesian reason, which has been derided as the ghost in the machine, turned out to be too weak a support for the autonomy of language over against reality. The existence of Cartesian reason, if not refuted, is generally dismissed today while the existence of language which appears to be hardier has been absorbed among the physically existent things, at least in the sense that most people would hesitate to deny that it is in principle impossible to give a mechanical counterpart of the competent speaker.

A brief look at the practical linguistic work that was carried out by Cartesian grammarians will clarify the above problem as well as point

---

[7] Cf. Keith Gunderson, "Descartes, La Mettrie, Language, and Machines," *Philosophy*, XXXIX (1964), 193–222.

up a historical connection and parallel.[8] The linguists in the Cartesian tradition seemed to follow Descartes' rationalism in their willingness to depart from narrowly empirical data in devising grammatical rules and procedures which serve the sole purpose of leading to empirically given speech but are not themselves given in any empirically immediate way.[9] This rational, empirically invisible groundwork also articulates in certain ways how language can be so universal, flexible, and potentially infinite in its empirical shapes as Descartes had claimed it to be. It is apparent that these endeavors share the orientation of the authors of the Medieval speculative grammars. In both instances there is the realization that language has dimensions that are not given with the empirical strings of sounds, but are mandatory for the intelligibility of what is empirically given. The perspective and instrumentarium for this non-empirical investigation is furnished by Scholastic metaphysics in one case, by Cartesian rationalism in the other. What was to be rendered intelligible in the speculative grammars was the manner in which the parts of speech singly and jointly (in sentences) are modes of signifying. We saw that this enterprise failed if by signifying is meant presentation of reality in language, and that it partly succeeded if by signifying is meant construction of sequences which are intricately and systematically arranged and can therefore serve as flexible and powerful referential vehicles.

In the Cartesian grammars and logics, what is to be explicated is how language presents and conjoins ideas. This formulation of the problem leads to great advances in grammatical theory because the troublesome problem of reality is divorced from grammar. The ideas are of themselves the tokens of reality, and in such a way that reality is articulated in clearly delimited and easily manipulated units.[10] But on this view, the essential problem of how language can be the presence of reality is skipped; what remains is a formal system of combining units into larger wholes. In the 17th and 18th centuries, language may have been the only imaginable exemplification of this system. But this was an empirical argument for the uniqueness of language and man, the speaker, not the sort of necessary rational demonstration that Descartes had sought.

---

[8] See e.g. Antoine Arnauld and Claude Lancelot, *Grammaire générale et raisonée*, 3rd ed. of 1676, ed. Herbert E. Brekle (Stuttgart-Bad Cannstatt, 1966) and also Arnauld, *The Art of Thinking*, tr. James Dickoff and Patricia James (Indianapolis, 1964).

[9] Cf. Noam Chomsky, *Cartesian Linguistics* (New York, 1966).

[10] Arnauld's remarks on native wit, connotation, and the force of circumstances are attempts at overcoming the shortcomings of the view sketched. But the remedies are without a positive basis and more properly diagnoses than solutions. See, *Art of Thinking*, pp. 204, 236, 341–342.

27. The sciences and the humanities. Vico

Fiction, historiography, rhetoric, philology, all disciplines of great proximity to language, were dismissed by Descartes as relatively useless. For Vico (1668–1744), they are crucial powers and sources of meaning.[11] He develops his view of language, drawing from these forces and in opposition to Cartesianism.[12]

The context within which language displays decisive and far-reaching significance for Vico is initially sketched in *On the Study Methods of Our Time* (1709).[13] In this essay, Vico recognized that Cartesian thinking was the power to be reckoned with in his day.[14] Cartesian thinking is not the philosophy of Descartes, but the peculiar way in which Descartes' endeavors had become consequential and dominant. As an effective power, it had emancipated itself from the search for ultimate metaphysical fundaments and instead promoted the discovery of cogent theoretical knowledge.

In part, Vico's critique is bound to the narrow perspective of his time. Scientific theories, though on the whole much more technologically powerful than craftsmanship based on dexterity and experience, have a technological incubation period individually; and in the early 18th century, the entire scientific enterprise was still in its infancy though it showed definite technological aspirations. It could therefore seem at that time as if the new scientific theories, though indubitably certain, were practically inconsequential or at any rate inferior to traditional practices.[15]

But Vico went on to point out that region which is never investigated by the sciences and which at best moves into darkness when the sciences become the dominant force of an era. This is the domain where there can be no question of objective certainty and description since all endeavors proceed in a commerce with what is instantly and

---

[11] Cf. Tullio de Mauro, "Giambattista Vico: From Rhetoric to Linguistic Historicism," in *Giambattista Vico. An International Symposium*, ed. Giorgio Tagliacozzo and Hayden V. White (Baltimore, 1969), pp. 279–295.

[12] See Karl Otto Apel, *Die Idee der Sprache in der Tradition des Humanismus von Dante bis Vico.* Archiv für Begriffsgeschichte, vol. 8 (Bonn, 1963), pp. 318–380. For a survey of Vico's views on language and of Vico scholarship, see Bruno Liebrucks, *Sprache und Bewusstsein*, vol. 1 (Frankfurt, 1964), pp. 268–279.

[13] Giambattista Vico, *On the Study Methods of Our Time*, tr. Elio Gianturco (Indianapolis, 1965).

[14] Cf. Yvon Belaval, "Vico and Anti-Cartesianism," in *Giambattista Vico*, ed. Tagliacozzo and White, pp. 77–91 and Stuart Hampshire, "Vico and the Contemporary Philosophy of Language," *ibid.*, pp. 476–477.

[15] *Study Methods.*, pp. 21–33.

uniquely significant, moving, and convincing. Vico calls this domain the realm of the probable.[16] We come to be at home and efficacious in it through the study of the repositories of past experience and wisdom, the so-called common places or τόποι, through the study of ethics, and through the exercise of our insight, thus gained, in eloquence. The poet gives immediate and forceful expression to this wisdom and so creates a reality which is more powerful than physical reality since it is the probable and poetical realm wherein we live, plan, mourn, and rejoice.

This early outline is not only sketchy but in parts also ambiguous. The characterization of the probable does not suffice to insure its autonomy. The probable seems much more readily characterizable as that which has *not yet* been explored scientifically than as the realm that will *never* be amenable to scientific investigation. Further, it is unlikely that topics with its schematic listing of probable arguments is a discipline that is either sufficiently cogent or sufficiently rich and vital to serve as a guiding force. Arnauld (1611–1694) was correct both in rejecting what topics in its traditional form had achieved and in recognizing that its task was nonetheless important.[17] His consideration of probable and circumstantial elements in reasoning was not too different from Vico's. But his narrow and rudimentary solution was all that his Cartesian orientation permitted, and there were characteristic attempts at bringing the probable under control through a calculus.[18] Vico's outline on the other hand was merely a starting point. He came to a fuller and indeed monumental treatment of this problem through laborious and sensitive attention to history, poetry, and language.

28. Vico's New Science. The principles of language

From these labors, new light was shed on the nature and origin of language. This came about through Vico's forceful reach beyond the metaphysical distinction of form and matter, theory and practice. This accomplishment, in turn, would have been frustrated had Vico merely trained the common scientific and scholarly instruments on new materials and problems. He proceeded more radically and developed and practiced a new kind of science, i.e. his New Science. It was intended to pursue at once the true (the theoretical and universal) that is studied in philosophy and the certain (the factual and historical) which

---

[16] *Ibid.*, pp. 12–20, 33–41.
[17] Arnauld, *Art of Thinking*, pp. 235–240.
[18] *Ibid.*, pp. 204, 236, 341–342, 354–357.

is investigated by philology. These two types of knowledge and disciplines could be illustrated in more exhaustive and contemporary terms. It would then become apparent that many of our cultural and technological achievements arose from just this division of the theoretical and practical. One might therefore look with scepticism on the feasibility and utility of Vico's project.

The standard and basis for Vico's new science was to be the principle that full knowledge could only be had of what we can make or do. This principle clearly emphasizes dimensions in our common concept of knowledge which are otherwise latent or suppressed.[19] To know is not to have a body of true propositions before one's mind, but to be in possession of (some segment of) reality. And to be in possession of something is not to have some abstract claim to it, but to have appropriated it in creating or transforming it.

Vico's principle entails in a less obvious sense a modification of our understanding of making and doing and, more importantly, of what can be made and done. These latter implications will ultimately determine the possibilities and limitations of Vico's enterprise. *The New Science* (1744) is consequently an event and exercise as much as the exposition of a doctrine.[20] It proposes to exhibit the principles of humanity, and in so doing it is the attainment of full humanity.[21]

When Vico treats of principles, the word principle presumably speaks to him and through him to us in its etymological power: the principle is the first *(primum)* and the dominant *(princeps)*.[22] This observation leads us to the first point of significance for the philosophy of language: Vico's reflection on language is at all times a response to what language discloses, a response which uncovers latent dimensions in language and is so itself a disclosure.

Vico's principle enjoins that the dominant nature of humanity is to be sought at the origin of man. The nature of man cannot be known abstractly, but only in re-doing and re-making humanity, i.e. in taking again the historical step from what is not yet man to what is man. The theory must begin where its subject matter begins.[23] This is Vico's methodological principle; and it is apparent how closely it hangs to-

[19] These dimensions were still alive in the Socratic and Platonic concept of (ethical) knowledge.
[20] *The New Science of Giambattista Vico*, 3rd ed. of 1744, tr. Thomas Goddard Bergin and Max Harold Fisch, 2nd ed. (Ithaca, 1968). References are to the paragraphs as numbered by Bergin and Fisch. Roman numerals refer to the Introduction by Bergin and Fisch.
[21] *Ibid.*, pp. xix and xli–xlii and paragraphs 365, 391, 661, 734.
[22] *Ibid.*, p. xx.
[23] *Ibid.*, paragraphs 314 and 740.

gether with his principle of knowledge and his principles of humanity.

It is clear by now that the origin of man is neither presented as theory, nor as a historical fact since that origin first makes something like historiography possible. The origin is taken as a primal event of many aspects. Religiously, it is the return of the descendants of Ham, Japheth, and Shem to humanity after they had roamed the great forests as beasts for 200 years following the great flood. Scientifically and sociologically, the event is the clapping of the thunder which is explained as a consequence of the vapors rising from the forest and which drives haphazardly formed couples of pre-human animals into the shelter of caves, thus giving rise to permanent abodes and social units. Metaphysically, it is the awakening of beasts to the awareness of divine powers whereby these animals become human beings, characterized by the attainment of an encompassing world view and the conscious establishment of an ordered world. These first human beings were no longer organisms, fully directed by instincts and fitted into the world; they rather made their world; they were founders or makers, in Greek ποιηταί.

All theories according to which language arises from convention or ostension are circular since conventions and ostensions presumably require language.[24] The only way out of this circle is to present an original situation which is articulate in the sense that it has definite dimensions and parts and which is transcendently significant in the sense that it is dominated by an event which is fully present in the situation and at the same time evidently consequential beyond this situation. In such a situation gestures can be performed which have reference to definite entities and in such a way that the pertinence of the gesture and the intended entities to the entire world of the beings in question is apparent. In fact, it is first in and through such a situation that pervasive meaning is lit up and that there is a world where there was formerly a mere aggregate of things. Here world and language co-originate.

We can take Vico's primal event of the thundering sky as the force which articulated the original situation (the sky, the earth, the caves), bestowed meaning on it (majesty, awe, insecurity), and called forth gestures of pervasive pertinence (adoration, flight, settling down). Vico is not at all concerned quickly to push the development to our discursive verbal language, but postulates an entire age, the age of the

---

[24] Cf. section 17 above.

gods, for this primal world with its grand regions and beings and for this mute language of rituals and ceremonies. His achievement lies in having shown that there is no need to be apologetic about the crudity of such beginnings and that this age may have had its own unsurpassed dignity.

The following age is that of the heroes where meaning is conveyed through signs which leads to a more versatile and explicit language. The last age, that of men, begins with verbal language which is said to originate from onomatopoeia and interjections.[25] This view which is otherwise easily ridiculed by its opponents because it is overburdened by its advocates here merely needs to explain how the process of assigning oral noises to entities, attitudes, and goals is triggered.

What necessarily escapes a discussion such as this is the scope and power of Vico's presentation. Since any theoretical argument would have violated the principles of the New Science, Vico was committed to presenting each of his points in its historical reality. In this endeavor, he organized and integrated an immense number of facts in the history of literature, language, law, politics, and religion, and he opened up vistas which enriched and transformed scholarly disciplines over many generations.[26]

In Vico's view, then, language has a depth that extends from the awesome and entirely unified world expressions in the age of the gods down to the explicit and facile verbal discourse of today. Poetry, on this view, is not an unusual and parasitic use of language, but the concomitant expression of the *making* (Greek ποιεῖν) of the world. But this is not a total re-definition of poetry; it rather preserves and indeed lends new life to what we commonly call the poetic qualities and forms of language: metonymy, synecdoche, metaphor, and irony.[27] Synecdoche, e.g., is the naming of the whole after a part, say in Latin the naming of the sword after its point.[28] Such naming seems to be secondary in that it apparently requires the prior names *sword* and *point*. But for one who wields and seeks to escape a sword, the point is the first and decisive reality with which he contends.

The original making of the world is, as we saw, the response to an event. Language arises not just when man comes to signify, but when

---

[25] *New Science*, paragraph 135.
[26] See Fisch's Introduction to *The Autobiography of Giambattista Vico*, tr. Bergin and Fisch (Ithaca, 1944), pp. 61–107. The symposium which gave rise to Tagliacozzo's and White's anthology is eloquent testimony in this regard.
[27] *New Science*, paragraphs 406–411.
[28] *Ibid.*, paragraph 407.

the world has come to be eloquent. Hence poetry, although a making, is not arbitrary construction, but an answer to the call and demand of reality; and Vico, in emphasizing that poetry is imitation, again gives a new profounder meaning to a traditional dictum.

Though Vico frequently refers to the threefold division and sequence of ages, beings, and languages, he does not strictly adhere to these delimitations; and at times, these three segments appear to be simultaneous aspects of one development.[29] Consequently, although the divine and heroic languages are said to be mute, Vico repeatedly characterizes them with reference to words, stemming presumably from these eras. But what seems to be carelessness can be taken positively as a reflection of the fact that in our verbal language the heroic and divine powers are still alive.

This vitality of language and its ultimate mooring in a transcendently meaningful situation are the basis of what Vico calls his Mental Dictionary. It is not a lexicon in the ordinary sense, but a method of tracing the history and relations of a word so that the historical and international dimensions of humanity become apparent. Vico's concept of the Mental Dictionary provides both a new foundation and a new purpose for etymology.

It is at this point that the *New Science* makes good its maxim that to know truly is to be able to do and make. The search for the knowledge of the principles of humanity reaches its goal in providing the basis for a more profound realization of human existence. Language and poetry served Vico as "the master key" to the principles of humanity; i.e. language and poetry not as they were conceived in Vico's time, but in their original power. To find this key or rather to recognize that what we believed to be thoroughly familiar with was in fact the index of the true principles of humanity was therefore the decisive and the most laborious stage of the New Science.[30]

29. The New Science and the natural sciences

But why has the *New Science* remained so relatively silent and ineffective beyond the disciplines of the humanities? We have noted before that the principle of knowledge in the New Science establishes a connection between knowing and making or doing which modifies our common concept of knowledge, and we asked whether the converse

---

[29] Cf. *ibid.*, paragraph 446.
[30] *Ibid.*, paragraphs 34 and 338.

might not also be true. If we know something, does that mean that we can do or make that thing in a certain sense? If the New Science does provide new and fundamental knowledge, does that entail that there is a basic remaking of what there is new knowledge of? Vico excludes nature from the domain of which there is such knowledge. He sees his enterprise as parallel and not basic to the new natural sciences.[31] The possibility remains then that all the major points of the new science can be stated alternatively in terms of the natural sciences. The rapid development of these sciences seems indeed to require such alternative statements; for many of Vico's observations and explanations were soon found to be erroneous not only in the light of scientific discoveries, but through work carried out by the humanities in the new scientific spirit. The modern reader finds himself correcting Vico's (quite natural and excusable) mistakes automatically and constantly. In the instance of Vico's original event, he knows that if there were manlike beasts, they were the result of evolution and not of the dispersion of the dissenting sons of Noah after the great flood.[32] He knows that thunder does not arise from dry exhalations at the end of a process of evaporation that takes two centuries. Hence the original event can certainly not have been a unique one meteorologically.[33] As far as the workings of providence are concerned, Vico ruled out intrusions by insisting on immanent providence, one that works in harmony with the laws discovered by natural and the new science.[34]

But Vico is quite undecided as to the status of the gods who represent decisive powers in the first age. The dignity of this age and the spirit of Vico's principles require that they be autonomously real. But Vico's Christian heritage and the force of the Enlightenment lead to metaphorical explanations, i.e. to dissolutions of the gods.[35]

Finally, Vico's approach is in one respect so scientific in the Cartesian sense that it threatens the very significance of his achievement. Vico insists that the nature and succession of the three ages is at least basically the pattern for all peoples and all times, and such universality is also claimed for the Mental Dictionary. This claim undermines the other maxims according to which a theory is bound to its (historically unique) subject matter and that true knowledge is lived and acted out.

---

[31] *Ibid.*, paragraphs 42, 331, 722, 498, 779; cf. pp. xxii, xxxi, xxxiii.
[32] *Ibid.*, paragraph 13.
[33] *Ibid.*, paragraph 62.
[34] Cf. *ibid.*, p. xxxii.
[35] *Ibid.*, paragraphs 689, 917, 949, 1098.

The claim ascribes to the result of the *New Science* the very abstract universality that is typical of the laws of Cartesian science.

These ambiguities and contradictions are indications that Cartesianism has not been fully understood and integrated in Vico's science. They make it understandable why modern science proceeded unaffected by, and in apparent triumph over, the *New Science*. And the relative failure of the *New Science* obviously reflects on the insight into language that it promised and seemed to provide.

But there remains a problem with the Cartesian world, and Vico's promise of a solution is not empty. This can in conclusion be brought into focus once more by considering one remark that Vico makes regarding the relationship of his science to natural science.[36] Vico claims there that "the world of civil society" alone can be fully known by men since they have made it. The world of nature can be fully known by God who has created it. But do not our progressive discoveries of the natural laws approximate this divine knowledge? Vico's investigations enable us to see that the enigma of scientific laws is precisely that they give insight into the world without at all telling us of themselves what to make the world like. Scientific laws open up ever more extensive possibilities of manipulation; but the forces that could guide us in creative actualizations recede in the face of the expanding possibilities.[37]

Applied to language, this means that the scientific approach and attitude give us ever greater knowledge of, and proficiency in speaking, but the possibilities and reasons for saying anything at all grow ever paler. There is more and better speaking, but the question of whether anything is being said becomes increasingly diffident. The final question is whether or not we should accept the restriction of our inquiries to speaking. Vico, at any rate, lets us see this question more clearly.

30. The origin and progress of language. Rousseau and Herder

We can pursue some of the strands that developed from Vico's work by considering briefly the treatises on the origin of language written by Rousseau (1712–1778) and Herder (1744–1803).[38]

---

[36] *Ibid.*, paragraph 331.

[37] Cf. sections 43–45 below.

[38] Jean-Jacques Rousseau, *Essay on the Origin of Languages*, tr. John H. Moran (New York, 1966); Johann Gottfried Herder, *Essay on the Origin of Language*, tr. Alexander Gode (New York, 1966). The two essays are published in one volume. Not all of Herder's essay is

Rousseau's treatise (1755) is an illustration of the difficulty that even an acute observer and versatile thinker has in attaining or maintaining the level of incisive investigations that we found in Vico's work.[39]

The stages of development which in Vico are not merely successive, but designate pervading powers which are all present in today's language, are taken by Rousseau as mutually exclusive possibilities with a typical decline in their succession. The original fullness and liveliness of language gives way to clarity and paleness. But thus the possibilities that by implication are open to us who live in the final stage differ greatly from those that Vico's work suggests. If Rousseau is correct, we must abandon the present and return to the past. Following Vico's insight, we ought to attend to those powers in our language that have their roots in the origin of humanity, but are now modified and covered up by new forces. Vico looks at the past with perceptive awe and sometimes with horror. For him, the historical change entails fundamental changes which make nostalgia and a desire to return impossible. Thus the present itself is given us as a task, and yet as a task for which the past is of significance.

That Rousseau's basic position does not attain the scope and depth of Vico's is further evident from the former's remarks on music. Rousseau connects these remarks with those on language by pointing out that originally music and language were closely connected. He then proceeds to elaborate on the power of what he calls the representative and moral elements of music which he finds to be neglected in favor of the mechanical and formal aspects. The point may be important, but it is not related by Rousseau to the problem of the origin of language.[40] Yet there is a connection on a deeper level. Language in its original stage had a power of eloquence that closely resembles the representative and moral efficacy of music, and this further explains the original affinity of music and language. Language has lost this power in attaining rigor and clarity; music is just in that phase of its development where it may suffer a similar fate of deterioration. This parallelism, had

given in the translation; when I refer to the remaining passages, I will quote from "Abhandlung über den Ursprung der Sprache" in *Sprachphilosophische Schriften*, 2nd ed., ed. Erich Heintel (Hamburg, 1964), pp. [1]–87. As regards the intellectual environment of Rousseau's and Herder's investigations of language, cf. Pierre Juliard, *Philosophies of Language in Eighteenth-Century France* (The Hague, 1970).

[39] Regarding the question to what extent Rousseau was acquainted with Vico, see *Autobiography*, pp. 72–73.

[40] An external reason for the discontinuity may be the earlier date of composition of these parts. Cf. Moran's Afterword to the *Essay*, p. 80.

it been noted, would have permitted further significant elaborations and explorations. But it escaped Rousseau since his investigation did not proceed on a sufficiently deep and fruitful level.

We find in Herder's *Treatise on the Origin of Language* (1770) an explication of some of the important points in Vico's work, an explication that draws from the increase in scientific knowledge and the greater sophistication in philosophical reflection.[41]

The focus of Herder's arguments is the thesis that the problem of the origin of language is the problem of man's humanity. On that view it does not make sense to try and grasp the nature of language by resorting to what is less than human or more than human. At the same time, it is through a discussion and critique of these mistaken views that Herder succeeds in giving some form and force to the otherwise elusive positive aspect of the problem. Positively we can never do less than presuppose the existence and intelligibility of human language and never more than describe various aspects and stages within the total domain.

Herder is in agreement with Descartes that animal language is something in principle different from human language and that therefore the latter cannot be derived from the former. But Herder gives detailed observations where Descartes is content with hints. Herder points out that man, in comparison with animals, is quite destitute of instincts.[42] He lacks all the automatic and reliable guiding devices which enable animals, at least as a species, to cope perfectly with the world. Language is one such device by means of which information, useful to the species, is transmitted in preestablished and efficient ways from one specimen to another. Man is without language in this sense.[43]

In language, the entire world with a fundamentally unlimited number of possibilities is opened up to man.[44] For the correlative openness in man, Herder uses the word *reflection (Besonnenheit)*.[45] Reflection radically distinguishes man from animals. It is given with man's humanity and is already present in the infant.[46] In language learning, the infant does accordingly not receive something in essence novel to, and

---

[41] A more detailed account of Herder's relation to Vico is given by George A. Wells, "Vico and Herder," *Giambattista Vico*, ed. Tagliacozzo and White, pp. 93–102.

[42] Herder, *Origin*, pp. 103–107; "Ursprung," pp. 56,62.

[43] *Origin*, pp. 105–107.

[44] *Ibid.*, pp. 107–111.

[45] *Ibid.*, p. 112. – Cf. Lohmann who holds that language first arose from *Besonnenheit* in Herder's sense *(Philosophie*, pp. 83–84).

[46] *Ibid.*, pp. 112–113. This point has been substantiated by Eric Lenneberg in *Biological Foundations of Language* (New York, 1967), pp. 125–187.

separate from, the child; rather the child strengthens and articulates his own nature.[47] "If I could ... make at once visible," Herder says, "the woven texture called human nature – in all its parts a texture for language."[48]

It follows from this account that it is an empty proposition to say that language has been given to man by God. Either man, as language was bestowed on him, was truly a human being; but this he could have been only in possessing language. Hence God gave man what was already his. Or the being to which language was given existed in a pre-human state. In that case, God's gift amounted to the creation of man; and the original position does not explain anything, but rather raises a question that may be unanswerable as Herder suggests.[49]

In these arguments, Herder deals with a position which today is of limited interest. But given appropriate modifications, these reflections constitute a refutation of any claim that conceives of language as an extrinsic addition to man. This type of claim is involved in any argument according to which language is a matter of convention or has the nature of a tool.[50]

In his positive discussion of language, Herder follows Vico's and Rousseau's lines, characterizing language in its early stages as poetic, vigorous, and synthetic over against the later stages where language becomes prosaic, concise, and analytic.[51]

The terminology *synthetic-analytic* is somewhat later than Herder's essay.[52] But Herder is clearly aware of the problem, and he credits its discovery (though not its elucidation) to Rousseau; and as we have seen, the entire phenomenon was already present in Vico. The distinction has a semantic and a morphological aspect. Morphologically the synthetic stage is illustrated by the Latin sentence

(1) *Habitabimus Romae.*

The analytic stage is exemplified by the English equivalent of (1), namely

(2) We will live in Rome.

Obviously, what is expressed and compounded (synthesized) in two

---

[47] *Ibid.*, pp. 121–122.
[48] *Ibid.*, pp. 146–147.
[49] "Ursprung," p. 58.
[50] Cf. *Origin*, p. 100.
[51] *Ibid.*, pp. 91–92, 135–136, 152–163.
[52] The distinction in this sense, which goes back to Friedrich Schlegel, must of course not be confused with Kant's distinction which has its own linguistic significance. See Quine, "The Problem of Meaning in Linguistics," *From a Logical Point of View*, 2nd ed. (New York, 1963), pp. 47–64.

words in Latin is unfolded and separated (analyzed) into three and two words respectively in English. The semantic implication is that in Latin meaning is present in an involuted and compact way whereas in English it is explicated and divided into separate but combinable units.

The distinction, as explained above, is a real, but not a radical one because we can isolate within the compact Latin words those elements that are rendered as separate words in English. Thus *we* roughly corresponds to *-mus*, *will* to *-bi-*, *live* to *habita-*, *in* to *-e*, *Rome* to *Roma*. Herder presumably has the above sense of the distinction in mind; but there is a further significance conveyed by it. As the properties *poetic* and *vigorous* indicate, Herder refers by *synthetic* to a power of eloquence and presentation that is not found in analytic languages so that the transition from the synthetic to the analytic is not merely a reorganization, but a fundamental change and possibly a loss.

However Herder, just like Vico and unlike Rousseau, refrains from passing a definitive judgment on the present stage of language. He rather emphasizes that the openness of the world and to the world which belongs to man from his infancy, remains in force throughout an individual's life and indeed throughout human history.[53]

31. Ontological and ontic language. Humboldt

The essential lines of Western reflection on language since Heraclitus converge and culminate in Wilhelm von Humboldt's (1767–1835) investigations of language.[54] The depth and influence of Humboldt's achievement can be gathered from he fact that both Noam Chomsky, a linguist who has opened up new ways of coming to grips with the formal structures of language through concise and comprehensive methods, and Martin Heidegger, a philosopher who has sought to penetrate the history and destiny of being, acknowledge Humboldt to be one of the decisive forerunners in their particular concern with language.[55]

[53] *Origin*, pp. 163–166; "Ursprung," pp. 58–60.

[54] For a discussion of some of the more immediate predecessors of Humboldt, see Roger Langham Brown, *Wilhelm von Humboldt's Conception of Linguistic Relativity* (The Hague, 1967).

[55] Chomsky, *Cartesian Linguistics*, p. 2; Heidegger, *Unterwegs zur Sprache*, 2nd ed. (Pfullingen, 1960), pp. 246–249, 267–268 *(On the Way to Language*, tr. Peter D. Hertz [New York, 1971], pp. 116–119, 136). – Weisgerber and his school also understand their enterprise as a continuation of Humboldt's intents. Cf. n. 56 of Chapter Three above and for discussion see Robert Lee Miller, "The Linguistic Relativity Principle and Humboldtian Ethnolinguistics," (Diss. Michigan, 1963). – Ernst Cassirer is another important follower of Humboldt. See his discussion of Humboldt in *Language*, pp. 155–163.

Both writers also allude to the obscurity and ambivalence of Humboldt's thought.[56] These traits stem in part from the discursive manner of Humboldt's presentation, but more importantly, from the interpenetration of two procedures which Humboldt follows. On the one hand Humboldt speaks from a position of extraordinary competence, from his command of classical and modern literatures and languages, from philological and philosophical training, from a mastery of history, and from first hand research of so called primitive languages. On the other hand he speaks as one who leaves behind the security of such learning and attempts to gain unprecedented insight into language. Thus he speaks unevenly and sometimes confusingly as a virtuoso and as a pioneer.

Let us try to find the main direction and the most radical level of Humboldt's inquiries. A helpful clue is the topic of the preceding section, the problem of the origin of language. We saw in that section that according to Herder the origin of language cannot be understood as an event where a certain talent is given to, or acquired by, man. Such an account takes too much for granted. Humboldt seeks to illuminate and question these presuppositions in a more radical and resourceful way. He puts the problem aporetically by emphasizing that any investigation of the origin of language finds language to be there always and already. If the notions of language and origin are basically conceived, the origin of language is unsearchable.[57] Human language, to be sure, originated at some point in (evolutionary) history. But the persistent difficulty is not just that we have almost no information of the developments of that period.[58] Rather the problem is to fathom an event which first opened up perspectives and capabilities within and by means of which one can set out to investigate, among other things,

---

[56] Chomsky, *Cartesian Linguistics*, p. 86, n. 37; Heidegger, *Sprache*, pp. 246, 267–268 (*Language*, pp. 116, 136).

[57] The following references are to Humboldt's fundamental and final essay on language, "Über die Verschiedenheit des menschlichen Sprachbaues und ihren Einfluß auf die geistige Entwicklung des Menschengeschlechts," *Werke*, ed. Andreas Flitner and Klaus Giel (Stuttgart, 1963), III, 368–756. There is a competent partial translation in *Humanist Without Portfolio. An Anthology of the Writings of Wilhelm von Humboldt*, tr. and ed. Marianne Cowan (Detroit, 1963), pp. 251–298. A nearly complete translation has been furnished by George C. Buck and Frithjof A. Raven, *Linguistic Variability and Intellectual Development* (Philadelphia, 1972). The translation is inadequate because (1) it contains serious errors of translation, (2) it takes unwarranted and confusing editorial liberties, (3) it substitutes the definite and narrow terminology of modern linguistics for Humboldt's varying and highly connotative terms. For convenience I refer to all three editions whenever possible. – "Verschiedenheit," pp. 285–286, 400–402, 410–412; *Variability*, pp. 2, 13, 20–21; *Humanist*, pp. 254, 265–266, 273–274.

[58] Lenneberg, *Foundations*, pp. 227–266.

cosmology, evolution, and the evolution of human language in particular.

Consequently the origin of language is, according to Humboldt, not essentially a certain event at a certain time and place in history. It is a problem of a systematic sort and a continuous event. Language establishes, creates, and recreates itself persistently.[59] It does so, however, historically in the sense that its constant self-renewal is an interaction with its prior creations. Language does not re-establish itself ever and again from the ground up, but by reworking and revitalizing the material it has already accumulated.[60] Language is so bound to historically given speech communities for which Humboldt uses the somewhat misleading term "nation".[61]

From these considerations it appears that what Humboldt deals with under the title of the origin of language could be called the presence of language. It is the dynamic presence of language as a constant generative process.[62] Not being confined to a static structure, it must be acknowledged as infinite; but its infinity is articulate; it is based on finite means, and its endless unfolding is guided by definite sounds and concepts.[63] Hence although language is infinite, it can be present totally and simultaneously in every act of speaking.[64] It sustains in its totality every speech, and every particular speaking affects the totality of language.[65] Correspondingly, to be able to speak is to be open and attuned to the totality of language. This precursive openness manifests itself in the speaker's innate linguistic capacity. Any actual speaking or acquisition of language proceeds within the totality of language which is native to man so to speak.[66]

Relative to this total presence, any particular use and aspect of

[59] "Verschiedenheit," pp. 416–417, 417–418; *Variability*, pp. 26, 27; *Humanist*, pp. 278–279, 280.

[60] "Verschiedenheit," pp. 384–392, 548–550; *Variability*, pp. 1–6, 121–122; *Humanist*, pp. 253–260.

[61] "Verschiedenheit," pp. 385–387, 395–397, 408–410, 414–416, 469–470, 561–562; *Variability*, pp. 2–3, 9–10, 19–20, 24–25, 64, 131–132; *Humanist*, pp. 254–255, 263–264, 272–273, 276–278.

[62] "Verschiedenheit," pp. 416–417, 417; *Variability*, pp. 26, 27; *Humanist*, pp. 278–279, 280.

[63] "Verschiedenheit," pp. 426–428, 430–431, 445–446; *Variability*, pp. 34–35, 37, 48; *Humanist*, pp. 287–289, 291.

[64] "Verschiedenheit," pp. 398–399, 430–435, 446, 560, 594; *Variability*, pp. 11, 37–40, 48, 130–131, 153–154; *Humanist*, pp. 264–265, 291–294.

[65] "Verschiedenheit," pp. 408–409, 423–424, 438–440, 445–446; *Variability*, pp. 19, 31, 43, 48; *Humanist*, pp. 272, 285. Cf. the discussion of two eminent cases, pun and metaphor, in sections 3, 7, and 23 above.

[66] "Verschiedenheit," pp. 412–414, 430–434, 449–450; *Variability*, pp. 22, 37–39, 50; *Humanist*, pp. 275–276, 292–294.

language is partial; and conversely when we focus on such a definite use or aspect, much of language must seem redundant, excessive, and capricious.[67] It is in fact impossible to reach that totality by way of distinguishing and enumerating all of its parts.[68]

Language so ambitiously conceived clearly is no longer an item in, or an aspect of, the world, but is rather the disclosure of the world itself. It is language taken ontologically, not ontically.[69] Heraclitus approached ontological language in the ambiguity of the λόγος; Vico displayed the rise of ontological language in grand mythic simplicity. Humboldt's approach is philosophically more circumspect, more aware of the empirical data, more responsive to the challenge of scientific orientation. He treats of ontological language not because he has a clear and forceful grasp of it, but because he is driven to it from ever new directions. Hence the movement of his approach is more compelling to us than Heraclitus' and Vico's, but it is also far less certain of its direction. In important cases, the movement is entirely deflected from its goal and surrenders to the main intellectual currents of its time.

Thus an important vocable of Humboldt's is *intellect* or *spirit* (German *Geist*). In Humboldt's time, the era of German Idealism, the word has as an important and ever present meaning, the one which is well-known through Hegel. In this sense, "intellect" or "spirit" is often used by Humboldt to designate ontological language.[70] But "intellect" can also designate the particular human or subjective capacity.[71] When Humboldt so uses the term, he does not sever its close tie to language. But the latter's meaning then also shifts toward the particular and subjective. Language is then no longer the disclosure of the world itself; it becomes one aspect of the world or a medium through which reality appears in a certain way.[72] Reality itself becomes inaccessible.[73]

Another important pivot of Humboldt's wavering is the problem of meaning. When language is taken ontologically, meaning is as precursive, omnipresent, and total as language itself. There can be no dis-

---

[67] "Verschiedenheit," pp. 388–389, 393–394, 462–463; *Variability*, pp. 4, 8, 59; *Humanist*, pp. 256–257, 261.

[68] "Verschiedenheit," pp. 419–420; *Variability*, pp. 28–29; *Humanist*, pp. 281–283.

[69] For convenience I will use "ontological language" synonymously with "language taken ontologically" and so with "ontic language".

[70] "Verschiedenheit," pp. 382–384, 426–428; *Variability*, pp. xix–xx, 34–35; *Humanist*, pp. 251–253, 287–289.

[71] "Verschiedenheit," pp. 382–384 *et passim*; *Variability*, pp. xix–xx *et passim*;*Humanist*, pp. 251–253 *et passim*.

[72] "Verschiedenheit," pp. 433–435, 469–470, 565–566; *Variability*, pp. 39–40, 64, 134; *Humanist*, pp. 293–294.

[73] "Verschiedenheit," pp. 468–469; *Variability*, p. 63.

embodied meaning, nor can there be anything that is of itself meaning-less; in particular there can be no basically meaningless sound.[74] The point deserves elaboration. The sounds through which we have com-merce with the world are always sounds of this or that, warning, threatening, reassuring sounds.[75] They are indeed the presence of the world. The sounds of language are normally so *im*mediately and radi-antly meaningful that it takes a laborious and skilled effort to hear them as mere sounds. Even then the "mere" sound has meaning, i.e. a definite physiognomy as a phoneme, allophone, an instance of a certain pitch, etc. A sound can have various meanings to various people and various meanings to one person at different times. But it is therefore of itself no more meaningless than a thing that may be under-stood variously. Meaningless sounds can only be had by stipulation; such meaninglessness is clearly not basic or original.

Given Humboldt's ontological notion of language, we can see why signification, i.e. the bestowal of meaning, can never be radical, i.e. the primal provision of meaning for initially and basically meaningless sounds. But radical signification is a problem that exercises Humboldt continuously.[76] It is an eminently traditional and contemporary prob-lem, but clearly one that arises only once ontological language has been lost sight of.[77]

Though we can now see the ambivalences in Humboldt's thought which were concealed to himself, there is no thought on language today which has been able to resovle them. Humboldt's work on language remains singular since it is equally open to language in its strongest sense and to all the linguistic data and endeavors which, while expli-cating language, bar access to its strongest sense. As we shall see, the two pivots of Humboldt's ambivalence, the intellect and radical signifi-cation, are the ones around which an adequate understanding of our world and of man's place in it revolves to this day.

---

[74] "Verschiedenheit," pp. 430–435; 478, 560, 594; *Variability*, pp. 37–40, 71, 130–131, 153–154; *Humanist*, pp. 291–294.

[75] Cf. Martin Heidegger, *Being and Time*, tr. John Macquarrie and Edward Robinson (New York, 1962), p. 207.

[76] "Verschiedenheit," pp. 419, 440–441, 452–454, 475–476, 477; *Variability*, pp. 28, 44–45, 52–53, 69, 70; *Humanist*, pp. 281–282.

[77] Relative signification remains a legitimate and important problem.

PART TWO

CONTEMPORARY ISSUES IN THE PHILOSOPHY OF LANGUAGE

LANGUAGE AND PRECISION

32. The linguistic turn. Wittgenstein's "Tractatus"

It has been said that philosophy in the twentieth century is characterized by "the linguistic turn."[1] This means generally that in our century
all philosophy (or at least philosophy in the Anglo-Saxon countries)
has become essentially philosophy of language. More specifically, this
linguistic turn implies that fruitful talk about reality is possible only
if first of all we concern ourselves with the language in which that
reality is accessible to us.

Wittgenstein (1889–1951) in his *Tractatus Logico-Philosophicus* (1921)
is credited as the author of the linguistic turn.[2] Though the major
theses of this work are frequently rejected as untenable, Wittgenstein's
method has been most influential. The *Tractatus* is a slender work of
aphoristically formulated theses. Apart from the intrinsic difficulties
of the subject, there is a spirit of austerity and solitude in the *Tractatus*
which accounts for its celebrated obscurity and for an extensive body
of interpretive literature.[3] In the main, discussions revolve around "the

[1] See Richard Rorty, "Metaphilosophical Difficulties of Linguistic Philosophy," in *The Linguistic Turn*, ed. Rorty (Chicago, 1967), pp. 1–39. – It should be emphasized here that there is a definite and original speculative concern with language *between* Humboldt and Wittgenstein, e.g. in Nietzsche and Hegel; regarding the latter see Werner Marx, *Absolute Reflexion und Sprache* (Frankfurt, 1967) and Josef Simon, *Das Problem der Sprache bei Hegel* (Stuttgart, 1966).

[2] Ludwig Wittgenstein, *Tractatus Logico-Philosophicus*, German text with English tr. by D. F. Pears and B. F. McGuiness, 3rd ed. (London, 1966). References will be to paragraphs as numbered by Wittgenstein. In view of the brevity and crossreferential organization of the text, references are given only in very specific cases.

[3] See G. E. M. Anscombe, *An Introduction to Wittgenstein's "Tractatus"* (London, 1959); Max Black, *A Companion to Wittgenstein's "Tractatus"* (Cambridge, 1964); Irving M. Copi and Robert W. Beard, eds., *Essays on Wittgenstein's "Tractatus"* (New York, 1966); David Favrholdt, *An Interpretation and Critique of Wittgenstein's "Tractatus"* (Copenhagen, 1964); James Griffin, *Wittgenstein's Logical Atomism* (Oxford, 1964); Alexander Maslow, *A Study in Wittgenstein's "Tractatus"* (Berkeley, 1961); James C. Morrison, *Meaning and Truth in Wittgenstein's "Tractatus"* (The Hague, 1968); Erik Stenius, *Wittgenstein's "Tractatus"* (Oxford, 1960).

picture theory of language." This expression indicates clearly enough that the central question of the *Tractatus* is that of the relationship of language and reality. We want to discuss this problem by first outlining Wittgenstein's ontology, then his theory of language, and finally his view as to the interconnection of the two realms.

According to his ontology, the basic constituents of the world are not objects, but facts. They are basic in that they alone are the case. Objects are the elements of facts, but of themselves they are never the case. Facts are the case within the scope (logical space) afforded by the objects. The objects delimit the space through the (logical) form that is proper to each object and which predetermines the possible ways in which some object can be combined with others into facts.[4] The objects attain reality through their combination in facts. Among facts *(Tatsachen)* we can single out the irreducible ones (atomic facts: *Sachverhalte)*. The objects are by definition simple and irreducible; it is clear that they differ from what we ordinarily call objects (chairs, trees, rocks) since these are never simple and necessary.

Language, in Wittgenstein's view, initially appears to be quite parallel to reality. Names correspond to, and have *meaning*, in standing for objects. They are, however, just as unreal in isolation as objects are. Names properly have reference only in the context of propositions.[5] Propositions correspond to facts, more specifically elementary propositions correspond to atomic facts. A proposition has *sense* in referring to a *fact*.

Although a host of technical problems is attached to every technical term of Wittgenstein's that we have mentioned, these complications can be disregarded for our purpose, and then the ontology and theory of language that emerge are rather clear and largely conventional. Wittgenstein's thought becomes significant and systematically complicated when his views regarding the connection of language and reality are considered. Names are held to be associated with objects by convention. The decisive move is made by Wittgenstein in his explanation of how propositions and facts are related. They are related in sharing their logic. Logic in this sense can be tentatively explained as structure or arrangement. An illustration that Wittgenstein himself uses is that of the score, the performance, and the recording of a piece of music

---

[4] An ontological predecessor of this theory can be found in Plato's *Theaetetus*, a grammatical counterpart can be seen in Thomas of Erfurt's *Grammar*. See sections 8 and 20.

[5] This is closely parallel to Buridan's position where *supposition* corresponds to reference. See section 16.

where the three renditions obviously differ in many respects but share some essential feature which enables us for instance to convert one rendition into another.[6]

This common logic or structure, according to Wittgenstein, is exhibited, but not described and, in fact, not describable. This is fairly clear in the case of facts.[7] When I see a book lying on the desk, I see two objects in a certain arrangement, but I do not see the arrangement in the way that I see the objects. Now if a proposition and a state of affairs share their decisive structure, a proposition must present its structure (logic) in as implicit a fashion as the arrangement of objects is implicit in a state of affairs. Wittgenstein contended therefore that genuine, i.e. fully analysed propositions contain names only; the logic of the proposition is not named or expressed, but exhibited.

Any attempt at expressing the logic of a proposition will result precisely in obscuring this logic. A fortiori, a description of the entire system of logic is impossible. The limits of logic and the world are also the limits of what is thinkable, i.e. of thought. The ego or subject, conceived as the locus and actuality of thinking is therefore coextensive with logic.

It is apparent that in a strange and striking way, Wittgenstein comes close to Heraclitus' reflections where language, logic, (the fundamental law of) reality, and reason are also one, and are simultaneously considered and presented as the λόγος. In moving forward (or back) to this point, Wittgenstein appears to have overcome the fundamental difficulties that arise from the radical distinction between language and reality. They already come to the fore at the beginning of metaphysics, i.e. in Plato's thinking. Plato distinguishes between language and reality through reference to the language-independent ideas. But this basis of reference and distinction cannot serve to explain how language can present reality, i.e. how it can be meaningful. (Plato's etymology ends in resignation.) On Wittgenstein's account, there is at least a

---

[6] *Tractatus*, 4.014. Wittgenstein gives as a fourth alternative the "musical idea." If this refers to the singular event of the piece of music passing through my mind (an event that could be further specified experientially or neurologically), then it would indeed constitute an alternative. If "musical idea" refers to the abstract structure of this piece of music (if it is its *eidos* phenomenologically speaking), it would be what Wittgenstein calls the logic of this piece of music. This point brings out a definite kinship between phenomenology and the *Tractatus*, one that emerges again in the problem of solipsism. Cf. also Paul Ricoeur, "Husserl and Wittgenstein on Language," *Phenomenology and Existentialism*, ed. Edward N. Lee and Maurice Mandelbaum (Baltimore, 1967), pp. 207–217.

[7] Except where there is danger of confusion, I will use "fact" in the sense of *state of affairs* as opposed to *proposition* (a proposition can also be regarded as a fact).

partial answer to this question: Language presents reality in being logically identical with (ideally representative of) reality.

These difficulties are again present towards the end of metaphysics, i.e. in Kant's philosophy.[8] Kant in his transcendental move shows that reality is not given ready made either in tangible units or in compounds with objectively specifiable metaphysical elements. Reality is rather (and perhaps decisively) co-constituted by reason. He attains again a level where there is an original unity (through interaction) of reason and reality-in-its-fundamental-structure. But Kant's analysis fails to be truly radical since language (and formal logic) remain untouched by, and unrelated to, the analysis which is in fact guided and sustained by language.[9] Wittgenstein is very explicitly concerned with the inter-relation of reality, language, and logic; and accordingly the problem of how language not only serves as a theme but also as a basis of analysis is at least explicitly posed if not fully solved.

33. The conflict of precision and expression

We have said before that the *Tractatus* posits more than it argues. But this attitude is elliptical rather than apodictic. The *Tractatus* gives hints and outlines of arguments and demands and invites argument through its practice though not in its pronouncements.

A more detailed discussion is thus called for and is required in light of the parallel between Wittgenstein and Heraclitus. For the discussion of Heraclitus has shown that his unified and comprehensive reflection on language and reality is fraught with systematic ambiguities which make his thought vulnerable and abusable. Wittgenstein brings the precision of modern logic to bear on the fundamental problem, and this approach promises to provide the cogency that heretofore always seemed to be purchased at the expense of letting language in its funda-mental power provide the formulation of the problems of language while that fundamental dimension of language was at the same time left unexplored and even unrecognized.

Wittgenstein's presentation seems to be most rigorous and tangible where he elucidates the notions of atomic fact and atomic proposition. He seems to have reached here a level of compounds constituted of

---

[8] Cf. Stenius, "*Tractatus*", pp. 214–226.

[9] Herder, following his teacher Johann Georg Hamann, criticized the *Critique of Pure Reason* on these grounds. See *Sprachphilosophische Schriften*, pp. 183–227. Cf. also the Con-clusion below.

irreducible and necessary elements. And it is just on this level that the striking structural identity of language and reality becomes apparent. But Wittgenstein never gives an example of either an object or a name, a fact or a proposition. On the other hand, he nowhere asserts that these entities are separated by an unbridgeable gap from our ordinary objects, names, facts, and propositions. On the contrary, he points out the directions in which we have to move if we want to attain or at least approximate the primary entities.

Ordinary language and script, Wittgenstein tells us, obscure the basic elements and configurations of which they consist. The analysis and notation of symbolic logic are more perspicuous though not perfect. It is tempting then to try and construct a proposition that is perfect in Wittgenstein's sense. An atomic proposition, he says, consists of names only, predicates and properties being exhibited by the arrangement of names. Take *a* and *b* as names and form the sentence: *a b*. What is the minimal sense of this sentence? "There are two objects, *a* and *b*." But this interpretation is neither true nor false, but senseless on Wittgenstein's account. A proposition asserts a fact which is a configuration of objects. A fact is the case and the corresponding proposition is true, or the fact is not the case and the corresponding proposition false. In either instance a fact presupposes the existence of objects which provide the possibilities of facts, but to assert the existence of objects is not to claim a fact and hence does not imply a truth claim. If *a* and *b* are to be the case, then they must be the case in a definite configuration. If "*a b*" is a proposition, then according to Wittgenstein the configuration is already exhibited in the proposition. And there are at least two relational configurations exhibited in "*a b*", namely: *a is to the left of b* and *b is taller than a*. This interpretation faces two immediate difficulties: (1) The explicated relations and analogous ones (e.g. relations of color, figure, etc.) form a very small subset of all possible relations. The intended interpretation of configuration is therefore too narrow (too weak). (2) It is impossible for a proposition to exhibit just one configuration (and there are certainly contexts where the intelligibility of discourse depends on my ability to single out and present just one configuration even if I do not thereby intend to deny other compatible configurations). For on the intended interpretation there is always more than one configuration exhibited. The intended notion of configuration is therefore too wide.

It is usually assumed that a proposition *pictures* the logic of a fact, and in so doing it is said to have sense. The sense of a proposition is therefore not assigned to the proposition, but inheres in it; or in traditional terminology, the sense of proposition is based on nature, not on convention. The objects of the fact, however, are *named* in the proposition, and the names are assigned to the objects by convention, i.e. the reference of names is conventional. But there is a conflict here because closer investigation shows that the propositional logic cannot be the same as the factual logic if propositional sense is natural and reference of names conventional. The possibility of a configuration of objects into facts, Wittgenstein says, is determined by the form of the objects. Configuration in this sense can be exhibited in *propositions* only to the extent that names too are pictures of the objects' features, relevant for the configuration. The names picture the objects' spacial discreteness if the configuration is side-by-sideness, they exhibit size if the configuration is *larger-than*, etc.

Names in this sense would be crude pictures, to be sure, but no cruder than maps, for instance, which are likewise pictures, reduced to the relevant features. More precisely, crudeness in the sense of reduction is a necessary condition for something to be a picture, and to the extent that a picture attains greater physical likeness with its object, it ceases to be a picture and comes closer to being a duplicate.[10]

If names are said to have reference by convention, the function of names is not so much explained as it is made a problem because one wants to know how the assignment is made and what sustains and guarantees the representative power of a name. But this unsolved problem, one might say, is better than a spurious solution to it. A picture theory of names would in fact be spurious. It would explain the referential power of a name through the likeness of name and object, but likeness is always counteracted by crudeness or by a duplicative tendency. Pictures of themselves are referentially ambiguous or indifferent. A picture requires a relating instruction that tells us how and to what extent to relate some entity pictorially to another. Thus a map has an arrow, a scale, and a legend.[11] But these are again pictures, requiring relational instructions; and so ad infinitum.

It is clear that the present explication of the picture theory of language leads to an impasse. This may be due to the narrow and literal cast of the explication. Wittgenstein nourishes this suspicion through his refusal to give more than suggestive examples of instances of a

---

[10] Cf. Plato, *Cratylus*, 432 B–C; Goodman, *Languages*, pp. 3–43. Cf. section 9 above.

[11] Cf. David Keyt, "Wittgenstein's Notion of an Object," *Essays*, ed. Copi and Beard, pp. 289–303.

logically perfect language and through his contention that ordinary language is logically perfect though in a complicated and concealed manner.[12] A logically perfect language, not sharing this concealment, would be *the perspicuous language.*[13]

But the problem remains that language begins to fail us when we try to focus on its perspicuity. It has been said before that, since logic circumscribes the scope of the expressible, logic itself cannot be expressed. It can only be elucidated. There is then *some* kind of language in which Wittgenstein and we can talk about logic, i.e. about the nexus of language and reality. But with regard to the ordinary language which has properly expressive power it is a limitary and self-defeating type of language. Its main function is to prove itself superfluous. It is, in Wittgenstein's words, a ladder that is used to climb up a wall and is then thrown away.[14] This language has thus been called *the ladder language.*[15] The ladder language is used to talk about the unspeakable, the structure of the world as a whole. Since it is unspeakable, one's definitive attitude toward it should not be talking but silence.[16]

34. Formalized languages

For the Wittgenstein of the *Tractatus*, the logic of the perspicuous language was also and already the logic of reality. This Wittgenstein endeavored to show in a rigorous way by rendering reality and especially language perspicuous. But it appeared, at least in our explication of an instance of a perspicuous language, that the identity of the logic of reality and of the logic language fails to obtain because it is and must be abandoned at the level where objects and names are connected. Wittgenstein's endeavor ends in silence. But this outcome need not indicate that the task was inappropriately approached, but only that it was too ambitiously or naively conceived. Thus one can maintain his allegiance to rigor and perspicuity. But the task must be addressed more circumspectively. Rather than revealing the very structure of reality in the structure of the perspicuous language, one might first expend more care on the construction and specification of a perspicuous

---

[12] *Tractatus*, 3.323, 4.002, 5.5563.

[13] See Richard J. Bernstein, "Wittgenstein's Three Languages," *Essays*, ed. Copi and Beard, pp. 231–247 and Wilfrid Sellars, "Naming and Saying," *ibid.*, pp. 249–270.

[14] *Tractatus*, 6.54.

[15] Cf. Bernstein, "Three Languages."

[16] *Tractatus*, 7. – *Schweigen* can be attentive, concerned, and even eloquent, which is precluded in Pears' and McGuiness' translation ("pass over in silence").

language and then use it as a heuristic, therapeutic, or recording instrument in dealing with definite and limited problems of reality, philosophy, or ordinary language.[17]

What might a perspicuous or ideal language be like? Roughly speaking, the rigor and perspicuity of an ideal language are attained through a total specification of all items and features of the language in question.[18] This specification proceeds under two titles, *syntax* and *semantics*.

The syntax has in turn four parts.[19] The first is the *vocabulary* which lists all the irreducible elements of the language. The second part consists in the *formation rules* which specify how the elements can be combined. Third, there is a set of element combinations, produced from the vocabulary in accordance with the formation rules. These combinations are usually called *axioms*. Fourth and finally there are rules which permit the transition from one or more element combinations of a specified form to another combination of a specified form. These are the *rules of inference*. In these four parts, syntax defines the notion of *calculus*.

A calculus or strictly formal system is applicable in the sense that it can be interpreted. Of itself it has no meaning if by meaning we understand reference to the empirical world. Such reference is established through the second part which together with the syntax constitutes a formalized language, namely through semantics.[20]

What sort of syntax and semantics could serve to throw light on the nature of language? One application of these disciplines consists in the development of a calculus which, properly interpreted, mirrors the ways in which the truth or falsehood of compound propositions is determined by the truth or falsehood of the constituent propositions and by the nature of connectives such as *and, or, if – then*.[21]

More precisely but still very informally, a calculus as sketched above becomes a propositional calculus if it is given the following interpre-

---

[17] Rorty, "Metaphilosophical Difficulties," pp. 4–7.

[18] More precisely, rigor is a function of total specification, perspicuity a function of rigor; hence perspicuity is a rather more metalinguistic and subjective property of the language in question.

[19] A calculus, constructed in a slightly different terminology, but with a view to elucidating what language is, can be found in Rudolf Carnap, "Foundations of Logic and Mathematics [1938]," *The Structure of Language. Readings in the Philosophy of Language*, ed. Jerry A. Fodor and Jerrold J. Katz (Englewood Cliffs, 1964), pp. 429–431.

[20] With regard to the problem what role the notion of calculus plays in the structure and method of the sciences, cf. Henry E. Kyburg, *Philosophy of Science. A Formal Approach* (New York, 1968).

[21] Cf. Carnap, "Foundations," pp. 422–428, 431–436.

tation: The vocabulary contains variables (which stand for propositions) and constants (i.e. symbols for negations and connectives such as *and, or, if – then*). The formation rules specify the possible connections of the items of the vocabulary (they will for instance permit a sequence of a proposition, a connective, and a proposition, but not provide for a sequence of a proposition, a connective, and another connective).

The axioms will be certain sequences of propositions and connectives which in the tradition would have been called self-evidently true sentences. But here they have the sole function of providing starting points and constituents for series of proposition sequences which mirror the formal characteristics of what we intuitively call valid arguments. This amounts to giving a formal presentation of some of the Medieval doctrines regarding syncategorematic terms.

However, series of proposition sequences are perspicuous and rigorous only if the transitions from one or more proposition or proposition sequences to another proposition or proposition sequence is regulated by rules, which correspond to and are called rules of inference. Such a rule will for instance specify that given two propositions ("p" and "q") concatenated by the connective "if – then", and given the proposition "p", we can make the transition to (i.e. we can infer) the proposition "q".

Such a propositional calculus allows us to reconstruct argumentative pieces of language in a formalized way which would lay bare the logical structure of the arguments and possibly expose fallacies. It thus serves to elucidate an important dimension of language; and Wittgenstein's *Tractatus* contained in fact something like a propositional calculus which was to show how one gets from the elementary propositions to the more involved types of discourse that we find in ordinary language.[22]

35. *Russell's theory of definite descriptions*

An example of the benefits that can be derived from the confrontation of ordinary with a formalized language is Russell's theory of definite descriptions.[23] The theory was not originally attached to any particular

---

[22] *Tractatus*, 4.3–5.32. For a critique of the value of calculi and of symbolic logic for significant philosophizing see Brand Blanshard, *Reason and Analysis* (La Salle, 1962), pp. 92–307 and Günther Jacobi, *Die Ansprüche der Logistiker auf die Logik und ihre Geschichtschreibung* (Stuttgart, 1962).

[23] Bertrand Russell, "On Denoting," *Contemporary Readings in Logical Theory*, ed. Irving M. Copi and James A. Gould (New York, 1967), pp. 93–105. The following account follows

formalized language though it was later incorporated into the *Principia Mathematica*.[24] Still it manifests the spirit of ideal language philosophy as it was designed to resolve some paradoxes of ordinary language through an explication of the logical structure of the paradoxes, a structure that Russell claimed to be disguised in ordinary language.[25]

The paradoxes result from phrases in ordinary language that seem to function like proper names and are recognizable by their form which is "the so-and-so" where "so-and-so" stands for some (qualified) singular term.[26] These phrases seem to describe some definite entity and are therefore called *definite descriptions*.[27]

One of the standard examples that Russell has introduced and the puzzle that is attached to it is the following. King George IV wished to know whether Scott was the author of *Waverley*. Now "Scott" and "the author of *Waverley*" are identical in the sense that they stand for the same entity; the name "Scott" and the definite description "the author of *Waverley*" would seem to be interchangeable when they refer to an entity. In the sentence

(1) George IV wished to know whether Scott was the author of *Waverley*.

I ought to be able to substitute "Scott" for "the author of *Waverley*". This substitution would yield the sentence

(2) George IV wished to know whether Scott was Scott.

But the result of the substitution is not equivalent to the original sentence because it is true that George wished to know whether Scott was the author of *Waverley*, but no one can want to find out what is trivially true, i.e. that Scott is Scott.

Where does the mistake lie? According to Russell it lies in the assumption that a definite description means in the same way in which a name means, that is in standing for the entity named or described. This false assumption is engendered by the form that a definite description has in ordinary language. An analysis and transcription of an ordinary definite description into a logically revealing language would, so

primarily this version of the theory which was first published in 1905. A later version (1919) by the title "Descriptions" is reprinted in Leonard Linsky, ed., *Semantics and the Philosophy of Language* (Urbana, 1952), pp. 93–108.

24 Alfred North Whitehead and Bertrand Russell, *Principia Mathematica*, 2nd ed., 3 vols. (Cambridge, 1925–1927), I, 66–71.

25 The theory can be put to much wider use for the purpose of creating a canonical language which is both structurally simple and semantically powerful. See Quine, *Word and Object*, pp. 181–190.

26 "On Denoting," p. 93; "Descriptions," p. 93.

27 Russell distinguishes these from "indefinite or ambiguous descriptions" such as "a man". We will disregard the indefinite descriptions.

Russell holds, show that a name and a definite description properly understood are not equivalent and interchangeable.

What is the proper logical analysis of a definite description according to Russell? First we must explicate more precisely the distinction between names and definite descriptions, for it is our failure to see this distinction which is at the bottom of the puzzle. A name, Russell says, "is a simple symbol, directly designating an individual which is its meaning, and having this meaning in its own right, independently of the meanings of all other words."[28] Definite descriptions lack this autonomy and immediacy; they have meaning in a complex and dependent fashion which is brought out when we reflect on the general form of the contexts in which they can occur. There are two such contexts. The first asserts or denies existence of the so-and-so, the second ascribes or denies some property to the so-and-so. An example of the first is "the Queen of England exists", and example of the second is "the author of *Waverley* was Scotch". The salient point is now that we can give for each definite-description-plus-context a new proposition which, Russell claims, is logically equivalent to the initial proposition, but does not contain a group of symbols that could be called a definite description. For the initial proposition

(3) The Queen of England exists.

Russell provides

(4) There is one and only one individual that reigns over England and is female.

The initial proposition

(5) The author of *Waverley* was Scotch.

Russell translates into

(6) One and only one individual both wrote *Waverley* and was Scotch.

(4) is said to be true (false) whenever (3) is true (false), and so with (6) and (5). However the definite descriptions of (3) and (5) disappear once (3) and (5) are analysed into (4) and (6). There is then no temptation in (4) and (6) to mistake a group of symbols for a name. This is easily applied to our puzzle. (1) is properly rendered as

(7) George IV wished to know whether one and only one individual both wrote *Waverley* and was identical with Scott.

It seems that (7) preserves the unique reference of (1), but in terms of the existence or non-existence of some indefinite entity ("individ-

---

[28] "Descriptions," p. 102.

ual") which has some property ("wrote *Waverley*") and as such has another property ("was identical with Scott"); and there seems to be no implication or even suggestion (as in (1)) that we are dealing here with two separable verbal entities ("the author of *Waverley*" and "Scott") that have the same meaning in standing for the same thing. There is, then, no possibility in (7) of substituting one verbal entity ("Scott") for the other ("the author of *Waverley*"); and thus if we spoke the language manifested in (1), the puzzle that we started from could never arise.[29]

36. Limitations of the theory of definite descriptions

Though this is a brief and informal exposition of a part of Russell's theory of descriptions, it is a sufficient basis for a discussion of some of the problems involved in such theories.

The first question here regards the identity of the specific problem that the theory is to deal with. Russell seems to claim that definite descriptions are recognizable by their grammatical form.[30] But "the so-and-so" is a form shared by expressions which we would not call definite descriptions and mistake for names. An example is: "The table is the most important article of furniture in a dining room."[31] There is no unique reference here in Russell's sense.[32] Neither is it possible to prove the presence of a definite description in a proposition by an argument to the effect that the proposition in question which is overtly true and informative would become either false or trivial unless a certain expression is taken as a definite description. Such would seem to be the case if in

(8) Scott was the author of *Waverley*.

the expression to the right of the "was" were to be taken as a name, naming either the individual denoted by "Scott" ((8) is then trivially true) or some other individual ((8) is then false). But an argument which so establishes the presence of a definite description is, as a syntactic analysis, never more than an informal interpretation of that

---

[29] There are two more puzzles in "On Denoting" that Russell uses as test cases for the theory.

[30] This claim is at any rate attributed to him by Peter Frederick Strawson in "On Referring [1950]," *Readings*, ed. Copi and Gould, pp. 105–106 and by Leonard Linsky, *Referring* (London, 1967), pp. 62–64.

[31] This example is Linsky's who adduces still other cases illustrating the same point. See *loc. cit.*

[32] More precisely, there is not necessarily a reference to some particular table. But one might argue that "table" is a disguised definite description of a unique class.

proposition; syntactically this interpretation carries no more weight than one which disallows the definite description at the expense of interpreting the proposition as being either false or trivial.[33] Moreover, this account is not exhaustive since two names may (in a certain sense) name the same thing, but in different modes, the difference being informative. Unique reference, to be sure, always characterizes definite descriptions. But this trait is not sufficient for their identity since it is shared by other linguistic entities such as "today", "I", "this", "Robert", and the like.

If the difference between names and definite descriptions is granted according to Russell's intentions, another difficulty follows just from this difference. A name has for its meaning the bearer of the name; to understand the name is roughly to be acquainted with the thing named. A definite description has no separate meaning; rather the proposition into which it is analyzed conveys meaning through its constituents and their configuration. Assume that someone has a colleague by the name of Robert. He knows Robert; "Robert" is a (logically) proper name for him. His wife, however, never met Robert; all she knows is that he is her husband's colleague. For her "Robert" is a disguised definite description. So when the man and his wife speak of "Robert", that expression functions in different ways for them; this follows from Russell's theory, and the theory cannot give an account of how communication about Robert is possible in this case.[34]

A third type of difficulty arises from the fact that the definite description of (1) does not occur in a main clause, but in a subordinate clause. The subordinate clause ((8) above) is the proposition "Scott was the author of *Waverley*." Syntactically, (8) occurs as a complement to the verb phrase ("wished to know") of (1); semantically (8) functions in (1) as the object of George's curiosity. That dependence could take formally similar variants: (8) could be the object of George's hope, anger, concern, fear, etc. There are characteristic verbs for each such dependence; they have been called *verbs of propositional attitude*.

An adequate comprehension of (1) presupposes a twofold understanding of (8):

    (a) we must understand what (8) means as a main clause;
    (b) we must understand that and how (8), as found in (1), is dependent relative to the main clause of (1).

---

[33] Cf. Linsky, *Referring*, pp. 53–54.
[34] This difficulty is raised by Max Black, "Russell's Philosophy of Language [1944]," *Linguistic Turn*, ed. Rorty, p. 145 and by Linsky, *Referring*, p. 59.

Assume now that

  (c) we understand (8) in the sense of (a) and find (8) to be true,

and assume that

  (d) we understand the dependence in (1) according to (b) and find
      that it does obtain;

we are now in a position to affirm the truth of (1). If (1) and (7) are to
be equivalent, then (7) should likewise be true according to the (suit-
ably modified) criteria (a)–(c). More particularly, conditions (a) and (c)
must be met for

  (9) One and only one individual both wrote *Waverley* and was
      identical with Scott.

rather than for (8), and conditions (b) and (d) for (9) and (7) rather
than for (8) and (1). (7) indeed is true on these conditions.

The difference in formulation between (8) and (9) suggests however
that in a different and quite conceivable historical setting (8) would
have satisfied (c) while (9) would not have done so, namely if *Waverley*
had not been written by one individual, but had been co-authored.[35]
On that assumption (1) and (7) would not be equivalent in the sense of
(a)–(c). Yet (7) is still true, if

  (e) George asked in all seriousness whether (8) was the case, and
      he accepted the equivalence of (8) and (9).

What is sufficient for (7) to be true is not that (9) be true analogous to
the sense of (c), but that (9) was in fact a possible formulation of the
object of George's curiosity. The same holds true for (1) and (8) respectively. Condition (c) is illicit for all clauses that depend on verbs of
propositional attitude (with the possible exception of *know*); it is precisely the absence of such a condition which is one of the characteristics
of intensional propositions.[36] The equivalence of (1) and (7) is therefore
not impaired merely through the difference in formulation between (8)
and (9).

But it has been argued that under certain circumstances (1) and (7)
are not equivalent even if condition (c) is dropped.[37] The thesis is that
condition (e) may not be met. The argument is one from illustration,
and it is this: George IV says to a courtier: "I wonder if Scott is the
author of *Waverley*." The courtier cannot help his sovereign in this
matter. He goes to see an expert in literary matters and explains the

[35] Linsky's point, *ibid.*, pp. 69–70.

[36] In Russell's terminology: an intensional proposition does not have primary occurrence;
see "On Denoting," p. 102.

[37] The argument is Linsky's in *Referring*, pp. 71–74.

problem to him. They then go to the King, and the expert begins by saying: "Sir, I understand that you wish to know whether one and only one individual wrote *Waverley* and is identical with Scott." George replies: "No, this is not what I wanted to know. I *do* know that just one person wrote *Waverley*. What I *wish* to know is whether Scott is the author of *Waverley*."

Does this argument suffice to show that condition (e) may conceivably not be met? The answer seems obvious in light of the illustration.[38] If we accept this answer, we have to conclude that (7) is not the only possible explication of (1). (1) is ambiguous and can also be explicated thus:

> (10) George IV knew that one and only one individual had written *Waverley*, and George IV wished to know whether Scott was that individual.

(7) and (10) are not equivalent; for (10) is false if *Waverley* was co-authored whereas (7) would not be false merely on that assumption.

Still another explication of (1) can be given the truth value of which (like that of (7)) is independent of whether *Waverley* had one or more authors and which nonetheless fails to be equivalent with (7). It would run as follows:

> (11) George IV believed that one and only one individual had written *Waverley*, and he wished to know whether Scott was that individual.

But (11) is itself ambiguous. It could be the report of the following:

> (12) George IV said: "I believe that one and only one individual wrote *Waverley*, and I wish to know whether Scott is that individual."

(12) is either inconsistent since the first part of George's statement merely assumes the existence of a single author while the second part presupposes that the single author in fact exists. Or (12) is elliptical for the statement:

> (13) George IV said: "I believe that one and only one individual wrote *Waverley*, and, assuming that I am correct in my belief, I wish to know whether Scott is that individual."

---

[38] Linsky does not insist on the validity of this argument and goes on to produce one which he holds to be valid even if the first fails *(ibid.*, p. 72). But it seems that either the first argument is valid, and then the second is not needed; or the first is invalid, and then so is the second since the first is contained in the second and invalidates the second; for Linsky cannot and would not argue a thesis that he knows to be invalid. In the terminology of section 38, the first argument, if invalid, does not fall within the scope of what is arguable by Linsky.

(13) is not equivalent with (7) because the single authorship of *Waverley* is said to be the object of belief in (13) whereas (7) reports it to be the object of curiosity.[39]

Although (11) is true or false independently of whether *Waverley* had in fact a single author if (11) is taken in the sense of (13), (11) can also be given an interpretation such that (11) is false (as is (10)) on the assumption of multiple authorship. In that case (11) is obviously not equivalent with (7), but neither is it with (10). (11) in this sense reads as follows:

> (14) George IV said: "One and only one individual wrote *Waverley*
> [we know that this is not the case], and I wish to know whether
> Scott is that individual."

The verb "believed" in (11) is here explicated not as indicating an attitude of belief, which the believer holds knowingly (this is the interpretation of (13)), but as designating an honest yet erroneous attitude on the part of the believer. If "believed" is understood in this latter sense, it is intensional in two ways at once: (a) It indicates that

> (15) One and only one individual wrote *Waverley*.

as it occurs in (11) is not to be taken as true or false of itself, but as true or false in its dependence on, and in conjunction with, "George IV said that". (b) It indicates that the negation of (15) is true in its dependence on, and in conjunction with, "we know that". Thus it indicates that the truth value of the compound proposition characterized in (b) overrides the truth value of the dependent proposition characterized in (a) with which it conflicts.[40]

37. *The explanatory status of logical analyses of language*

We want to leave aside the question whether the difficulties in the theory of definite descriptions just discussed derive from limitations of that theory or from the way it was applied and illustrated by Russell. Nor do we want to settle the question just what claims Russell made

---

[39] One might argue that (13) further differs from (7) in that the identity of the author is the object of unqualified curiosity in (7) whereas that curiosity is conditional in (13).

[40] Using Quine's terminology, "believed" of (11) in the sense of (14) is transparent but in such a way that the *negation* of the clause dependent on "believed" has purely referential occurrence. This transparency of "believe" is different from that mentioned by Quine, *Word and Object*, p. 145, and it can be accentuated colloquially thus: "George IV, believe it or not, believed that ..."

for his theory.[41] Instead we turn to more general problems to which the preceding section gives us access.

The first of the three difficulties, mentioned in the preceding section, illustrates the fact that logically reconstructed pieces of language cannot in a generally determined way replace ordinary locutions because no logical analysis contains a mechanical or rigorous device of spotting those pieces of ordinary language that are to be replaced. Hence the misleading or ambiguous feature of ordinary parlance that is to be corrected must be recognized as such prior to any logical analysis.[42]

The second of the above difficulties shows that a particular instance of a logical analysis of language needs an ordinary understanding of language not only to get under way, but for its intelligibility throughout. The demand that the theory of definite descriptions explain how mutual understanding is possible if for one person "Robert" is a logically proper name and for another a disguised definite description is justified only on the assumption that the theory does provide an explanation of mutual understanding if "Robert" is a disguised definite description for *both* partners of a conversation. But obviously the theory merely lays down some necessary conditions for such understanding. Beyond that, psychological, linguistic, and ultimately ontological conditions would have to be specified if (solitary or mutual) understanding were to be explained. Normally these specifications are informally supplied by our ordinary understanding of language as we apply it by way of empathy to the problem under discussion. If someone is said to learn of an individual that has the property of being her husband's colleague, clearly that information is at once and necessarily enriched with anticipations, recollections, presumptions. Or putting it differently, the definite description as a piece of information is instantly and intricately integrated into the recipient's world. To the extent that the recipient shares her world with her husband who uses a name where she has a definite description, communication is possible. That a difference with regard to "Robert" persists is correctly entailed by the theory. The difference must be obeyed by both partners.

Finally it is apparent from propositions (7), (10), (13), and (14) above

---

[41] There are at least shifts of emphasis. For instance, Russell makes more sweeping claims for his theory in "On Denoting" than he does in his reply to Strawson, "Mr. Strawson on Referring [1959]," *Readings*, ed. Copi and Gould, pp. 127–132. – Linsky goes perhaps too far in his ascription of claims to Russell.

[42] Cf. Rorty, "Metaphilosophical Difficulties," pp. 15–16 and P. F. Strawson, "Analysis, Science, and Metaphysics," *Linguistic Turn*, ed. Rorty, pp. 312–316.

that even after some ordinary sentence (e.g. (1)) has been found to require (in some situations) a logical analysis, there is still no unique and rigorous method of finding the correct translation; rather there may be competing and jointly incompatible explications.[43] The differences among the various explications all derive from the single fact that the verb of propositional attitude in (1) is ambiguous with regard to the number, types, and scopes of intensionality which it may designate.[44]

It now becomes apparent that the retreat from Wittgenstein's ambitious project in the *Tractatus* abandoned just that element which alone could have made a logical analysis of language an enterprise in its own right. A concept of logic as presented in the *Tractatus* would have provided guidance for corrective recourse to a logically perfect language. But without the guidance of such logic, logical analysis of language comes to no more than casting certain aspects of extralogically gained insights into the form of a logically perfect language.[45] This negative result still leaves us with the task of showing in more detail why the problem of guidance failed to assert itself openly in the circumspectively conceived task and of showing precisely why the problem, though present in the *Tractatus*, remained unsolved there also. We pursue this goal by pushing further the discussion of intensionality as it arises in the theory of definite descriptions.

38. The grounds of logical analyses of language

That a proposition is intensional can be explicated by saying that it is claimed to fall within the (intensional) scope that is proper to the respective verb of propositional attitude (the governing verb). Every such verb has a characteristic scope; for "believe" it is the believable, for "imagine" it is the imaginable, for "hope" it is what can be hoped for, etc.[46] That a dependent proposition fall within the scope of its governing verb is a necessary condition for the truth of the main proposition. Russell implicitly appeals to this principle when he rejects

[43] The requirement that a logically reconstructed sentence (one in canonical form) be in every sense logically equivalent to or synonymous with the initial ordinary sentence is too strong ever to be satisfied. See Quine, *Word and Object*, pp. 159–161.

[44] Problems of intensionality also arise for verbs other than those of propositional attitude, e.g. *look for, plan*, etc.; and problems of scopes arise for words other than verbs, e.g. indefinite singular terms such as *each, every, any*. See Quine, *ibid.*, pp. 138–141, 151–156.

[45] Cf. Irving Copi, "Language Analysis and Metaphysical Inquiry," *Linguistic Turn*, pp. 127–131. – This secondary aspect of a logical analysis of language deprives of cogency an attempt such as Carnap's in "The Elimination of Metaphysics Through Logical Analysis of Language [1932]," *Logical Positivism*, ed. A. J. Ayer (New York, 1959), pp. 60–81.

[46] These scopes correspond to Husserl's *doxic modalities*. See his *Ideas*, pp. 275–277.

"George IV wished to know whether Scott was Scott" as a true proposition. The tacit argument is that "Scott is Scott" is not within the scope of curiosity.

The intensional scopes differ in extension. More states of affairs are imaginable than are believable; and there are events that I can wish that they come true, but not hope that they come true. Furthermore in ordinary language, one dependent proposition may be subject to more than one intensional scope though there be just one governing verb. Proposition (1) is an example of this. As (10) shows, the scope of "wished to know" may not cover all of the dependent proposition, but only part of it. The remaining part then falls within the scope of a "knew" which is implied in "wished to know" and which, together with its dependent clause, is compatible with "wished to know" and *its* dependent clause, a necessary condition of compatibility being that the extension of the two intensional scopes is not claimed to overlap (it is impossible to wish to know what one does know and vice versa).

Explication (12) of (1) again points out two intensional scopes in the dependent proposition of (1). But here the two governing verbs together with their respective dependent clauses may not be compatible. The reason (as hinted at above) seems to be this: All propositions within the intensional scope of "wish to know" must (at least intensionally) imply the existence of that in regard to which one wishes to know something. But in (12), precisely that element which is to provide the basis for the *wish to know* (the single authorship of *Waverley*) is placed within the scope of what may not have existence and is merely believed. The incompatibility, in short, results from disregarding the fact that the extension of the scope of "wish to know" presupposes (but does not overlap or coincide with) some specifiable extension of the scope of "know".

What is asserted by propositions within the scope of believability is for the believer suspended between existence and non-existence. It may become apparent as existent or non-existent to the believer who then becomes a knower. If he knows something to be existent, he can wish to know more about it. This qualification is made in (13) which is therefore consistent.

In the discussion of (12) and (13), it has already become apparent that the intensional scopes are not opposed to the sphere of reality or existence which is rather the intensional scope of "know".[47] The scope

---

[47] This scope corresponds to Husserl's *protodoxa*; see *ibid.*, pp. 273–278.

of "know" is a limitary case of intensional scopes since all propositions within it must be true if they are to be dependent propositions in true main propositions. This is not a characteristic of any other intensional scope. The scope of "know" has the crucial function of mediating between the other intensional scopes and reality or truth. It seems initially at least disquieting that beliefs, hopes, and apprehensions can be valid without being true. However someone's intensional propositions (of belief, hope, and apprehension) are conditional on his scope of knowledge, and this scope is no longer accepted as valid apart from its truth or falsehood, but it is simply true or false.

Proposition (11) understood in the sense of (14) is an example where a proposition is located by a speaker (by the speaker within (11), not by the speaker who utters (11)) in his scope of knowledge. That proposition is then subject to the standard of reality or truth, which (granted the bracketed assumption of (14)) it fails to meet. This failure can be explicitly stated (as in (14)) or indicated by means of a governing verb within the proposition ((11) in the present case) such that the verb expresses both the claim to the scope of knowledge and the failure to meet the claim (this can be the meaning of "believed" in (11)).[48]

If knowledge has a decisive role in grounding and interrelating the intensional scopes, we must ask by what authority knowing has this power. Is it sufficient to say simply that the scope of knowledge coincides with what there is? We return here to the central problem of the *Tractatus*. The Wittgenstein of the *Tractatus*, we saw, gives an affirmative answer; and *logic* is the term which designates the way in which cognitive language and reality hang together. Warned by the failure of the picture theory of language, men like Carnap and Quine took the more circumspect position outlined in section 34. In conclusion of this chapter we want to examine the general justification of this view.

Carnap urges a distinction between the questions that pertain to linguistic frameworks as a whole (the external questions) and those that obtain within frameworks (the internal ones).[49] The frameworks afford conclusive answers to the internal questions. The external questions are of a practical nature and practically settled, i.e. by the "success or failure in practical use" of the linguistic forms in question.[50] Similarly Quine insists that in using a formal language (one in canonical

---

[48] Cf. note 40 above. – Some of these points and problems can be formalized. Cf. Jaako Hintikka, *Knowledge and Belief. An Introduction to the Logic of Two Notions* (Ithaca, 1962).

[49] Rudolf Carnap, "Empiricism, Semantics, and Ontology [1950]," *Linguistic Turn*, ed. Rorty, pp. 72–84.

[50] *Ibid.*, p. 83.

notation) we can tell exactly where and to what this language is onto-logically committed.[51] But this does not of itself determine what it is that warrants an ontological commitment.[52] This again is a practical matter, one of finding the most convenient myth.[53]

But if this is all that can be said, the primacy of knowing will remain opaque and inaccessible to principled discourse; all the distinctions and evaluations of propositional attitudes will rest on uncertain ground. One man's knowledge is another man's superstition or propaganda. Speaking more directly to Carnap's and Quine's positions, we must ask: In what type of language will we investigate, establish, and discuss "success or failure in practical use" and the convenience of our pres-ently employed myth? Clearly this is the decisive question which in the end decides on the value of the internal questions and of our concern with canonical notation. The decisive theory is the one which has for its problem and object not just the nature of some object language, but the connection of the object language to reality.[54] But this metatheo-retical problem is not only left unexplored, but is declared inaccessible and is thus occluded. The metatheoretical occlusion in turn makes meaningless any assertion that there is something like success or failure of (competing) linguistic frameworks or myths or something like onto-logical slum clearing.[55]

Why are such assertions advanced nonetheless? The reason seems to lie in an unquestioned confidence that the natural sciences reveal at least in principle a coherent and meaningful world composed of items sufficiently clear and distinct to admit of straightforward and incontro-versial tests of languages against the scientific world. But this assump-tion seems sufficiently strong and consequential to require explicit consideration. There is moreover some danger of misinterpreting the pragmatism of Carnap and Quine. One is inclined to infer from the

---

[51] Willard Van Orman Quine, "On What There Is [1948]," *From a Logical Point of View* (New York, 1963), pp. 12–14.

[52] *Ibid.*, pp. 15–17, 19. A discussion of Quine's notion of ontological commitment is just one way of making the present point. It could be similarly illustrated through a discussion of Quine's radical translation or semantic ascent; cf. *Word and Object*, pp. 26–35, 270–276. Cf. also "Ontological Relativity," in *Ontological Relativity and Other Essays* (New York, 1969), pp. 26–28.

[53] See "Two Dogmas of Empiricism [1951]," *From a Logical Point of View*, pp. 44–46; "On What There Is," pp. 17–18.

[54] The proper metatheory need not be what is usually called semantics since the latter may relate a formal language to a possible world or a stipulated domain of objects, not to reality in the inexorable sense.

[55] "Slum clearing" in "On What There is," p. 4 and "Semantic ascent," p. 275. Real slum clearing too has proven more involved and frustrating than was thought possible in the fifties.

rigor and perspicuity of the object language that it will reveal or reflect how the world is at its most rigorous and perspicuous, and further one is tempted to attribute a kind of force and clarity to the inference itself. But as has been argued such inferences move in an area that is meta-theoretically occluded; and hence such moves are unwarranted on the terms of the philosophy by which they are performed; if anything they are in contrast to the rigor and perspicuity of the object languages.

We can now see that in Wittgenstein's *Tractatus* the properly meta-theoretical problem is clearly present, but the appropriate language, the ladder language, begins to falter and ends in silence. The meta-theoretical problem in turn failed to assert itself independently of a corresponding metalanguage because words of themselves seemed in-inconceivable as the presence of things. Things had already fallen silent and so could not be seen to issue in words. Words need to be connected to things through a depicting relation which would have secured radical signification. But the attempt at establishing such a relation ends in an infinite regress and thus from a different direction leads to the impasse already discovered in section 31.

When language is rendered precise, it seems to get severed from the world which is of itself alive and eloquent. Rigor in the end is *rigor mortis*.

CHAPTER TWO

ORDINARY LANGUAGE

39. Access to reality through ordinary language.
Wittgenstein's "Philosophical Investigations"

In the preceding chapter, we have repeatedly had occasion to refer to the ordinary understanding of language as that realm from which a logical analysis of language departs and which in important though not exclusive ways sustains such an analysis. It is plausible to expect that a turn to ordinary language would enable one to understand and overcome the limitations and impasses to which one is led in the pursuit of rigor and precision in language. Wittgenstein, who had been one of the most influential representatives of this pursuit, was also the one who criticized this approach most incisively and was most consequential in providing alternative investigations of language.

The fundamental impetus for the change in Wittgenstein's attitude seems to have been his realization that language displays aspects more subtle, variable, and contextual than are apparent in a formal structure.[1] Ordinarily, we command the subtle powers, rules, and ramifications of language without difficulty. In philosophical reflection, however, prejudices and illicit simplifications lead us into seemingly inescapable and unresolvable problems. We get caught like a fly in the fly-bottle. This then calls for another liberating kind of philosophy. In Wittgenstein's words: "What is your aim in philosophy? – To shew the fly the way out of the fly-bottle."[2]

The positive force that sustains this enterprise is careful attention to the whole in which language realizes itself. Wittgenstein's attempts at

---

[1] See Norman Malcolm, *Ludwig Wittgenstein. A Memoir* (London, 1967 [first published in 1958]), p. 69 and Ludwig Wittgenstein, *Philosophical Investigations* [1953], 3rd ed. (New York, 1968), p. x. In the sequel, references will be to sections in the first part and to page numbers in the second.

[2] *Ibid.*, section 309.

securing such a broad vision are signaled by the recurring terms "language-game" and "language as a form of life". An adequate understanding of his work requires therefore that we enter into his investigations and perhaps carry them further. Let us by way of an example go through the movements and stages of Wittgenstein's analysis of "seeing".

The subject is introduced immediately and simply. "Two uses of the word 'see'."[3] The one: I see an object as such. The other: I see an aspect of an object; or: I see something as ... There is a distinct difference between the two. Consider the drawing of a certain plane figure. I can see it as the head of a rabbit or as the head of a duck.[4] The two long appendages can be seen as the rabbit's ears or as the duck's bill. In spite of these differences, I cannot say that anything physical has changed in the drawing as I see it in different ways.

Should I say that the differences do not lie in the physical drawing, but in the inner (mental) picture that I have of it? But either the inner picture has the same ambiguity as the physical one (as I recollect the physical drawing I can see it in my recollection as a duck or a rabbit), or it is a useless and even confusing postulate (for how do I see the inner picture? in having before me an inner picture of *it*?).

There are instances where "seeing as" becomes altogether inapplicable, and we are still not left with an uninterpreted object as such. Seeing the silverware laid out on the supper table, I cannot say: "Now I am seeing this as a knife and fork."[5] This expression is simply wrong (in its presuppositions). Or in looking at a landscape, I may suddenly see a rabbit running by. I exclaim: "A rabbit!" The exclamation is not the result of (among other constituents) the perception of an object and the interpretative addition of an aspect.[6]

When I see an appropriate drawing either as a duck or a rabbit, nothing physical in the picture changes. Similarly in drawings which can be seen as concave or convex steps or boxes or in puzzle-pictures where from among branches suddenly a human figure emerges. But after such a change has taken place, I can rightly say that the picture is no longer the same as before. I see something *different in the picture.* What has changed is its organization.[7]

[3] *Ibid.*, p. 193.
[4] *Ibid.*, p. 194. These aspects are most readily suggested, but are not the only ones. I could see the drawing as a sketch of a lake or bay, as a misshaped clothes pin or gingerbread man.
[5] *Investigations*, p. 195.
[6] *Ibid.*, p. 197.
[7] *Ibid.*, pp. 203, 208.

In cases where an aspect is difficult to grasp, we can imagine people who are incapable of seeing a certain aspect and suffer from what Wittgenstein calls aspect-blindness.[8] But such people would not see nothing. Do they see the object free of aspects? Or do they see just one particular (basic) aspect? Do we always see some aspect and never the thing as such?

Wittgenstein emphasizes that investigations of the above sort do not seek the psychological or physiological causes of seeing, but attempt to clarify the concept of seeing which would remain genuinely problematic even if all scientific problems had been solved.[9] The problematic nature of this concept must be recognized. "The concept of 'seeing' makes a tangled impression. Well, it is tangled." The difficulties that lie hidden in it at once come into relief when in a given situation we ask for a "description of what is seen." But the difficulties are only perverted if the problem of *seeing* is dissected into a list of fine distinctions. "What we have rather to do is to *accept* the everyday language-game, and to note *false* accounts of the matter *as* false."[10]

Articulating the idiosyncrasy and interrelatedness of a word in its language-games is what Wittgenstein calls giving the grammar of a word. Wittgenstein's delineation of the grammar of the word "seeing" is richer and more suggestive than our sketch indicates, and there is a definite gain for the reader in his understanding of the word "seeing". But completeness of the data and substantive results are not overriding desiderata. "In giving all these examples I am not aiming at some kind of completeness, some classification of psychological concepts. They are only meant to enable the reader to shift for himself when he encounters conceptual difficulties."[11]

40. Speaking and doing. Austin

Austin, just as Wittgenstein, was convinced that many philosophical problems resulted from a misunderstanding and misuse of ordinary language; but in addition his investigations were motivated by the realization that ordinary language, apart from being a living force and the standard of all speaking, was in itself a region of great surprises and gratifying discoveries. Austin had the imagination and persistence

---

[8] *Ibid.*, pp. 213–214.
[9] *Ibid.*, pp. 193, 201, 203, 212.
[10] *Ibid.*, p. 200.
[11] *Ibid.*, p. 206.

of an explorer, and the results of his explorations confirm his view that "evidently, there is gold in them thar hills" of ordinary language.[12]

Perhaps his most celebrated discovery is the distinction between constative and performative sentences.[13] Constative sentences are those that state a fact. Where the distinction between language and reality is made in a facile manner, language appears primarily as a reflection of reality, and a constative is then the paradigm of language. On that view, there are to be sure, deviant types of sentences, such as questions, exclamations, imperatives; but they seem arbitrary since they do not fall under the criterion of truth or falsehood. This view takes its point of departure from Aristotle as we have seen.[14]

What Austin teaches us to see is that there are sentences which are of the subject-predicate form, but are so far from being reports of facts that they rather and primarily constitute facts or events. In

(1) I give and bequeath my watch to my brother.

an event first comes about (a bequest) and may then be reported. Neither is it accidental to the event that it occurs in language, nor is such use of language incidental or arbitrary. Austin shows that performatives are governed by definite and intricate rules because we can measure them by the criteria of success and failure.[15]

To distinguish between constatives and performatives is to give genuine insight into two dimensions of speaking. But it also leads to problems because every type of speaking is a doing. Austin attacks this problem by pointing out that a given instance of speaking constitutes one of three possible modes of doing. It can be the *simple saying* of something meaningful (locutionary act); it can be exertion of some force *in saying* something (illocutionary act), and it can be the achieving of certain effects *by saying* something (perlocutionary act).[16] Examples:

(A) Locution
   (1) He said to me "Shoot her!"
   (2) He said to me "You can't do that".

---

[12] J. L. Austin, "A Plea for Excuses [1956]," *Ordinary Language*, ed. V. C. Chappell (Englewood Cliffs, 1964), p. 46.
[13] This is the central topic of *How to Do Things with Words*, ed. J. O. Urmson (New York, 1965 [first published in 1962]).
[14] Cf. section 11.
[15] Plato had used this argument to *establish* validity in language against the Sophists. Austin appeals to it in order to *extend* the scope of validity.
[16] *Things*, pp. 94–107.

(B) Illocution
    (1) He ordered me to shoot her.
    (2) He protested against my doing it.
(C) Perlocution
    (1) He persuaded me to shoot her.
    (2) He stopped me.[17]

Again, these distinctions give us a definite insight, but in turn open up new problems. For apparently there is no such thing as a simple disinterested saying of something. As a rule I say something in order to inform, warn, admonish, threaten, etc. Every locution also seems to be an illocution. Again, I can speak of an illocutionary force only if the illocution has certain effects such as being understood, responded to, and the like. In that sense, every illocution is perlocutionary. But these overlaps do not erase the central points of the distinctions. Locutions are at least abstractly separable from illocutions. Illocutions, in turn, owe their force to conventions while perlocutions do not. Bringing about an effect is a matter of efficiency simply; exerting a force on someone verbally requires that I avail myself of locutions (or alternatively or more broadly of gestures) which have come to possess the signifying power which suits my purpose.

We can now return to the constative/performative distinction and explain it in terms of the locutionary/illocutionary distinction, the latter being more general and flexible than the former. Obviously both constatives and performatives are locutions and illocutions. But constatives are relatively free of illocutionary implications while performatives are strongly and primarily illocutions. It follows from the above remarks on locutions that pure constatives or statements are abstractions to the extent of their purity, and so are their unique criteria of truth and falsehood as Austin takes pains to show.[18]

Throughout these considerations, Austin lets himself be guided by a fine feeling for the power of words, by attention to the recurring and pervasive syntactic behavior of the words under investigation, and by a desire to catch the typical features and groups of words in an informative terminology. An example of terminological diligence can be seen in the introduction of *il*-locutions as expressions conforming to the blank in: "*in* saying such and such I..." Similarly, *per*-locutions satisfy the blank in: "*by* saying such and such I..." But Austin is properly scrupulous with his own techniques and points out the many

---

[17] Adapted from *ibid.*, pp. 101–102.
[18] *Ibid.*, pp. 139–144, 150.

counter-examples to both heuristic devices.[19] But the formula "to say such and such is to ..." turns out to be a reliable detector of illocutionary verbs. As such it is a suitable instrument for field work, that is for the kind of concrete exploratory activity that Austin prized highly.[20]

41. The radicalism and cogency of Ordinary Language Analysis

Initially, at least, it is puzzling why Ordinary Language Philosophy has had such a wide appeal. It has, after all, none of the unassailable rigor of logic, nor does it possess the immediacy and poetic quality of existentialism.

But work in ordinary language philosophy is rewarding in much the same way in which phenomenology in its initial phase gratified its followers. It permits detailed and painstaking investigation which is seemingly free of the regimentation and tyranny of a highly developed tradition. At the same time, results are solid and verifiable; an original discovery or laborious investigations can count on recognition.[21] Connected with this is the insight that ordinary language is the medium in which human activities take place first and most of all. It is in ordinary language that I make friends and enemies, plan my future, influence others, make commitments, receive assurances. And novel, unheard of phenomena become intelligible and can be dealt with when they have left their native surroundings or jargon and entered the realm of ordinary language (or perhaps when ordinary language has extended itself and embraced them).[22]

Being well-versed in this decisive region, its student is rewarded by being invested with rightful authority which permits him to undercut in modest and yet radical fashion the high-flown philosophemes of the academician. G. E. Moore, though not formally an analyst of ordinary language, strongly influenced the movement through his mastery of methodological naiveté by means of which he showed that recourse to the simple and ordinary views of daily life has its own rigor and cutting

---

[19] Ibid., pp. 122–131.

[20] "Excuses," p. 47.

[21] This comes close to the popular conception of phenomenology which is used by sociologists and political scientists and probably also by Austin when he calls his enterprise "linguistic phenomenology" ("Excuses," p. 47). It has little to do with Husserl's mature phenomenology. On the cogency and rewards of Ordinary Language Philosophy, cf. further Austin, ibid., pp. 41–42, Stanley Cavell, "Austin at Criticism [1965]," Linguistic Turn, ed. Rorty, pp. 256–257, and Rorty, "Metaphilosophical Difficulties," pp. 11, 14, 33.

[22] Cf. Austin, "Excuses," p. 49.

edge.[23] Austin, to give an example, employed this method to combat the notion "that whenever a 'material-object' statement is made, the speaker must have or could produce evidence for it."

The situation in which I would properly be said to have *evidence* for the statement that some animal is a pig is that, for example, in which the beast itself is not actually on view, but I can see plenty of pig-like marks on the ground outside its retreat. If I find a few buckets of pig-food, that's a bit more evidence, and the noises and the smell may provide better evidence still. But if the animal then emerges and stands there plainly in view, there is no longer any question of collecting evidence; its coming into view doesn't provide me with more *evidence* that it's a pig, I can now just *see* that it is, the question is settled.[24]

But cogent demonstration and refutation are no more important than the region to which they apply. Obviously they do not apply to the realm of ordinary language because this is the power that sustains them; if ordinary language were itself in need of rigorous investigation, we could not appeal to it as a standard. Indeed the problems that ordinary language philosophy attacks are to be found, as hinted above, in the misuses of language perpetrated in traditional philosophy. Here again, G. E. Moore is an important forerunner of the movement:

I do not think that the world or the sciences would ever have suggested to me any philosophical problems. What has suggested philosophical problems to me is things which other philosophers have said about the world or the sciences. In many problems suggested in this way I have been (and still am) very keenly interested – the problems in question being mainly of two sorts, namely, first, the problem of trying to get really clear as to what on earth a given philosopher *meant* by something which he said, and, secondly, the problem of discovering what really satisfactory reasons there are for supposing that what he said was true, or, alternatively, was false. I think I have been trying to solve problems of this sort all my life, and I certainly have not nearly been so successful in solving them as I should have liked to be.[25]

But if recourse to ordinary language is legitimate, it cannot be the case that ordinary language is in any significant way influenced by traditional philosophy. However, if ordinary language is thus immune, then traditional philosophy has failed to exercise influence in an area which, in the sense indicated previously, is most decisive for human existence and which, at the same time, is the one field where philosophy would most readily be expected to be effective. It follows then that

[23] See Malcolm, "Moore and Ordinary Language [1942]," in *Linguistic Turn*, ed. Rorty, pp. 111–124. All of Austin's *Sense and Sensibilia*, ed. G. J. Warnock (New York, 1964 [first published in 1962]) is an exercise along these lines.

[24] *Sense*, p. 115.

[25] G. E. Moore, "An Autobiography," *The Philosophy of G. E. Moore*, ed. Paul Arthur Schilpp (Evanston, 1942), p. 14.

traditional philosophy may well be in error with regard to the nature and importance of its problems; its entire enterprise might at any rate be inconsequential and negligible; and it is difficult to see why a correction of the error should be of significantly greater consequence and significance.[26]

42. The limits and further possibilities of Ordinary Language Analysis

There are, however, deeper implications of Ordinary Language Analysis. But these implications, if accepted, will lead that type of analysis beyond its present limits.[27]

To show this, we begin with the fact that it is not at all clear what ordinary language, the standard and object of all analysis, is. One might take it to be a collective term for the ways in which people ordinarily talk. Ordinary parlance could then be analyzed according to its vocabulary, its external shape (sounds), its formation rules, and its methods of signifying. But all these problems are pre-empted by lexicography, phonetics, syntax, and semantics. One might reply that what we need is precisely a type of investigation that draws on the specialized and fragmented results of these disciplines, and in focusing on the entire speech act or situation, shows in a more flexible and comprehensive way how language is typically and concretely used. One might think of Wittgenstein's "language-game" and "language as a form of life" as controlling concepts of such an approach.[28]

But here a new problem arises. Does not such an investigation require the experimental and statistical methods of, say, psychology and sociology? Are not such methods presupposed in the locutions, frequently used by ordinary language philosophers, such as: "we do say ..., but we don't say ...", "we would normally say ...", "we say ... when ..."? Gilbert Ryle has argued against this view that the ordinary *use* is not a matter of frequency of occurrence (this is true of *usage*), but represents in a normative way what can be said at a given occasion and what not. The opposite of *ordinary use* is *misuse*, the opposite of *ordi-*

---

[26] For further criticism see Blanshard, *Reason and Analysis*, pp. 308–421 and Benson Mates, "On the Verification of Statements about Ordinary Language," *Ordinary Language*, ed. Chappell, pp. 64–74.

[27] These limits have already been transgressed e.g. by Ryle's work on Plato, Toulmin's in the philosophy of science, Strawson's in Kant. The decisive question is whether this and similar work is adequate to the extent that it relies on Ordinary Language Analysis, and whether it relies on that sort of analysis where it is indeed insightful.

[28] Cf. also Austin's concern with "the total speech act" in *Things*, pp. 52, 136, 147.

nary usage is *non-stock use.*[29] This has been further explicated by Stanley Cavell. Ordinary language is in his sense the common and basic constitution in which all speakers of a speech community share. If I have a legitimate claim to membership in that community, I am in a position to articulate this constitution without need of gathering empirical evidence. Statements describing features of ordinary language are therefore not reports of (generalizations of) empirical facts, but presentations of conditions, delimiting the possibilities of facts, but also of fictions, attitudes, theories. Hence such statements are called "instances (not of Formal, but) of Transcendental Logic."[30] This is a legitimate and enlightening allusion to Kant, and it gives an alternative, perhaps more incisive, account of the peculiarly privileged and radical approach of ordinary language analysis. But clearly the present problem directs us to, and the quotation above depends for its force on, Kant's critical enterprise. Hence if ordinary language philosophy means to ground and understand itself it must at least recognize Kant's enterprise as legitimate and urgent. This would in turn force one to forego application of linguistic analysis to Kant. His problems would have to be accepted at face value.[31]

Such a discussion of Kantian problems could take many turns; and as the philosophical experience of nearly two centuries has shown, it would not even encounter all its foundational problems in Kant. Kant, e.g., not only did not deal with the question of history in his critiques; it is hard to see how he could even have posed it appropriately in the framework of his critical philosophy. The identification of ordinary language with the transcendental structures is in itself a fruitful step beyond Kant because it lets us see that these structures qua ordinary language have changed in the course of history, and it at least suggests ways of attacking this problem. We can for instance see that there are

[29] See his "Ordinary Language [1953]," in *Philosophy and Ordinary Language*, ed. Charles E. Caton (Urbana, 1963), pp. 108–127.

[30] "Must We Mean What We Say?" *Ordinary Language*, ed. Chappell, p. 86. Cf. also Strawson, "Analysis," in *Linguistic Turn*, ed. Rorty, p. 318.

[31] Rorty, e.g., says in "Metaphilosophical Difficulties," p. 17, n. 28: "The unfortunate side effects are due to the fact that if we accept Kant at face value (rather than reading him as a linguistic philosopher born before his time), we have to start worrying about his claim that physical objects are 'appearances,' about the status of the 'transcendental standpoint,' etc." It seems that once these claims are understood one cannot help but be deeply concerned with them, and this is in fact P. F. Strawson's attitude in *The Bounds of Sense. An Essay on Kant's "Critique of Pure Reason"* (London, 1966). However, one might find even here some evidence of a debatable appeal to ordinary language in Strawson's use of *the intelligibility of experience*, a notion that is used to criticize Kant's transcendental subjectivism, but is itself a quite straightforward if not naive concept and thus not as critical or radical as its object of criticism. This objection is not to derogate the unusual competence and force of the book.

not merely alterations in the history of language, but there is a continuity which preserves older features in assimilating new ones. Thus a word becomes a depository of collective and progressive experiences. Such observations are at the bottom of Austin's remarks:

> ... our common stock of words embodies all the distinctions men have found worth drawing, and the connections they have found worth marking, in the lifetimes of many generations: these surely are likely to be more numerous, more sound, since they have stood up to the long test of the survival of the fittest, and more subtle, at least in all ordinary and reasonably practical matters, than any that you or I are likely to think up in our armchairs of an afternoon – the most favored alternative method.[32]

But if we are to propose and utilize such principles with confidence, we must turn to further problems. We must establish more definitely what is permanent and what is variable in languages, what is a variation within existing structures and what is to count as a basic restructuring. We must ask what the formative powers in the changes of various kinds are. *Prima facie* at least, the great works of literature are such forces, and possibly the major philosophical systems. Ordinary language analysis would here have to expand into the philosophy of history and the theory of literature.

Related questions of special significance are these: How are the formative powers of the past present in the language I speak? Are they effective subliminally and inevitably or as a result of my free encounters with them? Are there today original formative powers? When Austin speaks of the totality of the speech acts and situations, as he does frequently and emphatically, he surely delimits the locus of these questions.[33] But in concrete investigations he no more than touches on these problems although the very direction he gives his investigations appears to call for a more incisive procedure. Under the general topic of "excuses", e.g., Austin makes the important observation that certain adverbs, falling within the scope of that topic, do not have their semantic opposite in their negative counterpart as we would naively expect ("involuntary" is not the opposite of "voluntary").[34] And in the case of "inadvertently", the positive form "advertently" is not even used. Austin points out that in performing actions we supervise their concomitant and auxiliary actions to a certain degree of attention

---

[32] "Excuses," p. 46.
[33] Cf. note 28 above.
[34] "Excuses," pp. 53–54; cf. Gilbert Ryle, *The Concept of Mind* (New York, 1968 [first published in 1949]), pp. 69–74.

to detail below which supervision is not expected. If something goes wrong on a level beneath the mark of expected supervision, we are *eo ipso* excused though we did commit the act, *inadvertently* as we say. To say that all acts, not done inadvertently (in the sense explained), are done advertently would suggest that they are all supervised which would never be true of actions below supervision and not necessarily true of actions, that one would expect to be supervised.

Although this account is informative and conclusive as far as it goes, it rests on presuppositions which clearly fall within the domain of philosophical investigation. Austin himself points out that inadvertence is disallowed in actions that seem essentially similar to others in which inadvertence is readily granted as grounds for excuse (I can say that I inadvertently stepped on a snail, but not on a baby).[35] The first group of questions that arise here is this: Why are clues, roughly equal in size, intensity, familiarity, and number still not regarded as equivalent in fixing the limits of inadvertence? Is this a matter of psychology or philosophy? What factors fix the limits? These questions are closely related to Wittgenstein's observation on "seeing as". Am I free in choosing my perspective? With what powers do I have to contend? What is the interpretative power of "as" in the phrase "seeing something as something"? Is the "as" inevitable in seeing?

A second group of questions goes further and challenges not merely the limits, but the possibility of ordinary language analysis. With what right do I appeal to the legitimacy of using "inadvertently" assuming that I have succeeded in delimiting its domain? When I claim that of a certain action it can be said that it was done inadvertently or when I state that this cannot be seen as that, am I not appealing to an average kind of agreement as to what is and what is not worth supervising and what are the limits of intelligent seeing? Could not those agreements amount to irresponsible destruction (cf. the problems of traffic, drugs, and pollution) and to the unthinking elimination of significant experiences (e.g. seeing the mountain as majestic)? If these questions are not to be pushed aside by reverting to a statistical method and if it is true that, as Austin says, to learn about words is to learn of things, then one must address himself through the words to the powers which make them mean.[36] One might argue that Heidegger's treatment of the hermeneutic *as* and of the *they* (the average opinion) is inadequate, but at least he has raised the questions, and his enterprise is

---

[35] "Excuses," p. 56; the example is ill chosen because the objects are physically so distinct.
[36] On getting to things through words cf. "Excuses," p. 47.

misunderstood if it is taken as a way of practicing ordinary language analysis.[37] What is at stake, and inevitably so, is the foundation of ordinary language analysis.

To attack the problem from yet another angle, it is in the above case possible to *establish the use* of "inadvertently" or of "seeing as" without investigating the attitudes and encounters from which this use springs; in short, it seems that I can avoid the problem and shifts of *meaning*. But my description of some use will be intelligible only because it avails itself of meaningfully characterizing terms. To define meaning as use is not to settle the problem, but to make it inaccessible. A certain use prevails or does not prevail, but since it does never more than that on its own account, it is of itself speechless. In bringing some use into relief, in probing it, in opening up regions of new uses we go beyond use though we do not go beyond language; indeed language may be eminently meaningful and consequential in just these extraordinary events where use is left behind.[38]

The emphasis on use and the analysis of ordinary language in general have the great virtue, as we have seen in various ways, of exploring the medium in which things are ultimately important and in which they constitute our world. If we acknowledge science and technology as important formative powers of our world which however are fully understood in a technical sense by just a few experts, we must admit that ordinary language is amazingly vigorous and successful in integrating the advances of science and technology into the web of readily intelligible and manageable terms and experiences. No innovation has up till now been able to rend this fabric. But not only has the problem of science and technology in fact received little attention by the ordinary language philosophers. There are dimensions to the problem which appear to lie in principle outside of the basic methods of this discipline. The point in the scientific enterprise in which all the endeavors of ingenuity, discipline, and ambition are to issue and find fulfillment and from which all the power of technology flows is the scientific law, i.e. the severely tested scientific theory. These laws, if taken in their scientific rigor and purity, are without use, and they are true without regard

---

[37] What Rorty says of Kant (note 31 above), Nakhnikian says rather more circumspectively of Heidegger in "Martin Heidegger. Introduction," *Readings in Twentieth-Century Philosophy*, ed. William P. Alston and George Nakhnikian (New York, 1963), p. 682. Regarding Heidegger on the *they* and on the hermeneutic *as* see *Being and Time*, pp. 163–168, 188–195.

[38] See Ricoeur's criticism of Wittgenstein in "Husserl and Wittgenstein" and Marcus B. Hester, *The Meaning of Poetic Metaphor. An Analysis in the Light of Wittgenstein's Claim that Meaning is Use* (The Hague, 1967).

to ideology, social circumstances, practical goals. It has been argued by Austin and P. F. Strawson that there are no statements which are true simply and of themselves.[39] And these arguments are important and illuminating because they let one see how often, and how many, abstractions and presuppositions remain unquestioned when statements are said to be true. But scientific laws are not touched in their autonomy by these particular arguments; they are free of the ambiguities, intricacies, and subtleties and thus are quite impenetrable to the tools of ordinary language analysis. But rightly or wrongly, scientific laws are increasingly exerting influence on ordinary parlance, chiefly in two ways. They are coming to be regarded as paradigms of true statements generally; and they are sought out as authorities and terminal points in disputes about ordinary problems, e.g. in the areas of health, morality, economics.[40]

We can summarize these considerations as follows. Ordinary language in its most important sense is to be understood as the central and integrating sphere of human existence. It is this status which gives ordinary language analysis its privileged rank. But if one indeed turns to ordinary language in its most important sense, one is driven to inquire what the ordinary world is which comes to the fore in ordinary language, and what the forces are that shape the ordinary world. But if the ordinary language philosopher takes this turn, he shares his privilege with other types of philosophical inquiry.

---

[39] Austin, *Things*, pp. 132–146, Strawson, "On Referring," pp. 110–114.
[40] Cf. also Grover Maxwell and Herbert Feigl, "Why Ordinary Language Needs Reforming," in *Linguistic Turn*, ed. Rorty, pp. 193–200.

CHAPTER THREE

THE EMINENCE OF LANGUAGE

43. The structure of language and the presence of language

Scientific and philosophical investigations of language are usually confined to one aspect or level of language; but such restrictions carry with them the implication that the formal subject of investigation is on its level proper to the entire language. Language is here taken as a structure or system of which only a part is examined; but this part has reference to the whole structure or system. Due to this reference, individual investigations can be understood as tributaries of a cooperative effort which has for its goal the explication of the total structure or system. The ideal result of this effort would constitute a definition of the respective language in delimiting all its formal regularities and referential possibilities.[1] It would represent an ideal grammar that would tell us univocally and comprehensively how to speak that language. It seems then that this complete linguistic science would contain everything one could wish to know about this language.

But in an important sense this is not true. The systematic account of language does not tell one what would constitute an exemplary realization of the possibilities, delimited in their full extension by the systematic account. Since the possibilities are infinite, the ideal grammar tells one nothing about a particular piece of language in its particularity. The same limitation of the ideal grammar is apparent in another way. The claim that it would teach one to speak all and only the correct sentences of the language is true only in the sense that the grammar would contain rules such that if I were to follow them I would generate only well-formed sentences and such that no well-formed sentences could not be generated by one who followed the rules. But

---

[1] See section 51 for how, in principle, the infinite possibilities of language can be represented finitely.

all this is, as far as it goes, analytic. The terms "rules" and "well-formed" and the terms "ideal" and "comprehensive" entail one another. Thus the claim that the ideal grammar teaches one to speak is empty. One can properly speak a language if he produces well-formed sentences in the *appropriate circumstances*. Investigation of these conditions is usually done in an informal and incidental manner or is explicitly excluded. This is a legitimate and fruitful restriction. But one ought to realize that it is not as clear and simple a matter as it is often implied to be.

The account of language given by the ideal grammar seems unsurpassably complete, and yet the account is unintelligible unless we acknowledge additional features and forces of language which have always and already interacted with those described by the ideal grammar. More concretely, it is impossible to envisage a situation which on the terms of the ideal grammar is language free and into which language as described by the ideal grammar is first inserted. Whenever we conceive of a situation wherein a speaker begins to speak by following rules we can do so only by (tacitly) presupposing that the speaker has already followed rules. In any situation, the reasons for speaking must somehow be present to the speaker; they must be articulate; the articulation to be intelligible must be rule-governed; and these rules, which have been (implicitly) followed, would coincide with important parts of the grammar the rules of which the speaker was about to employ explicitly.

One might object to these observations that their basic assumption (i.e. "the task of the ideal grammar is to teach one how to speak") is false since obviously someone, who can be taught in the sense that he can be told about rules, already has mastered some language and *its* rules. On the other hand, teaching of a first language (to children) is obviously possible without a prior command of a language on the part of the pupil *and* without the command of an explicit grammar (ideal or other) on the part of the teacher.

We know, to be sure, that language begins radically for every speaker at one time, and we know that such first language acquisition is essentially bound up with the employment of rules. This is not the problem. But what remains concealed in such an account is the question to what degree of completeness our theoretical understanding of language can be brought by expanding scientifically and systematically our knowledge of the general structure of language. Whatever can be said generally of a language, including the lexicon, grammatical exceptions, deviations, etc., is part of the structure or system of language in this wide sense. Linguistic rules are an instance of that general structure, and the problem of their employment pertains to the general question how complete and self-sufficient the description of a language by way of an ideal grammar is. The incompleteness of the ideal grammar appears not just when one considers rules and the subsequent difficulty of original employment. One might alternatively formulate the problem by saying that the conceivability of grammatical types being converted into tokens of language requires the antecedent presence of some sort of tokens in which the motive force and direction of the conversion is realized. Similarly with the correlation of grammatical possibilities and actual pieces of language. It appears then, again taking the notion of rule as a paradigm, that the linguistic sciences can specify the rules of language, but the rules alone are not yet language, and correspondingly an understanding of these rules is always an understanding of something more than these rules. Thus the linguistic sciences constantly recollect and anticipate language. But they never present language itself. Where they give examples, one is not to pay attention to the message of the example, but to the rule it embodies. And the message of the language which the linguistic sciences speak in direct discourse is bound up with the meaning of the rules which it exhibits. Since that meaning is precisely in question, the presence of language insofar as it is embodied in the ideal grammar is itself conditional.

One might reply that there is a level of life and language which cannot be questioned without futility.[2] It may be argued that the presence of language, since it eludes the linguistic sciences, is in principle elusive, or that the presence of language is pseudo-elusive in the sense that *any* piece of language is obviously an instance of its presence and that clearly, if we are dissatisfied with instances and want *the* presence of language *itself*, we are after a systematically elusive entity. But recognizing *this* difficulty, one might say, is also to be done with it.

44. The exemplary presence of language in literature. The theory of literature

However, this conclusion is unwarranted. Language is not so amorphously and indifferently present. It overpowers us in drama, it en-

---

[2] Cf. Gustav Bergmann, "The Glory and the Misery of Ludwig Wittgenstein [1961]," *Essays*, ed. Copi and Beard, pp. 344, 349.

thralls us in poetry, it engages us in fiction.[3] In such events, language stands out and is eminently present. Here the rules of language are not simply and in fact employed; they are well employed; their possibilities are forcefully realized; and here is the presence of a force which does not decisively depend on a prior setting, but envelopes and transforms its essential antecedents and establishes itself of its own power. It does not refer us to prior or future uses of rules, but is present in employing them here and now.

It is at once clear that an elucidation of language *par excellence* requires a mode of argument different from that of a treatment of language as a system, and that such elucidation is nonetheless a *desideratum* for a full understanding of language. It is furthermore apparent that the history and theory of literature are just those disciplines which are concerned to aid our understanding of drama, poetry, and fiction. They are then in a definite and indispensable sense part of the philosophy of language.

Surely this thesis requires further argument. The theory of literature usually is not taken, nor does it take itself, to constitute a philosophy of language.[4] If it has a unique contribution to make to our understanding of language, it is certainly quite unclear about its own concept of language, for the dictionaries and the introductory foundational works in this discipline have little that is novel and usually nothing at all to say about language itself.[5] One might take this as a symptom of the low level of methodological sophistication in the theory of literature and generalize this view to the effect that the kind of informal, historical, and variable approach to be found there, disqualifies the theory of literature from the status of philosophical investigation.

This view seems further confirmed when we consider the nature of the subject matter of this theory, namely literature. It is a factually specifiable body of writings; and such a coherent and sharply delimited subject seems to call for an empirical and positive, rather than a specu-

---

[3] These examples are slanted towards literature. Other examples would be political speech, philosophical discourse, religious meditation, and a revolutionary scientific treatise. But what these examples have in common is or used to be eminently and paradigmatically present in literature.

[4] For convenience, I will use this shorter expression "theory of literature." It will become clear in section 45 that a theory of literature must also and always be the study, criticism, and history of literature.

[5] See my "Sprache als System und Ereignis. Über linguistische und literaturwissenschaftliche Sprachbetrachtung," *Zeitschrift für philosophische Forschung*, ed. G. Schischkoff, XXI (Meisenheim: Anton Hain, 1967), 580–581. – In this article, I first developed some of the subsequent arguments regarding the theory of literature (pp. 580–589) and linguistics (pp. 570–580).

lative or theoretical approach. But when we go beyond the mere fact that there is indeed an amazingly strong consensus as to what constitutes the corpus of literature and when we ask what the foundation of this agreement is, we are led back to language as the controlling concept. For it is not the factual content of literature which is distinctive; anything may be its subject. And all other likely criteria turn out to be symptoms or consequences, but not the grounds of something being a piece of literature. Such elements are authorship, public acceptance, cultural effect, and the like.

Literature is language *par excellence*, but it does not speak about itself as language. The scholar of literature is similarly implicit; he does not speak expressly of literature as language. Yet clearly his work is a reflection on literature; and if it is true that language is the controlling concept of literature, then a reflection on the nature of the theory of literature ought to bring out the way in which language is present in literature and governs the perspective of the theory of literature.

If we take any piece of literary scholarship and try to determine its method, we find that instead of one method there is always a conglomerate of fairly distinct methods. These are borrowed from philology, linguistics, semantics, historiography, and mythology; in addition to these definite tools, there are more informal ones, loosely associated with psychology, sociology, philosophy. Some of these methods are combined or specialized to form auxiliary disciplines which are proper to the theory of literature, but not methodologically autonomous. The resulting disciplines are metrics, rhetoric, stylistics, poetics, and the history of literature. Even where the auxiliary disciplines are historically prior to those first mentioned, they are systematically derivative of the latter.

In addition to these *methods*, the study of literature avails itself for the elucidation of its subject of *factual knowledge* drawn from whatever scientific or practical discipline may be of service. The explicator of Thomas Mann's *Doctor Faustus* will draw on musicology, the student of Shakespeare's history plays should be familiar with history and constitutional law.

All this operative and illustrative knowledge is spread out before the student of literature, but it is not given or used systematically. There is no overall program that would indicate the sequence of steps to be taken in the analysis of a piece of literature; far less is there a set of criteria application of which would establish mechanically whether a given body of writing is literature or not. One could certainly devise such procedures; but the result would not be an explication of what students of literature in fact do, but a way of eliminating the need for such people and their endeavors.[6]

Programmatic statements are always greeted with suspicion in the study of literature. The norm in this field enjoins to explore the great works of literature ever anew without preconceived norms. If such ventures are successful, there is a precipitation of interpretive techniques which gain a certain currency and can be taught. But new discoveries are made only when these methods are left behind, modified, or essentially supplemented. The impetus for such innovation does not come from a precursive refinement of the tools; rather a new insight into, say an epic, may call for new ways of articulation and demonstration.

Innovation of this kind is not in all respects proper to the theory of literature or even to the study of art in general, nor to the arts themselves. In the natural sciences, the great feats consist in carrying out tasks for which the decisive methods have been previously unknown. Discovery of the thing and discovery of the way in which it can be approached coincide here. Scientific activities, for which the methods are fully prescribed, are really matters of routine or of technological application; at best they are preparatory (and hence frequently useless) steps. But there is this great difference that scientific investigations, though they venture into the unknown, securely connect the new territory, once it is conquered, to the previously known region even if this region undergoes a partial transformation through the conquest. Although it is a difficult problem to determine precisely and transparently the grounds of scientific cogency, any scientist uses, and can count on, workable criteria of acceptance.

But the student of literature cannot expect such cogency for his results because he could not tell what would count as a criterion of cogency. And yet in his endeavors he advances for his results a claim of more than subjective pertinence. How is this possible?

45. Literature and reality. The difficulty of a theory of literature

The great works of literature are presentations of reality in language. This definition puts them in definite relations to other phenomena. But

---

[6] Cf. Keith Gunderson's proposal in "Poetics [abstract]," *Journal of Philosophy*, LXIV (1967), 688–689 and Archibald A. Hill's in "A Program for the Definition of Literature," *Studies in English*, XXXVII (1958), 46–52.

they differ from the latter in important respects. (1) The great works of literature are intimately connected with their time. Faithfulness to their time distinguishes them from epigonic fabrications. (2) Their significance is not confined to the time of their origin. As works of art, they do not become outdated. (3) Form and content cannot be separated. Isolation or alternative rendition of a poem's content does not of itself preserve anything poetic. (4) They are not factual, or at any rate they are more than factual reports of events or prescriptions for practical endeavors. (5) It follows from (3) and (4) that they are inexhaustible in the sense that they do not have an adequate cognitive, factual, or operative counterpart. We may entitle these features the (1) historicity, (2) timelessness, (3) ontological indivisibility, (4) semantic autonomy, and (5) inexhaustibility of literature.

These are fairly non-controversial features, accepted by most people who accept something like literature. Yet they are fairly opaque as well, and even paradoxical. Hence, an elucidation of these features will quickly lead to controversy. Tentatively, an elucidation can only recommend itself by promising to shed some light on literature and its theory and give some account of an area which we are led to by the linguistic sciences, but which must remain unexplored by these sciences.

In every era, there are fundamental norms which determine not merely how certain goals can be achieved, but what constitutes a goal in life and what not. These norms, then, are not elements or episodes in that era's life, but the foundation and definition of human life in those times. They are therefore unique to that era; more properly they are ultimate and incomparable since there is no higher authority to appeal to and no more comprehensive frame within which these norms would stand out as unique.[7] Since they are comprehensive, they cannot be formulated from any explicitly defined point of view, be it moral, scientific, or social. Their presence can therefore not be cognitively or conceptually formulated. But they may be prominent in some reality that displays the fundamental features of that era's reality and addresses the decisive sensibilities of the people of that time. The changes from one epoch to another are changes of these norms. These epochal changes are revolutions and leave nothing untouched except the prior norms which are no longer in force since the times which they shaped have past. But the preceding norms have not been transcended with regard to their ultimacy. To do this, subsequent norms would have to

---

[7] Our all-comprehensive and all-equalizing attitude is presumably a late and in itself unique development. Cf. below.

recast the shape of the past. This is impossible. On the contrary, however, past norms in their ultimacy remain a challenge and thus a force that reaches into the present, if only as a possibility that had gained actuality and is now no longer an open possibility, but remains a basis of rejection, reaction, and innovation. Ultimacy itself cannot be overcome, but only brought to renewed prominence. The norms of an era are prominent in its literature.[8] This proposition correlates the five traits of literature listed above with the account that follows the list.

Any more explicit correlation necessarily undoes the unitary power of literature aimed at in the preceding account. But in at least one respect, such unravelling is called for. It has been said that the norms, though never exhaustively explicable, can attain prominent reality. We can now ask further in what kind of medium this is likely to come about most successfully. Language then suggests itself quite readily since it is more sensitive and pervasive than music or figurative media. In introducing the question of media, we return to the problem of language which is the primary subject of our reflections. But in regaining language, we are losing the relative fullness of its presence that we sought. Language as medium is intelligible only in relation to abstract or ideal forms which it embodies. These forms are presumably the epochal norms. But the norms, as abstract or ideal forms, are no longer the fundamental and comprehensive forces that they were claimed to be. This claim is already misunderstood or disregarded when the question of media is raised and an answer is given by way of arguing that language is of itself the most suitable medium of the norms. For this we could never establish had not the norms already addressed us forcefully in literature which as language, i.e. as medium, has answered the question of media before it was raised. Language is an abstraction from literature, and it is ultimately misleading to suggest that literature is a specific use or application of language.

Once language is abstracted from literature, the fullness of language is present only as an irretrievable *desideratum*. This is where the limit of the linguistic sciences lies. It is, on the other hand, entirely consistent that the consequential step of isolating language incisively is never taken by the theory of literature.

[8] But not necessarily exclusively. They may be present in other forms of language as indicated in note 3 above, and they may be present in non-literary works of art. Questions of priority are awkward in the realm of ultimate norms. The same awkwardness dominates the question whether the prominent literary locus of epochal norms is one (the greatest) literary work, or the great works of the time or the great ones focally and the minor ones marginally though indispensably. – On the structuring power of art cf. Goodman, *Languages*, pp. 31–33.

It is now also clear why the theory, history, and study of literature must all essentially coincide.[9] The concern with literature turns to its subject matter without criteria higher than literature; yet all of literature unfolds itself in historical sequence. Hence the study of literature is the history (historiography) of literature and vice versa. The term *theory of literature* can accordingly not designate an *a priori* system of dealing with literature; it merely emphasizes a relatively higher degree of generality and reflection in the concern with literature.[10]

The work of the student of literature is wholly in the service of the norms which literature represents. He therefore finds himself in the midst of the conflicting demands of preserving the integrity of literature and of aiding the understanding of literature which requires explication and abstraction. In our times, the task is rendered more difficult by the widespread lack of any need for something like literature. This lack results from the preoccupation with interacting, rule-governed systems which makes us overlook the (dignity of the) question what the ultimate powers are that move and guide the systems. For that reason that task is all the more urgent; for that reason too it requires such simple and in a sense selfcontradictory reflections as the foregoing ones. Presumably, our time has its uniqueness in its apparent power to evacuate all prior epochs of their uniqueness by analysing, understanding, and surpassing them in every essential respect. But this appearance, though overwhelming, is deceptive. Yet even to pose the question whether under those circumstances literature is truly possible any longer, requires a novel and a radical reflection on literature.

Thus the student of literature today does his work in response to three forces which, though essentially inseparable, have claims of different strengths on that work which should first of all be open to the powers of literature itself, second must be aware of the uncanny and hidden illiteracy of our era, and third must take care to avail itself of all the substantive and methodological knowledge which it has developed as an academic discipline and which is available from so many other sources.

---

[9] Cf. René Wellek and Austin Warren, *Theory of Literature* (New York, 1949), pp. 30–31.

[10] Morris Weitz's book, *Hamlet and the Philosophy of Literary Criticism* (Chicago, 1964), is an example, it seems to me, of how easily a metacritical enterprise (one concerned with "the logic of criticism") resorts to a concept of language (qua standard and tool of the metacritique) which is quite derivative compared with the concept of language which is at the bottom of literary criticism. Weitz is correct, I believe, in arguing that metaphysics (through the "classical theory of language") has been a threat to the proper self-understanding of literary criticism. But I do not think that this is the central issue in the philosophy of literary criticism. See especially pp. vii–xii, 215–227, 316–319.

The works in what is usually and technically called "theory of literature" are overtly intended to provide a foundation and introduction to specific investigations of literary works of art. Let us, in conclusion, look at some traits of these theories of literature in order to illustrate some of the preceding points. The examples are chosen so as to give an idea of the variety of starting points and of the kinship of insights in the theory of literature.[11]

46. The practice of the theory of literature. Wellek and Warren

All of these theories respond to the tension of epochal uniqueness and conceptual explication in constantly moving between examples and theses. Thus they stay close to the untranslatable power of literature and expose themselves to the charge of hasty generalization since to every thesis one could find a counter-example. They are further strongly and consciously historical in their attitude. Whatever innovation and re-organization they may propose, they are always intent on bringing to fuller clarity and force insights that have guided concern with literature since Aristotle. Finally, we can discern in them an impetus that comes from without literature and thus testifies to the fact that the power of literature is eclipsed today. Though the resulting darkness is itself a kind of presence of literature, the situation is ambiguous and requires a resolution, issuing from independent forces. Let us take as focuses of this impetus the treatment of the literary genres in three theories of literature.

In the *Theory of Literature* (1949) by René Wellek and Austin Warren, the three genres, drama, epic, and lyric, are "distinguished according to 'manner of imitation' (or 'representation'): lyric poetry is the poet's own *persona*; in epic poetry (or the novel) the poet partly speaks in his own person, as narrator, and partly makes his characters speak in direct discourse (mixed narrative); in drama, the poet disappears behind his cast of characters."[12]

The discussion moves informally from systematic problems to sketches in the history of genre theory. Occasionally, there are important original observations, such as the likening of the genres to institutions, the analogy consisting in their formative and restrictive power and in their living and evolving nature. But the consistency and

---

[11] A survey concentrating on the main issues in Anglo-Saxon literary criticism is provided by John Casey, *The Language of Criticism* (London, 1966).
[12] *Theory*, p. 237.

uniqueness of the *Theory* do not lie in such scattered insights, but in the cosmopolitan and genteel attitude of the entire book, an attitude which intends to be "not eclectic like the Germans [Walzel and Petersen] or doctrinaire like the Russian [Tomashevsky]" and to "beware of both false relativism and false absolutism."[13] The work of all times and tongues seems to be brought under control and spread out before the reader. The guiding concept in this presentation is a functional view of the literary artwork. The view has two aspects. It contends on the one side that the literary work of art must be approached as having a function and on the other that the approach is practiced by determining the function of certain devices within the literary work of art. The second part of this view asserts itself in the recurring condemnations of dogmatism *and* relativism, in the advocacy of the descriptive approach, and in the preference of the intrinsic over the extrinsic study of literature.

A function, in our present context, is the performance of a certain task by a certain literary entity. The entity is decisively defined in relation to its task; the task in turn has its place and significance within a higher literary entity, characterized by its own function. In light of the initial considerations of this chapter, it is clear that the functional view is in great danger of missing the significance of literature, which is that of being the origin and goal of all functions, but never that of having itself a function. The *Theory of Literature* is at least implicitly aware of this danger when it says of the function of poetry: "... poetry has many possible functions. Its prime and chief function is fidelity to its own nature."[14] The question is, whether such noble reserve is sufficient today.

47. The practice of the theory of literature. Frye

A book of a different temper is the *Anatomy of Criticism* (1957) by Northrop Frye, the fourth essay of which deals with the theory of genres.[15] "The basis of generic distinction in literature appears to be the radical of presentation."[16] The radical of presentation is the basic mode in which literature is given presence, and there are three possibilities: (1) The external mimesis, the acting out of literature in drama.

---

[13] *Ibid.*, pp. v–vi, 35.
[14] *Ibid.*, p. 28.
[15] *Anatomy of Criticism. Four Essays* (Princeton, 1957).
[16] *Ibid.*, pp. 246–247.

(2) The central area of literature where the poet addresses his listeners directly as in the epic proper or where the direct address is mediated by the printed page as in fiction. (3) The internal mimesis by the poet who sings to himself and is merely overheard by the listener. This is the radical of lyric.[17]

The three genres derive further idiosyncrasy from pre-literary symbolic unities. Thus drama reflects the ritual, epic reflects scripture and and myth, lyric draws on dream and vision.[18] Moreover, each genre is internally integrated by a characteristic rhythm: epos is structured by the rhythm of recurrence, prose (which is rhythmically distinct from epos) by that of continuity, drama by the rhythm of decorum, lyric by the rhythm of association. Finally each genre falls into species which are not to be taken as distinct sub-classes but as cardinal points which together delimit a certain configuration such that a given drama for instance finds a characteristic place in relation to them.

Beyond the scope of this essay, there obtain a great number of intricate interconnections with other essays. The first essay deals with the theory of modes, a mode being a "conventional power of action assumed about the chief characters in fictional literature, or the corresponding attitude assumed by the poet toward his audience in thematic literature."[19] Depending on the degree of grandeur that we assign to the hero in the fictional modes, there result different types of drama, epos, and prose fiction.

The second essay is devoted to the theory of symbols which elaborates the ways in which we can isolate and understand components within a literary work of art. These methods apply with nearly equal pertinence to all genres though a formal (intrinsic) analysis seems to favor poems while the recognition and comparison of recurring patterns of presentation and experience (archetypes) is more fruitful in epic and drama.

Myths are narratives that represent or reflect basic experiences and events of human life in one of four basic forms, namely comedy, romance, tragedy, and irony, which are associated with the seasons of spring, summer, autumn, and winter. In each mythos, the narrative moves through two groups of three phases each, and each mythos

---

[17] *Ibid.*, pp. 246–251.
[18] *Ibid.*, p. 250.
[19] *Ibid.*, p. 366.

shares each group with one other mythos so that there are four different groups with altogether twelve phases.[20]

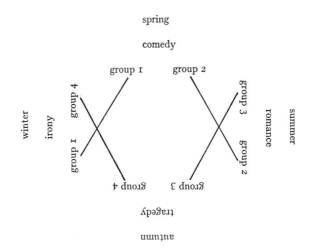

The above configuration is clearly present in the third essay; but its formal properties and possibilities are not fully exploited. For instance, no indication is given why the connecting lines cross only at the right and left and not at the top and bottom or why, alternatively, the lines cross at all. Nor is there any argument to show why there are no more or less phases than twelve, and why just these phases and not different ones.

Still, there is a strong classifying and interrelating power at work in the *Anatomy of Criticism* which makes it readily vulnerable to criticism of details and exposes it to easy ridicule with regard to the bold sweep of its theses.[21] But this expansive approach is intended to substantiate the claim that literary criticism is a systematic and continuous science.[22] Though at times it seems as if, after reading the *Anatomy*, all we can ever expect to find in literature are the structural elements expounded in the *Anatomy*, Frye, as we saw, exercises restraint in his

[20] The four groups have roughly the following phases. Group 1: (1) Society triumphs. (2) The hero escapes society. (3) The old ruler of society yields to a young man. Group 2: (4) One society supersedes another. (5) Society appears in a pensive perspective. (6) Society dissolves into small and esoteric units. Group 3: (7) The hero's birth. (8) The hero's innocent youth. (9) The hero's quest. Group 4: (10) The hero's fall. (11) The hero moves into a reduced ironical perspective. (12) The hero is overtaken by a world of shock and horror.

[21] See W. K. Wimsatt, "Northrop Frye: Criticism as Myth," in *Northrop Frye in Modern Criticism*, ed. Murray Krieger (New York, 1966), pp. 75–107.

[22] Cf. Casey, *Criticism*, pp. 140–152.

systematizing. The final source of authority and elucidating power is literature itself. It represents ultimate values; and where it does so, it cannot be approached with value judgments. Frye is furthermore clear in his formulation of the role of literary criticism today which follows from his conception of literature: It is central to the preservation of humanity in a technological world.[23]

48. The practice of the theory of literature. Staiger

In conclusion Emil Staiger's work should be mentioned at least to call attention to a further important paradigm and possibility of literary theory. Staiger was early influenced by Martin Heidegger, and hence the problem of time has always played a large role in his investigations.[24] In his *Basic Concepts of Poetics* (1946) he explicated the three genres as three modes of time.[25] The lyrical poet remembers time present, past, and future in the sense of bringing the ravishing flow of time back to the restful integrity of memory. The epic poet presents time as abiding; it manifests itself as ever the same in recurring and leisurely episodes, fully absorbed in the pleasure of regular passage, without being haunted by the past or fascinated by the future. The dramatist, finally, projects a goal of time that lies ahead of all action, structures it, and passes judgment on it. Time is characterized by the tension towards the project. Lyric as remembering, epic as presenting, and drama as tension are not attitudes towards particular phases of chronological time; they are modes in which man appropriates his world and which thus first give rise to the world and *its* time. The three genres are grounded in original time, i.e. time which is the origin of the world and its being and which for Staiger is the same as being.[26]

Staiger too has had his share of critics and doubters.[27] But he is not exposed to the danger that we noted in the case of the earlier theories of literature; he does not lose the uniqueness of the literary work of art in the generality of his theory. For Staiger, the three genres mark a historical development such that they arise successively and then re-

---

[23] *Anatomy*, pp. 350–354.

[24] See his *Die Zeit als Einbildungskraft des Dichters* (Zürich, 1939). – Beyond Staiger's work, Heidegger has given important impetuses to the theory of interpretation (i.e. hermeneutics) generally. See Richard E. Palmer, *Hermeneutics* (Evanston, 1969), pp. 124–161.

[25] *Grundbegriffe der Poetik*, 3rd ed. (Zürich, 1956).

[26] Not necessarily for the early Heidegger for whom time is the possible horizon of being. See *Grundbegriffe*, pp. 219–223.

[27] See Staiger's Postscript to the *Grundbegriffe*, pp. 229–256.

main available as possibilities, but in various degrees of vitality.[28] The epic, e.g. ceased to be a genuine possibility with the advent to Christian teleology. Further, every epoch realizes its literature in an irrepeatable and unpredictable form, i.e. in a style.[29] If the three genres and literature in general are ways in which man delimits and appropriates his world, then the study of literature is ultimately concerned with man; it is anthropology in a profound sense.[30]

It is worth noting that the three theories of literature stem from original and mutually independent efforts. It is thus quite remarkable that there is considerable agreement among them; and where such agreement is lacking, we can certainly conceive of a fruitful and principled disputation of the various positions. This in turn shows that there is indeed a scholarly discipline, concerned with language in its eminence.

[28] Frye makes a similar point in the first essay of the *Anatomy*, but more incidentally. Cf. section 47.

[29] See *Die Kunst der Interpretation*, 3rd ed. (Zürich, 1961), p. 14 and *Stilwandel* (Zürich, 1963), pp. 7–25.

[30] *Grundbegriffe*, pp. 12, 219–220, 252; *Stilwandel*, pp. 13–14.

CHAPTER FOUR

THE STRUCTURE OF LANGUAGE

49. *The historical and the systematic aspects of language. Saussure*

There is a privileged situation in which language becomes apparent as both elusive and systematic; it is the situation in which someone is to be taught formally how to speak. The language to be taught is in some sense a second language, either a foreign or a literary idiom. Language shows itself to be elusive in that the object language can rather easily be taught in bits of actual usage, but is very recalcitrant to attempts at giving a systematic and economical account of it. Yet language appears to be highly systematic; its rules are frequently and patently violated by the student even after he has acquired a certain competence and can make himself understood. Such learning situations presumably have arisen as soon as two different languages came in contact or a distinction between ordinary and elevated usage came about within one language. Such situations can be coped with in an informal way through rote and practice. But success is then achieved without insight.

These two features of language, its elusiveness and its systematic nature, and the two definite purposes, the practical one of teaching language and the related theoretical one of gaining insight into language have very early given rise to a particular study of language. We have already come across some of the stages in the development of this approach to language.[1] Perhaps the most consequential step in this development was taken in the invention of writing; the form which this invention took for the Western world was in turn significant, namely the interpretation of words as sound sequences and the representation of sounds through letters, Greek γράμματα. This step greatly limited the elusiveness of language and provided a reliable basis for all

---

[1] See sections 11, 14, 15.

subsequent studies of language. We have seen that the practical aim of grammar, that of finding a useful tool for instruction, was attained for Greek and Latin by the classical grammarians already.[2] The relative success of their endeavors led to almost total stagnation in that area for a millenium and a half, and it made it at least seem as though the question of insight was answered along with the practical achievement.

In the 19th century a historical view of language gained great momentum and precision, externally through the acquaintance of European scholars with Sanskrit and systematically through the vigorous scientific spirit of that era. The coincidence of the two events led to a novel and thorough investigation of the ancestry and development of that family of languages, now called Indo-European. Astounding discoveries were made, both of data and regularities in development which were, in the spirit of the time and in analogy to the natural sciences, called laws; formerly dissociated results fell into place; many misconceptions were dispelled. There seemed to be a tremendous advancement of our understanding of language. But in spite of the magnitude and the variety of those accomplishments, a curious and unchallenged fallacy pervaded much of the linguistic work of that century. To trace the development of a feature of language is not to explain that feature; and even if it is traced back to the oldest, irreducible, and laboriously reconstructed language (Proto-Indo-European), the question as to what the nature and function of that feature is has simply been evaded. Such historical investigations rather presuppose some understanding of the systematic structure and features of language. But due to the preoccupation with the (mostly phonetic) facts of development, the scholars of the 19th century settled for rather vague and at times misleading structural concepts.[3] That languages exhibit family relationships and change so remarkably is in itself a fact worthy of reflection. But the question what it means that languages are so deeply historical and relational was never raised.

At the beginning of this century, Ferdinand de Saussure (1857–1913) took a decisive step in providing more adequate principles for the organization of the material.[4] He recognized that language is not only quantitatively prevalent in everyday talk, but is present in such talk as a finely balanced and self-sufficient system. Common speech is not

---

[2] Section 14.

[3] Documents and discussions regarding this development can be found in Hans Arens, *Sprachwissenschaft* (Freiburg, 1955), pp. 135–337. Cf. also Cassirer, *Language*, pp. 167–176.

[4] See his *Course in General Linguistics*, ed. Charles Bally, Albert Sechehaye, and Albert Riedlinger, tr. Wade Baskin (New York, 1966 [first published in French in 1915]).

just the rough prelude or the inept sequel to literature, nor is it merely the source of materials for historical investigations; it is rather at every point in time a fully developed and adequate system of signs in a society. To become aware of this, one must rigorously exclude the historical perspective and look at language as it exists at one moment. Saussure called this static or systematic approach somewhat misleadingly *synchronic*; the investigation of the changes of language through time he called *diachronic*.[5] In an era where every linguistic feature spoke eloquently of its past to every linguist, it required great effort and ingenuity to resist the historical pull and exhibit language in its atemporal, systematic autonomy.

The language of which the historical philologist treats is never actual at any one time. It is rather an evolving and limited entity that exists primarily in the reconstructive scholarly activity of the philologist. In the synchronic perspective, language is much more immediately present. Saussure had difficulty in characterizing this kind of presence directly and favored a crudely psychological parlance according to which the form and locus of language are to be taken as "a sum of impressions deposited in the brain of each member of a community."[6] A much more incisive characterization resulted from the emphasis on the opposition of language to speaking. For Saussure, the total linguistic phenomenon, *speech* (French *language*), has two aspects: (1) the immediately observable and recordable linguistic activity of speakers, *speaking* (French *parole*), and (2) the abstract system which underlies, and is the same in all acts of, speaking, but is explicitly present in none of them, i.e. *language* in the concise sense (French *langue*) which is the proper object of linguistics.[7]

Saussure was a historical philologist of competence and accomplishments himself. He never denied the significance of historical investigations, but rightly insisted on the priority of the synchronic approach; We must be clear about what language is in itself before we can securely establish what language is in its historical development. Thus Saussure secured the important systematic insight which was a matter of course to the classical and Sanskrit grammarians as well as to the inventors of the phonetic alphabet. But whereas the methodological soundness of

[5] *Course*, pp. 81–83, 98–100. – We have touched on this problem and its terminology in section 7.

[6] *Ibid.*, p. 19; cf. p. 23.

[7] *Ibid.*, p. 77; cf. p. 98; in the French ed., *Cours de linguistique générale* (Paris, 1965), see p. 112 and cf. p. 138. – In more modern parlance (1) *speaking* is analogous to *the native speakers' performance* and (2) *language* to *the native speaker's competence*.

the linguistic pioneers was in part the result of a lack of historical and interlinguistic sophistication, Saussure regained their approach in the midst of the most diversified and distracting historical material.

50. Language as empirically given.
Structural and descriptive linguistics

Saussure thus laid the foundation for a remarkable development in linguistics. The new approach was freed from the historical bias and permitted access to the *structure* of language. It was freed from the preoccupation with literature and the attendant exercise of linguistic value judgment; instead it insisted on the *description* of language as it exists immediately and predominantly. The new linguistics accordingly called itself "structural" or "descriptive." [8] It developed most vigorously in the United States; and its perhaps most important representative was Leonard Bloomfield (1887–1949).[9]

This development is sometimes said to have been caused in part by two accidents of civilization.[10] The first was the presence of a great many, greatly differing, and unrecorded languages on the Northern American continent, the American Indian languages. The second was the rapid disappearance of many of these languages, due simply and tragically to the extinction of the speakers. There was then in the first half of this century a possibility and in fact a need to capture and somehow save these languages.

In another sense, however, these historical circumstances were not so much the cause of a development as a welcome confirmation of an attitude towards language which has a significance in its own right. It takes its point of departure from Saussure's synchronic approach, but modifies Saussure's view in a consequential fashion. It seeks to give the Saussurean position an unassailable, strictly empirical foundation. It assumes that this foundation emerges only if we free ourselves from any and all preconceptions of language, except the seemingly self-evident fact that language is a means of communication. And there is an exemplary situation of linguistic research where restriction to the empirical evidence and the abandoning of all prejudices is a matter of necessity, in a situation namely where we undertake to describe the

---

[8] I will refer to this approach as "descriptive and structural linguistics" and occasionally use the shorter form "descriptive linguistics" synonymously.

[9] Cf. his *Language* (New York, 1933).

[10] See Bolinger, *Aspects*, pp. 189–193.

structure of language with which we are totally unfamiliar, where language is initially nothing but the presence of vocal noises of native speakers.

Let us look more closely at the procedure of the linguist in the fieldwork situation.[11] At first, the oral sounds seem entirely inarticulate and elusive. But gradually, it becomes apparent that the sound sequences consist of separable, recurring, and minimal entities. Moreover, the basic stock of these entities is relatively limited, a set of say 35 elements. These irreducible phonetic elements are called *phonemes*.[12] If we assign a written symbol to each of them, we can now record utterances of the speakers.[13] After we have gathered a fair sample of utterances, we are in a position to investigate the phoneme sequences. Close inspection will reveal that some phoneme sequences recur. Attention to the occurrence of these phoneme sequences in actual speech will further show that at least some of them are clearly and uniquely associated with a definite object or situation. This association confers meaning on the phoneme sequences. Meaningful phoneme sequences which cannot be broken up into meaningful component sequences (and which are in this sense irreducible) are called *morphemes*.[14]

From these starting points we can proceed to analyse the remaining phoneme sequences, dividing them, identifying their meaning or function, and thus converting them into morphemes.[15] We can then draw up a list of morphemes which, together with their English equivalents, would constitute a dictionary of the language under investigation.

The last step in our investigation consists in determining the rules according to which morphemes are concatenated. This presupposes an intuitive understanding at least of short morpheme sequences, an understanding which is aided, but not fully constituted by our lexical knowledge of the language. On the basis of this understanding, we will find that certain neighboring morphemes form relatively coherent meaningful wholes; they constitute relatively independent units which can be used in different contexts and which, in turn, can be replaced

---

[11] The linguistic attitude sketched in what follows is present in some way in most textbooks written in the United States in the forties and fifties. An excellent example which also takes note of what was to come is H. A. Gleason's *An Introduction to Descriptive Linguistics*, 2nd ed. (New York, 1961).

[12] These elements are really abstract entities, i.e. classes, the members of which are sufficiently similar and are called allophones. The sufficient condition of similarity is discussed in section 52.

[13] This is oversimplified. We also need a way to record intonational phonemes.

[14] This corresponds roughly to Aristotle's definition of "word". See section 11 above.

[15] "Morpheme" is roughly equivalent to "word"; many words, to be sure, can be dissected into independently meaningful components; the limits of such dissection are difficult to draw.

by another group of morphemes or even a single morpheme. Again, we expand this analysis and convert a given sequence of morphemes into groups of morphemes; these groups will then be seen to fall into higher groups (groups of groups), the highest and all-encompassing group being coextensive with the initially given morpheme sequence (usually a sentence).

The basic tool of this analysis is the relative distinction between groups and their members. A member is commonly called an *immediate constituent*, a term which reflects the fact that a certain member is immediate, i.e. irreducible, relative to its group although it may itself be a group, and if taken as such has its own immediate constituents. The immediate constituent structure is obviously hierarchical and can therefore be represented as a tree, nodes corresponding to groups, branches to immediate constituents. Cf. the following example:

(1)

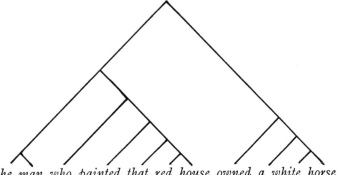

the man who painted that red house owned a white horse

The procedure just outlined, consists then of phonemics, morphemics, and syntax. It was unquestionably successful in recording languages. But here, as in the case of the classical grammars, the fallacious co-clusion was tacitly drawn that the solution of a practical problem was tantamount to gaining theoretical insight into that problem. The pro-grammatic restriction to the empirical stemmed from a mistaken view of the natural sciences and was awkward in at least two ways. First, it was not and could not be adhered to consistently. In all stages of the procedure, easily recognizable ideal concepts or hidden operations of a strictly conceptual or theoretical nature are at work. The concept of the phoneme, for instance, does not at all have a straightforward physical correlate; to be sure, it has *some* material correlate; but it requires a very intricate process of abstraction to isolate phonemes.

In the analysis of morphemes, strong intuitive, i.e. empirically opaque factors enter when those morphemes are identified that possess a meaning or function which cannot be pinpointed through straightforward association with a physically discrete entity. And even in the simpler cases, many tacit assumptions and operations are at work as pointed out elsewhere.[16] Finally, the immediate constituent structure of a sentence is nothing but a schematic representation of the knowledge that we somehow possess regarding the coherence of that sentence. What the basis and the most general form of this knowledge is does not become apparent in immediate constituent analysis.

In fact, the syntax of descriptive linguistics is not even able to reflect all the explicit insights that we naively possess. We know, for instance, that to most sentences in the active mood, there is a semantically near-equivalent one in the passive mood.

This brings us to the second and more important disadvantage that stemmed from the excessive empiricism of descriptive and structural linguistics. It failed to appreciate the interplay of theory and evidence in which the former is not the necessary result of the latter in that it is often a new theory which makes previously available evidence first come properly into focus and at times even makes us aware of, or search for, previously hidden evidence. Certainly, it is the evidence which in the end determines the fate of a theory. But the determining evidence, apart from being itself bound up with further theories, does not of itself give rise to the theory.

Descriptive and structural linguistics came to this impasse because it had, in spite of its debt to Saussure, disregarded Saussure's distinction between (empirical) speaking and (systematic and abstract) language, a distinction that would be without a real difference, were we able to read language immediately off from speaking.

51. The theoretical depth of language.
Generative and transformational grammar

Theoretical boldness and imagination were restored to linguistics by Noam Chomsky, whose first book, *Syntactic Structures* (1957), marked the beginning of a new phase in linguistics.[17] His most obvious contri-

---

[16] Cf. section 17.

[17] *Syntactic Structures* ('s Gravenhage, 1957). See also his *Aspects of the Theory of Syntax* (Cambridge, Mass., 1965). – In this section and in section 53, "generative (and transformational) grammar" will sometimes refer to the formal set of grammatical rules an example

bution is in the area of syntax. That our command of syntax does not primarily result from empirical data is not only apparent from immediate constituent analysis where, as indicated, the analysis is not a discovery of previously unknown structures, but the articulation of a competence that is present at the very inception of the analysis. It is also evident in the language learning of children, who, to be sure, require stimulation through actual discourse, but then quickly exhibit a command of grammar which goes beyond their empirical data in the sense that they not merely are capable of reproducing previously heard sentences but of generating and understanding sentences that they have never come across.[18]

Immediate constituent analysis reveals regularities in sentence structure in the form of a tree-like diagram. The problem is to formulate these regularities as a set of rules in the most economic and concise way. This Chomsky did by taking the most inclusive set of constituents (the sentence) as a starting point and by specifying how, beginning with this set (symbolized by the trunk of the tree), we can proceed from the trunk to branches, sub-branches, etc.). These rules are called rewriting rules. To generate the sentence in (1) *(the man who painted that red house owned a white horse)*, we need the following set of rules:

(a) Rewrite *Sentence* as *Noun Phrase* plus *Verb Phrase.*
(b) Rewrite *Noun Phrase* as *Noun Phrase* plus *Relative Clause* or as *Determiner* plus *Noun.*
(c) Rewrite *Relative Clause* as *who* plus *Verb Phrase.*
(d) Rewrite *Verb Phrase* as *Verb* plus *Noun Phrase.*
(e) Rewrite *Noun* as *Adjective* plus *Noun* or as *man* or *house* or *horse* or . . .
(f) Rewrite *Verb* as *painted* or *owned* or . . .
(g) Rewrite *Determiner* as *that* or *a* or *the* or . . .
(h) Rewrite *Adjective* as *red* or *white* or . . .

Using these rules we can generate the sentence in (1). The tree in diagram (2) reflects the process of using the rules.

The economy (and that is the explanatory power) of this approach is already apparent here in that rules (b) and (d) capture structural features which in the constituent analysis of (1) appear as separate and

---

of which follows below and sometimes to the research devoted to formulating and justifying such rules.

[18] Cf. Eric H. Lenneberg, "The Capacity for Language Acquisition," *Structure of Language,* ed. Fodor and Katz, pp. 579–603.

(2)

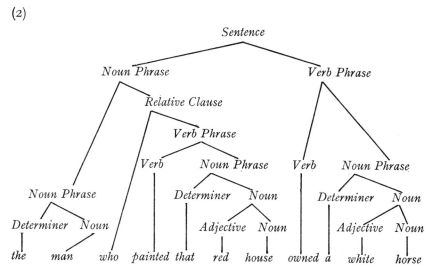

prima facie as unrelated. This virtue comes further into relief in the possibility of using the set of rules to generate many more sentences than just the one in (2), e.g. the following:

(3) That man painted the white house.
(4) The man owned a red horse.
(5) That horse owned a house.
(6) The man who painted that red horse owned a house.

An important further step was taken by Chomsky through the introduction of transformation rules which begin with a string of a specified structure and then permit transition to a string of a different structure, the difference stemming from reordering, adding, or deleting elements. The transformational rules permit formalization of syntactical relations that either elude or are very recalcitrant to branching rules. The active-passive relation in main clauses, for instance, that would fit the scope of the set of rules (a)–(h) can be represented thus:

(i) Rewrite *Noun Phrase₁* plus *Verb* plus *Noun Phrase₂* as *Noun Phrase₂* plus *was* plus *Verb* plus *by* plus *Noun Phrase₁*.

Rule (i) says, in other words, that whenever we find the sequence between "Rewrite" and "as" on any level of a derivation (construction of a tree) by (a)–(h), we can replace that sequence by the sequence which follows "as". E.g. from (3) *(That man painted the white house.)* we get by (i): *The white house was painted by that man.*

We have said above that generative and transformational grammar has great explanatory power. *Explanatory power* stands here for two (related) properties that a theory may have: (1) the theory may be capable of explaining a great number of initially disparate things; (2) the theory may be capable of explaining things with great explicitness. Both properties are relevant here. The range of phenomena covered by transformational grammars reaches from structural homonymy to the domain of possible subjects for verbs such as *love, hear, feel*.[19]

An example of structural homonymy is the sentence

(7) Flying planes can be dangerous.

(7) is homonymous, i.e. the sentence according to its external form has two possible meanings depending on whether in (7) "Flying planes" is replaced by

(8) Planes that fly

or by

(9) If someone flies a plane, that

If we understand (7) at all, one or the other replacement is somehow present in our understanding. In terms of generative grammar, we can say that (7) can be generated in two ways such that at one level of one of the two trees which represent the two ways of generating, (8) is present (or something resembling (8)), and (9) is similarly present in the other tree.[20]

The selectivity of the class of animate subject verbs can be handled by generative grammars through rewriting rules which prescribe the conditions under which the symbol of the next higher class of verbs (say that of transitive verbs) can be replaced by the symbol for animate subject verbs. These conditions take the form of stage directions; in the present instance they would specify that the rewriting can be carried out if the transitive verb symbol is preceded by the symbol for animate nouns. Another rule would then permit the replacement of the animate-subject-verb-symbol by *love, hear, feel, etc.*

The immense difficulties of the general problem here touched upon become apparent when we consider that the rules just suggested fail to handle metaphorical or ironical uses of these verbs. Moreover, we could not make the animate subject verbs a subclass of the transitive verbs since there are animate subject verbs which are intransitive, at least with regard to the active-passive relation (e.g. *live, die, sigh*). Finally and generally, it is clear that we are touching here merely a small segment of an intricate net of relations. Thus the noun-verb relation under discussion could be approached from the side of the noun. Other

[19] Cf. Chomsky, "A Transformational Approach to Syntax," *Structure of Language*, ed. Fodor and Katz, pp. 225–226.

[20] From Chomsky, *ibid.*, p. 237. – (9) is in turn ambiguous.

relations extend to the right of verb where further distinctions must be made since some of these verbs take only animate nouns for their objects *(talk to)*, others only physical objects *(buy)*, etc.

Generative grammar possesses explanatory power in the second sense in that it not merely exhibits the structure of a sentence in a vague way, but forces and enables us to relate every feature to a definite rule. In every application of a rule, moreover, two things are shown at once: (1) what kind of rule is being applied; (2) on what level the rule is being employed. While some rules are confined to a certain level (such as (a), (f), (g), (h)), others are not so limited. They are mediately ((c) by way of (b)) or immediately recursive ((b) and (e)) and thus explain how in principle infinitely long sentences could be generated by means of a finite set of rules.

52. The presuppositions of empirically oriented grammar

We must begin with a brief look at the philosophical implications of structural and descriptive linguistics. We have seen that this approach finds its natural setting in the field work situation because there presumably its objective and empirical orientation becomes most evident and fruitful. A deeper but related reason for this predilection is to be traced back to the view implicitly held by this type of linguistics regarding the relation of language and reality. The implication is that (1) the world is divided into discrete units of meaning; (2) the paradigmatic case of meaning is found in the common-noun/physical-object relation; (3) meaningful linguistic units can be combined additively into more complex units of language and meaning.

In phonetics the first implication is apparent in the definition of phonemes by minimal pairs. The definition says roughly that all actual variations of a sound belong to one phoneme as long as the variations do not interfere with the identifiability of two different meanings. Thus, the difference in the initial sounds of *think* and *sink* cannot be considered an insignificant variation; otherwise the two (distinct) meanings of *think* and *sink* could not be consistently identified. The two words constitute a minimal pair. However it makes no difference whether the initial sound of *proud* is heavily aspirated or not. The possible distinction between aspirated and plain /*p*/ is not utilized in English to convey meaning.[21]

---

[21] For a more technical account see Howard Maclay, "Overview," in *Semantics*, ed. Danny D. Steinberg and Leon A. Jakobovits (London, 1971), pp. 159–161.

A phoneme does not of itself have meaning, but it can make a difference in meaning. The phoneme /s/ plus /ink/ yields one meaning, the phoneme /th/ plus the same component /ink/ yields another. But close inspection shows that the one-to-one correlation between the (discrete) phonetic states and the (discrete) semantic states, i.e. the contention that the change of a definite sound (i.e. of a phoneme) is connected with a definite change in meaning, is quite doubtful. To be sure, the account is illuminating in an abstract way. But usually the force of this explanation is believed to lie in its immediate connection with plain and tangible facts.

The correlation is dubious on the strictly phonetic side in that, as noted earlier, the phonemes are far from being given in an empirically univocal way. Granting nonetheless the phonetic account, we come to recognize the highly conditional nature of the claim that there are discrete units of meaning. It is not the case that we connect discrete meanings with unique sequences of phonemes. Meaning is anchored in larger units of discourse and in the situation or scope of discourse. Due to these moorings, meaning remains firm even if phonemic details are changed. Thus if someone were to disregard the difference between /th/ and /s/ consistently either in favor of /s/ (as some foreign speakers of English do) or in favor of /th/ (as do people who lisp), misunderstandings, if any, would be minimal.[22] Conversely, an isolated word, even if given with complete phonemic accuracy, does not mean anything definite at all. A dictionary represents a rather restricted semantic situation because it obviously excludes all irony, wit, innuendo, literary or personal allusions; imagine an ironical dictionary, alluding to clannish jokes, etc. But these factors are often crucial in constituting meaning. And even in the dictionary's narrow world, most entries carry numerous and frequently diverging meanings.

Much of what has been said about phonemics applies to morphemics as well. Additionally, a consideration of morphemics shows with regard to the second implication above that there are certain privileged situations where a characteristic phoneme sequence can be directly associated with a distinctive physical object. And it is those situations which

---

[22] More precisely, the semantic core (the direct information) of the message would remain the same; but the total meaning of the message would indeed be changed through these phonetic changes. Due to the change, the message conveys the (indirect) information: "this is a foreign speaker" or "this man has a speech defect". Such indirect information may significantly modify the direct information ("he says this because/although he is a foreigner"). But the semantics of descriptive linguistics makes its claim strictly with reference to direct information. That claim is too strong and simple.

are favored and established in field work. But it is obvious how small the number is of morphemes so identifiable. Outside of the class of these morphemes, the concept of meaning changes radically and in a way that remains totally in the dark for descriptive linguistics.

Finally, the weakness of the third implication is apparent to anyone who has tried to translate out of a language to which a dictionary was his main access and who found that a collection of lexical meanings is not equal to a meaningful sentence.[23] To get beyond the simple acknowledgement of this fact, one needs a syntax that shows more than just how words hang together in the empirically given string. The discussion of sentence (7) has shown this. We must supplement the surface grammar which deals with the structures near the level of the empirically given string by a depth grammar which lays bare the underlying structures that are necessary for a perspicuous understanding of a sentence.[24]

Semantics is that discipline of linguistics which deals with the relationship of sound sequences to meanings. Meaning is always meaning *of* something in a double sense: it is the meaning of a word, and thus it means something other than the word qua sound sequence. Hence semantics presupposes an order of things and so an ontology.

But prior to this presupposition, linguistics quite generally presupposes an ontology which determines what kind of thing language itself is. We can call these ontologies semantic and linguistic respectively. In structural and descriptive linguistics, the two ontologies are both fairly explicit and definitely empirical. According to the linguistic ontology, one finds out what language is by simply looking at the facts whereupon he discovers phonemes, morphemes, and orders of immediate constituents. According to the semantic ontology, one relates the linguistic entities to reality by associating them in definite ways with distinct units of meaning which reflect or refer to reality in ways that can be left open.

Both ontologies, as we have seen, are, though illuminating in their own way, far too narrowly conceived and hence constantly violated. They exercised a restrictive influence nonetheless, and at least the

---

[23] The third implication designates a limit that descriptive linguistics has been unwilling or unable to go beyond and not a principle, positively advocated by descriptive linguistics.

[24] The distinction between surface and depth grammar, which is made in the standard theory of generative grammar, corresponds to the Medieval distinction between the accidents and the substance of grammar (cf. section 20). And just as the substance of grammar is identical with or close to the universal grammar, so depth grammar approximates universal linguistic structures. See Chomsky, *Aspects*, pp. 27–30 *et passim*.

linguistic ontology was attacked and rejected by generative and transformational grammar.

53. *The reach of theoretically oriented grammar*

Generative grammar draws a sharp distinction between the competence of the native speaker and his performance. His competence circumscribes what he can in principle say and understand, his performance consists of all those pieces of language that he has in fact produced or heard.[25] Chomsky insists that in linguistics and in psychological theory generally an explication of competence is required if performance is to be understood.[26] Once something like competence is granted, it is clear that it is very different in nature and scope from performance.[27] It follows in turn that in determining and formulating competence one cannot cling to the facts of performance and to what they seem to yield willingly. The question as to the empirical source of insights or hypotheses is properly declared irrelevant.[28] This attitude has led to the explication of competence in terms of the sort of abstract and powerful theory of which a simplified fragment was given in section 51.

But there must be some empirical checks on such theory construction. Indeed, the generative grammars have constantly been checked against, and developed in response to, two questions: (1) Are the pieces of language generated by a given grammar accepted by the native speaker as normal or correct? (2) Can a given (type of) sentence, produced by the native speaker, be generated by a certain grammar? Such empirical considerations are also regarded as decisive in the evaluation of competing grammars.[29] But the first question is obviously not answered satisfactorily if the grammar in question produces *some* acceptable sentences. As the second question suggests, the grammar should be able to generate a great number of sentences; in fact it should approach the infinite generative capacity that is comprised by the notion of competence. Even the sample grammar of section 51 shows that the properly syntactic part (rules (a)–(d), and (i)) is superior to the semantic part (rules (e)–(h)) in that it generates no deviant phrase

---

[25] Cf. section 49 above.

[26] *Language and Mind* (New York, 1968), pp. 63–64.

[27] *Ibid.*, p. 68.

[28] See Chomsky, *Structures*, pp. 50–51, 56, 59, 93–94, *Aspects*, p. 19; Katz, *Philosophy*, pp. 11–12.

[29] See Chomsky, "Deep Structure, Surface Structure, and Semantic Interpretation," *Semantics*, ed. Steinberg and Jakobovits, pp. 177–178, 187.

markers; and the phrase markers which it does produce cover many more actual English sentences than can be explicitly generated in conjunction with the semantic component.[30] Among these latter sentences, there are clearly deviant or unusual ones.[31] In section 51 we touched on the immense difficulties that one faces if such deviations are to be prevented. But even if they were prevented, the result would be limited for just that reason since the standard of normalcy would fail to sanction and explain the legitimate idioms of humor, poetry, fairy tales, dreams.[32] Much more sophisticated and powerful semantic theories have been proposed than our sample grammar could suggest.[33] But in light of the magnitude of the unsolved and unformulated problems, these proposals remain tentative and fragmentary also.[34]

Generative semantics is led to these problems in the attempt to bring the generative process to a conclusion which constitutes in phonetic transcription a sentence deemed normal by the native speaker, more precisely to a conclusion which reflects the general insights and capabilities of the speaker. As indicated such conclusions bear decisively on the evaluation and development of grammar. Such a grammar is to explicate the native speaker's competence. But whether this is the case can be established only if the grammar is made to perform. Performance in the sense of putting the grammar through its paces and showing how it generates a particular sentence is a matter of course for all generative grammarians. An instantiation of performance in the strong and narrow sense of giving a physical counterpart or a physiological location of a generative grammar and its rules is rejected by Chomsky as unobtainable at present and as unnecessary for the theoretical investigations of grammar.[35] Similarly Chomsky regards as of subordinate importance the question of performance regarding the sequence in which the syntactic, semantic, and phonological components of a grammar cooperate.[36]

---

[30] Due to the size of the lexicon there is a large number of instantiations of just the smaller syntactic structures (say of up to twenty terminal elements) that can be generated by the sample grammar. Moreover the grammar, since it contains recursive rules, can generate infinitely many different syntactic structures. But it is even intuitively clear that the capacity so described, is a small fragment of syntactic competence.

[31] Sentence (5) in section 51 is an example.

[32] See Uriel Weinreich, "Explorations in Semantic Theory," *Semantics*, ed. Steinberg and Jakobovits, p. 311.

[33] See e.g. Jerrold J. Katz and Paul M. Postal, *An Integrated Theory of Linguistic Descriptions* (Cambridge, Mass., 1964).

[34] See Weinreich, "Explorations," in *Semantics*, ed. Steinberg and Jakobovits, pp. 308–328; Chomsky, "Deep Structure," *ibid.*, p. 183 and *Language and Mind*, p. 50.

[35] See *Language and Mind*, pp. 83–84.

[36] See "Deep Structure," *Semantics*, ed. Steinberg and Jakobovits, pp. 187–188, 214.

The question is whether these senses of performance are ultimately separable. Performance in the first and apparently least problematic sense actually contravenes the spirit of generative grammar most because such performance conceals what precisely must be brought to the set of rules to make it yield an actual sentence. Overtly this contribution from without appears as a series of choices which are structured, but not decided, by the set of syntactic rules. The mere acceptability to the speaker of the result produced is not sufficient to justify such a procedure since parrots and taperecorders likewise produce acceptable results. What is required is that the procedure shed light on our understanding of language. But choices in the syntactic derivation are as such beyond motivation. What then motivates the speaker when he generates sentences? Broadly and tentatively, speaking is initiated and determined by the situation in which the speaker finds himself. But does this not entail that an explict account of performance would either lose all generality or else would have to capture the infinite variety of situations and speakers?[37] In the case of other scientific theories, the domains of explanation are delineated through abstraction of salient features to the exclusion of all others. But in human language all features and shades of reality come to be present. Attempts at bringing this infinite expressiveness of language under control have impressively shown how closely and finely textured the fabric of language is as it presents reality. But the systematic efforts of laying bare the basic pattern of the fabric have made little progress since from every knot that has been grasped indefinitely many threads run in obscure directions.[38] The more episodic and anecdotal efforts, though often striking, give no promise of converging into a coherent system.[39]

The infinite variety of language cannot be caught by a grammar formally and in advance of any actual speaking, i.e. performance, because this sort of variety is not of a formal sort. That variety constantly emerges in the questions formulated above, i.e.: Would we in fact say what the grammar generates? And: Can the grammar generate what we have in fact said? The adequacy of the formal explication of the expressive variety of a language could indeed only be evaluated if all the situations to be expressed could be anticipated.

[37] Cf. Maclay, "Overview," *Semantics*, ed. Steinberg and Jakobovits, p. 162.
[38] Cf. Weinreich, "Explorations," *Semantics*, ed. Steinberg and Jakobovits, pp. 308–328.
[39] Cf. Chomsky, "Deep Structure," *Semantics*, ed. Steinberg and Jakobovits, pp. 199–213; James D. McCawley, "Where Do Noun Phrases Come From?" *ibid.*, pp. 217–231. These two examples show in part that generative grammar can be extended to cover traditional problems as discussed in sections 16 and 35–37; they also show how extended and problematic the areas are that generative grammar is just entering.

This is the objective aspect of the impass. The subjective side of the very same problem appears when one remembers that speaking is grounded not just in a situation, but in the situation as the speaker finds himself in it. Spoken language arises from man's encounter with his world. Chomsky has not to any extent addressed the objective impass, but he has repeatedly proposed a positive answer to the subjective problem: A proper understanding of language will importantly advance our understanding of the human mind.[40] After more than fifteen years of effort the general implications from generative grammar for the nature of the human mind regarding freedom and creativity are primarily of significance in criticizing improperly restricted views of human behavior.[41] Chomsky has tried to argue more specifically that there are rules of grammar not explicable by the demands of efficiency which rules may therefore be typical and indicative of the nature of man's mind.[42] But there is not even a clue as to what such rules might indicate and whether the indications would be at all illuminating. Chomsky has spoken forcefully and admirably to problems of human freedom. But there is no substantive connection between such efforts and his linguistic work. *Problems of Knowledge and Freedom* is a distressing monument to the chasm that separates these two sorts of endeavors.[43]

Why has it been impossible to substantiate the thesis as to the significant relation between language and mind? The thesis presupposes that the mind as the seat of linguistic competence is, whatever else it may be, a rule using or rule governed entity. But on that view an agent that governs by or uses rules is assumed, but set aside in any investigation that merely seeks to explicate rules. Such an investigation is restricted to penultimacy unless it begins to consider man's mind as the embodiment of rules. Indeed the notion of competence suggests not just the availability of rules, but the ability to use them. As Kant has pointed out, it is futile to try and solve this problem by formulating rules of application of the first set of rules since this is but the first step of an infinite regress.[44] That such an infinity opens up is

---

[40] See his *Problems of Knowledge and Freedom* (New York, 1971) pp. 3–51 and *Language and Mind* for recent formulations.

[41] Chomsky, *Problems*, pp. 6–25, *Language and Mind*, pp. 1–4, 58–62, 70–76.

[42] *Language and Mind*, pp. 51–52, *Problems*, pp. 43–45.

[43] This is not to denigrate the value of Chomsky's work in the respective fields and the value of the book in that sense.

[44] Immanuel Kant, *Critique of Pure Reason*, tr. Norman Kemp Smith (New York, 1965), pp. 177–178 (A 132–134, B 171–174). The reference to Kant is not as incidental as it appears. The problem under discussion is a transcendental one and could so be developed and discussed. Cf. Conclusion below.

only the subjective correlate of the potentially infinite number of situations in and to which the rules are to be applied. Analogies to rule governed entities other than man's linguistic competence are misleading since some boundaries of application are always built into them.[45]

The second and third senses of performance, mentioned above, bear on the embodiment of competence; or using previous terminology, in the question of performance, linguistic ontology is at issue. But as remarked above, Chomsky thinks it possible and advisable to bracket the problem of embodiment, i.e. the problem of linguistic ontology. This is correct inasmuch as embodiment of rules explicated in terms of computing machines or brain physiology leads to Kant's regress and is, though important and enlightening, not a genuine solution of the problem.[46] But is there a genuine solution?

We have seen that there is no genuine solution to the problem of radical signification. Meaning is unsurpassably precursive. Any distinction between sound and meaning is relative to (acoustically or otherwise) embodied meaning which remains integral. The distinction of relative signification is axiomatic in generative grammar.[47] This is a corollary of the relative nature of generative grammar as a rule explicating enterprise. But what is it relative to? Generative grammar is at present a functional theory of human language. It has been shown that, given a system for which a functional account is to be given, the preferred state of the system can be determined in an indefinite number of ways, and correspondingly many functional accounts can be given.[48] In the case of human language, the indefinite number of situations in and for which it is used by the speaker seems to frustrate any attempt at fixing the level of description in a non-arbitrary manner. More precisely, a determinate level of description (syntactic, phonological, morphemic) at once reveals how much remains beyond the ken of such description. The overwhelming remainder appears loosely in the term "number and variety of situations in which the speaker finds himself" and is turned over to semantics. A sort of linguistics which is not troubled by the remainder (e.g. structural and descriptive linguistics)

---

[45] Chomsky alludes to this in *Language and Mind*, pp. 10–11.

[46] This is of course a controversial point. But it seems to me that the mind-body identity thesis in a strict physicalist ("physical$_2$") sense trivializes and dissolves problems of freedom, personality, and language. Cf. note 48 below.

[47] Cf. Maclay, "Overview," in *Semantics*, ed. Steinberg and Jakobovits, p. 178.

[48] Cf. Thomas Nagel, "The Boundaries of Inner Space," *The Journal of Philosophy*, LXVI (1969), 452–458; William Kalke, "What is Wrong with Fodor and Putnam's Functionalism?" *Nous*, III (1969), 83–93; Richard Rorty, "Functionalism, Machines, and Incorrigibility," *The Journal of Philosophy*, LXIX (1972), 203–220.

can proceed smoothly within its limits. The recent controversies in the semantics of generative grammar show both the ambition of the investigators and the prohibitive multiplicity of possible approaches.[49]

We have reached this point of relativism and agnosticism before, and essentially the same reply must be given as then.[50] The question at what level man is described most importantly and which situations are decisive and which trivial may be controversial, but it is not arbitrary. And indeed, Chomsky's research has been guided by a tentative but discernible substantive philosophy: the carefully reasoned and well informed humanism and libertarianism represented by men such as Descartes and Humboldt.

An air of excitement and promise has surrounded transformational grammar from the start. If it is to stay alive, there must be (1) detailed and technical reflection on the inherent limitations of generative grammar as presently pursued, (2) a formulation of an explict and substantive view of man and his world, (3) a mutual illumination of technical grammar and substantive philosophy. To illustrate the nature of the third part of the project, consider once more the sample grammar of section 51.

If we take a tree diagram which is the representation of the generating of some sentence and consider the dynamic aspect of the tree, how it grows and branches out, we can interpret this process as one of progressive explication. *Sentence* contains *Noun Phrase* plus *Verb Phrase, Noun Phrase* contains *Determiner* plus *Noun*, etc. The entire terminal string is contained and implicitly present in *Sentence*. This presence is a highly concentrated and involuted one, demanding an unfolding and clarifying explication. The generation of the sentence so understood recalls the generation of language as developed by Vico. It goes from a highly charged unitary situation to ever more explicit and relaxed stages. And this view recalls in turn Heraclitus' teachings on the λόγος.

The point, however, is not that the structure of today's language reflects in an odd way the historical evolution of language ("ontogeny reflects phylogeny"); as we have indicated in the discussion of Vico, the historically prior stages are not simply left behind, but rather remain the animating and cohesion bestowing force in the subsequent structures. We have emphasized in the discussion of the speculative grammars that the empirically one-dimensional (serial) form of sen-

[49] See Steinberg's and Jakobovits' anthology, pp. 155–482.
[50] See sections 43 and 44.

tences is misleading and that a sentence is essentially understood as a two dimensional entity. That means that the prior or upper parts of a sentence (i.e. of its tree diagram) must somehow be present for a hearer if he is to understand the sentence. This is sometimes expressed by saying that *the history of a sentence* (this expression has now a significant ambiguity) must be present to the speaker.

What is needed to come to grips with the two-dimensional nature of the sentence is a semantics of containment and involution which shows how a sentence (or its tree) is characteristically meaningful at every level and explains why all sentences, however different from one another as terminal strings, progressively resemble one another in their higher levels. This theory of meaning would also be a concomitant semantics and account for the increasing specificity of the decisions that are made in, but never explained by, the syntax and the semantics wherever the latter may set in.

The value of such an endeavor obviously depends on the value of the formal and substantive matters that are brought into contact here.[51] It favors at any rate a pedagogical separation of components of grammar in the sense of the standard version.[52] A combination of formal and semantic considerations from the start in the sense of generative semantics dissipates the force that a fruitful confrontation of the formal and substantive dimensions needs.

---

[51] Such an enterprise would in part explicate what Thomas of Erfurt calls *perfection*. See section 20.

[52] Cf. Maclay, "Overview," *Semantics*, ed. Steinberg and Jakobovits, pp. 163–181.

CONCLUSION

"I entitle *transcendental*," Kant said, "all knowledge which is occupied not so much with objects as with the mode of our knowledge of objects in so far as this mode is to be possible *a priori*."[1] We have seen how the spirit of Kant's enterprise is at work in most of the current concern with language. The predominant and explicit investigations of language, to use another of Kant's terms, inquire into the *conditions of the possibility* of speaking, setting aside the question what point there is to what actually has been said and the question what needs to be said.

In a radical turn away from objects to the conditions of their possibility, guidance by such objects in their unexchangeable dignity is abandoned and lost. Consequently an indefinite number of kinds of constitutive possibilities opens up. As we return to the objects, we are overwhelmed by the multiplicity of ways in which we can address them and by the failure of any mode of address to come forward with authority. Science is unable to guide us since if it is speaking globally and immediately it is but another voice among many; and as it speaks more rigorously, approaching the language of physics, it says less and less about the molar world in which we inexorably live. This is just an instance of the general difficulty. If one leaves behind without further obligation the normal world with its confusions and controversies for the world of atoms and nuclear particles, he is then unable without obliging himself to that world to rebuild it from the admittedly rigorous and fundamental level.

Having radically turned away from the normal world to constitutive possibilities, one faces in returning to the world with these possibilities a radical problem of how they can be actualized. This is the problem of radical signification. But in asking whether and how the possibilities

---

[1] *Critique of Pure Reason*, tr. Kemp Smith, p. 59 (A 11–12, B 25).

can be actualized, new conditions of possibility open up to an infinite regress. Kant felt the impass keenly when he addressed the question how in the so called schematism the a priori concepts of understanding were to be united with intuition in which the things themselves first announce themselves.[2] Kant all but despaired of a solution: "This schematism of our understanding, in its application to appearances and their mere form, is an art concealed in the depths of the human soul, whose real modes of activity nature is hardly likely ever to allow us to discover, and to have open to our gaze."[3]

The problem is indeed unsolvable; but it was possible for this to remain concealed as long as the encompassing natural language remained significatively intact and in constituting radical signification allowed the formulations of restricted constitutive possibilities to signify in a relative manner.[4] Can the transcendental approach be successfully taken to natural language itself? To the extent that this is possible, our world will lose what cohesion and direction it now has. Such losses are already taking place. They are not caused by, but reflected and acted out in current philosophy of language. If they continue, the result will probably not be conflict and chaos which require coherent and directed forces, but an entirely novel world, pallid and flat. The issue, at any rate, comes to a singularly sharp focus in the philosophy of language.

---

[2] A more implicit awareness of this problem on Kant's part was noted in section 53.

[3] *Critique of Pure Reason*, tr. Kemp Smith, p. 183 (A 141, B 180–81). It must be noted that this is not yet the truly radical problem since intuition does itself have a priori forms. The explicitly radical problem had already become inaccessible to Kant, at least in the analytic of the first *Critique*.

[4] That was a point already brought against Kant's critical philosophy by Hamann and Herder. Cf. section 32, note 9 in particular.

BIBLIOGRAPHY

Abelson, Paul. *The Seven Liberal Arts. A Study in Medieval Culture.* 2nd ed. New York, 1939.
Alston, William P. *Philosophy of Language.* Englewood Cliffs, 1964.
Anagnostopoulos, Georgios. "Plato's *Cratylus*. The Two Theories of the Correctness of Names," *Review of Metaphysics,* XXV (1972), pp. 691–736.
Anscombe, G. E. M. *An Introduction to Wittgenstein's "Tractatus".* London, 1959.
Apel, Karl Otto. *Die Idee der Sprache in der Tradition des Humanismus von Dante bis Vico.* Archiv für Begriffsgeschichte, vol. 8. Bonn, 1963.
Arens, Hans. *Sprachwissenschaft. Der Gang ihrer Entwicklung von der Antike bis zur Gegenwart.* Freiburg, 1955.
Aristotle. *On Interpretation,* tr. Harold P. Cook. Cambridge, Mass., 1962.
—. *Poetics,* tr. W. Hamilton Frye. Cambridge, Mass., 1965.
—. *Topics,* tr. E. S. Forster. Cambridge, Mass., 1966.
Arnauld, Antoine. *The Art of Thinking,* tr. James Dickoff and Patricia James. Indianapolis, 1964.
— and Claude Lancelot. *Grammaire générale et raisonnée.* 3rd ed. of 1676, ed. Herbert E. Brekle. Stuttgart-Bad Cannstatt, 1966.
Austin, J. L. *How to Do Things with Words,* ed. J. O. Urmson. New York, 1965.
—. "A Plea for Excuses," *Ordinary Language,* ed. Chappell, pp. 41–63.
—. *Sense and Sensibilia,* ed. G. J. Warnock. New York, 1964.
Barwick, Karl. *Probleme der stoischen Sprachlehre und Rhetorik.* Abhandlungen der Sächsischen Akademie der Wissenschaften zu Leipzig. Philologisch-historische Klasse, vol. 49, no. 3. Berlin, 1957.
Belaval, Yvon. "Vico and Anti-Cartesianism," *Giambattista Vico,* ed. Tagliacozzo and White, pp. 77–91.
Bergmann, Gustav. "The Glory and the Misery of Ludwig Wittgenstein," *Essays,* ed. Copi and Beard, pp. 343–358.
Bernstein, Richard J. "Wittgenstein's Three Languages," *Essays,* ed. Copi and Beard, pp. 231–247.
Black, Max. *A Companion to Wittgenstein's "Tractatus".* Cambridge, 1964.
—. "Russell's Philosophy of Language," *Linguistic Turn,* ed. Rorty, pp. 136–146.
Blanshard, Brand. *Reason and Analysis.* La Salle, 1962.
Bloomfield, Leonard. *Language.* New York, 1933.
Boeder, Heribert. "Der frühgriechische Wortgebrauch von Logos und Aletheia," *Archiv für Begriffsgeschichte,* IV (1959), 82–112.
Bolinger, Dwight. *Aspects of Language.* New York, 1968.
Borgmann, Albert. "Sprache als System und Ereignis. Über linguistische und

literaturwissenschaftliche Sprachbetrachtung," *Zeitschrift für philosophische Forschung*, XXI (1967), 570–589.

Brown, Roger Langham. *Wilhelm von Humboldt's Conception of Linguistic Relativity*. The Hague, 1967.

Buridan, John. *Sophisms on Meaning and Truth*, tr. Theodore Kermit Scott. New York, 1966.

Bursill-Hall, G. L. *Speculative Grammars of the Middle Ages. The Doctrine of "Partes Orationis" of the Modistae*. The Hague, 1971.

Carnap, Rudolf. "Empiricism, Semantics, and Ontology," *Semantic Turn*, ed. Rorty, pp. 72–84.

—. "The Elimination of Metaphysics through Logical Analysis of Language," *Logical Positivism*, ed. A. J. Ayer (New York, 1959), pp. 60–81.

—. "Foundations of Logic and Mathematics," *Structure of Language*, ed. Fodor and Katz, pp. 419–436.

Casey, John. *The Language of Criticism*. London, 1966.

Cassirer, Ernst. *The Philosophy of Symbolic Forms. Volume One: Language*, tr. Ralph Manheim. 7th ed. New Haven, Conn., 1968.

Caton, Charles E., ed. *Philosophy and Ordinary Language*. Urbana, 1963.

Cavell, Stanley. "Austin at Criticism," *Linguistic Turn*, ed. Rorty, pp. 250–260.

—. "Must We Mean What We Say?" *Ordinary Language*, ed. Chappell, pp. 73–112.

Chappell, V. C., ed. *Ordinary Language. Essays in Philosophical Method*. Englewood Cliffs, 1964.

Chomsky, Noam. *Aspects of the Theory of Syntax*. Cambridge, Mass., 1965.

—. "Deep Structure, Surface Structure, and Semantic Interpretation," *Semantics*, ed. Steinberg and Jakobovits, pp. 183–216.

—. *Cartesian Linguistics. A Chapter in the History of Rationalist Thought*. New York, 1966.

—. *Language and Mind*. New York, 1968.

—. *Problems of Knowledge and Freedom*. New York, 1971.

—. *Syntactic Structures*. 's-Gravenhage, 1957.

—. "A Transformational Approach to Syntax," *Structure of Language*, ed. Fodor and Katz, pp. 211–245.

Cleve, Felix M. "Understanding the Pre-Socratics: Philological or Philosophical Reconstruction?" *International Philosophical Quarterly*, III (1963), 445–464.

Colish, Marcia L. *The Mirror of Language: A Study in the Medieval Theory of Knowledge*. New Haven, 1968.

Copi, Irving M. and James A. Gould, eds. *Contemporary Readings in Logical Theory*. New York, 1967.

— and Robert W. Beard, eds. *Essays on Wittgenstein's "Tractatus"*. New York, 1966.

—. "Language Analysis and Metaphysical Inquiry," *Linguistic Turn*, ed. Rorty, pp. 127–131.

Crystal, David. *Linguistics, Language, and Religion*. New York, 1965.

Derbolav, Josef. *Der Dialog "Kratylos" im Rahmen der platonischen Sprach- und Erkenntnisphilosophie*. Saarbrücken, 1953.

—. "Das Problem des Metasprachlichen in Platons 'Kratylos'," *Lebendiger Realismus*. Festschrift für Johannes Thyssen, ed. Klaus Hartmann and Hans Wagner (Bonn, 1962), pp. 181–210.

Descartes, René. *Discourse on Method*, tr. Laurence J. Lafleur. 2nd ed. Indianapolis, 1956.

—. *Meditations on First Philosophy*, tr. Laurence J. Lafleur. 2nd ed. Indianapolis, 1960.

De Mauro, Tullio. "Giambattista Vico: From Rhetoric to Linguistic Historicism," *Giambattista Vico*, ed. Tagliacozzo and White, pp. 279–295.

Diels, Hermann and Walther Kranz, eds. *Die Fragmente der Vorsokratiker*. 11th ed., 3 vols. Zürich, 1964.

Duns Scotus, Joannes. *Grammaticae Speculativae Nova Editio*, ed. Marianus Fernandez Garcia. Quaracchi, 1902 (the treatise is falsely ascribed to Scotus and is in fact by Thomas of Erfurt).

Favrholdt, David. *An Interpretation and Critique of Wittgenstein's "Tractatus"*. Copenhagen, 1964.

Fink, Eugen. *Spiel als Weltsymbol*. Stuttgart, 1960.

Fodor, Jerry A. and Jerrold J. Katz, eds. *The Structure of Language. Readings in the Philosophy of Language*. Englewood Cliffs, 1964.

Freeman, Kathleen. *Ancilla to the Pre-Socratic Philosophers*. Oxford, 1948.

Frye, Northrop. *Anatomy of Criticism. Four Essays*. Princeton, 1957.

Geach, Peter T. *Reference and Generality. An Examination of Some Medieval and Modern Theories*. Ithaca, New York, 1962.

Gentinetta, Peter M. *Zur Sprachbetrachtung bei den Sophisten und in der stoisch-hellenistischen Zeit*. Winterthur, 1961.

Gleason, H. A. *An Introduction to Descriptive Linguistics*. 2nd ed. New York, 1961.

Godfrey, Robert C. "Late Medieval Linguistic Meta-Theory and Chomsky's Syntactic Structures," *Word*, XXI (1965), 251–256.

Goodman, Nelson. *Languages of Art. An Approach to a Theory of Symbols*. Indianapolis, 1968.

Grabmann, Martin. "Die Entwicklung der mittelalterlichen Sprachlogik," *Philosophisches Jahrbuch*, XXXV (1922), 121–135, 199–214.

Griffin, James. *Wittgenstein's Logical Atomism*. Oxford, 1964.

Gunderson, Keith. "Descartes, La Mettrie, Language, and Machines," *Philosophy*, XXXIX (1964), 193–222.

—. "Poetics [abstract]," *Journal of Philosophy*, LXIV (1967), pp. 688–689.

Hampshire, Stuart. "Vico and the Contemporary Philosophy of Language," *Giambattista Vico*, ed. Tagliacozzo and White, pp. 475–482.

Heidegger, Martin. *Being and Time*, tr. John Mcaquarrie and Edward Robinson. New York, 1962.

—. *An Introduction to Metaphysics*, tr. Ralph Manheim. Garden City, 1961.

—. *Frühe Schriften*. Frankfurt am Main, 1972.

—. *Die Kategorien- und Bedeutungslehre des Duns Scotus*. Tübingen, 1916.

—. *On the Way to Language*, tr. Peter Hertz. New York, 1971.

—. *Unterwegs zur Sprache*. 2nd ed. Pfullingen, 1960.

—. *Vorträge und Aufsätze*. 2nd ed. Pfullingen, 1959.

—. *What is Philosophy?* tr. William Kluback and Jean T. Wilde. New York, 1958.

Herder, Johann Gottfried. *Essay on the Origin of Language*, tr. Alexander Gode. New York, 1966.

—. *Sprachphilosophische Schriften*, ed. Erich Heintel. 2nd ed. Hamburg, 1964.

Hester, Marcus B. *The Meaning of Poetic Metaphor. An Analysis in the Light of Wittgenstein's Claim that Meaning is Use*. The Hague, 1967.

Hill, Archibald A. "A Program for the Definition of Literature," *Studies in English*, XXXVII (1958), 46–52.

Hintikka, Jaakko. *Knowledge and Belief. An Introduction to the Logic of Two Notions*. Ithaca, 1962.

Huizinga, Johan. *Homo ludens. A Study of the Playelement in Culture*, tr. R. F. C. Hull. New York, 1950.

Humboldt, Wilhelm von. *Humanist Without Portfolio. An Anthology of the Writings of Wilhelm von Humboldt*, tr. and ed. Marianne Cowan. Detroit, 1963.

—. *Linguistic Variability and Intellectual Development*, tr. George C. Buck and Frithjof A. Raven. Philadelphia, 1972.

—. *Werke*, ed. Andreas Flitner and Klaus Giel. 4 vols. Stuttgart, 1960–1964.

Husserl, Edmund. *Ideas. General Introduction to Pure Phenomenology*, tr. W. R. Boyce Gibson. New York, 1967.

Iseminger, Gary, ed. *Logic and Philosophy*. New York, 1968.

Jacoby, Günther. *Die Ansprüche der Logistiker auf die Logik und ihre Geschichtschreibung*. Stuttgart, 1962.

Juliard, Pierre. *Philosophies of Language in Eighteenth-Century France*. The Hague, 1970.

Kahn, Charles E. "A New Look at Heraclitus," *American Philosophical Quarterly*, I (1964), 189–203.

Kalke, William. "What is Wrong with Fodor and Putnam's Functionalism?" *Nous*, III (1969), 83–93.

Kant, Immanuel. *Critique of Pure Reason*, tr. Norman Kemp Smith. New York, 1965.

Katz, Jerrold J. and Paul M. Postal. *An Integrated Theory of Linguistic Descriptions*. Cambridge, Mass., 1964.

Katz, Jerrold J. *The Philosophy of Language*. New York, 1966.

Kaufmann, Walter. "Before Socrates," *Philosophic Classics*, ed. Kaufmann, 2nd ed. (Englewood Cliffs, 1968), I, 1–5.

Kayser, Wolfgang. *Das sprachliche Kunstwerk*. 8th ed. Bern, 1962.

Keyt, David. "Wittgenstein's Notion of an Object," *Essays*, ed. Copi and Beard, pp. 289–303.

Kirk, G. S. "Heraclitus's Contribution to the Development of a Language for Philosophy," *Archiv für Begriffsgeschichte*, IX (1964), 73–77.

— and J. E. Raven. *The Presocratic Philosophers. A Critical History with a Selection of Texts*. Cambridge, 1966.

Kneale, William and Martha Kneale. *The Development of Logic*. Oxford, 1962.

Kyburg, Henry E. *Philosophy of Science. A Formal Approach*. New York, 1968.

Larkin, Miriam Therese. *Language in the Philosophy of Aristotle*. The Hague, 1971.

Lenneberg, Eric H. *Biological Foundations of Language*. New York, 1967.

—. "The Capacity for Language Acquisition," *Structure of Language*, ed. Fodor and Katz, pp. 579–603.

Liebrucks, Bruno. *Sprache und Bewusstsein*. 4 vols. Frankfurt, 1964–1968.

Linsky, Leonard. *Referring*. London, 1967.

—, ed. *Semantics and the Philosophy of Language*. Urbana, 1952.

Lohmann, Johannes. *Philosophie und Sprachwissenschaft*. Berlin, 1965.

Lorenz, Kuno and Jürgen Mittelstrass. "On Rational Philosophy of Language. The Programme in Plato's *Cratylus* Reconsidered," *Mind*, LXXVI (1967), 1–20.

—. "Theaitetos fliegt. Zur Theorie wahrer und falscher Sätze bei Platon," *Archiv für Geschichte der Philosophie*, XLVII (1966), 113–152.

Maclay, Howard. "Overview," *Semantics*, ed. Steinberg and Jakobovits, pp. 157–182.

McCawley, James D. "Where Do Noun Phrases Come From?" *Semantics*, ed. Steinberg and Jakobovits, pp. 217–231.

Malcolm, Norman. *Ludwig Wittgenstein. A Memoir*. London, 1967.

—. "Moore and Ordinary Language," *Linguistic Turn*, ed. Rorty, pp. 111–124.

Mann, Thomas. "The Making of the Magic Mountain," *The Magic Mountain*, tr. H. T. Lowe-Porter (New York, 1965), pp. 719–729.

Manthey, Franz. *Die Sprachphilosophie des hl. Thomas von Aquin und ihre Anwendung auf Probleme der Theologie*. Paderborn, 1937.

Marx, Werner. *Absolute Reflexion und Sprache.* Frankfurt, 1967.
Maslow, Alexander. *A Study in Wittgenstein's "Tractatus".* Berkeley, 1961.
Mates, Benson. "On the Verification of Statements about Ordinary Language," *Ordinary Language*, ed. Chappell, pp. 64–74.
Miller, Robert Lee. "The Linguistic Relativity Principle and Humboldtian Ethnolinguistics." Diss. Michigan, 1963.
Maxwell, Grover and Herbert Feigl. "Why Ordinary Language Needs Reforming," *Linguistic Turn*, ed. Rorty, pp. 193–200.
Moody, Ernest A. *Truth and Consequence in Medieval Logic.* Amsterdam, 1953.
Moore, G. E. "An Autobiography," *The Philosophy of G. E. Moore*, ed. Paul Arthur Schilpp (Evanston, 1942), pp. 3–39.
Morris, Charles W. *Foundations of the Theory of Signs.* International Encyclopedia of Unified Science (Chicago, 1938–1962), vol. 1, part 2.
Morrison, James C. *Meaning and Truth in Wittgenstein's "Tractatus".* The Hague, 1968.
Nagel, Thomas. "The Boundaries of Inner Space," *The Journal of Philosophy*, LXVI (1969), 452–458.
Nakhnikian, George. "Martin Heidegger. Introduction," *Readings in Twentieth-Century Philosophy*, ed. William P. Alston and George Nakhnikian (New York, 1963), pp. 679–687.
Palmer, Richard E. *Hermeneutics. Interpretation Theory in Schleiermacher, Dilthey, Heidegger, and Gadamer.* Evanston, 1969.
Perreiah, Alan R. "Buridan and the Definite Description," *Journal of the History of Philosophy*, X (1972), pp. 153–160.
Pinborg, Jan. *Die Entwicklung der Sprachtheorie im Mittelalter.* Beiträge zur Geschichte der Philosophie und Theologie des Mittelalters, vol. 42, no. 2. Münster, 1967.
—. "Die Erfurter Tradition im Sprachdenken des Mittelalters," *Universalismus und Partikularismus im Mittelalter*, Miscellanea Mediaevalia, vol. 5, ed. Paul Wilpert (Berlin, 1968), pp. 173–185.
Plato. *Cratylus*, tr. H. N. Fowler. Cambridge, Mass., 1963.
—. *Epistles*, tr. R. G. Bury. Cambridge, Mass., 1952.
—. *Parmenides*, tr. H. N. Fowler. Cambridge, Mass., 1963.
—. *Phaedo*, tr. H. N. Fowler. Cambridge, Mass., 1938.
—. *The Republic*, tr. Paul Shorey. 2 vols. Cambridge, Mass., 1953.
—. *The Sophist*, tr. H. N. Fowler. Cambridge, Mass., 1961.
—. *Theaetetus*, tr. H. N. Fowler. Cambridge, Mass., 1961.
Popper, Karl R. "Back to the Presocratics" with an appendix "Historical Conjectures and Heraclitus on Change," *Conjectures and Refutations* (New York, 1962), pp. 136–165.
Quine, Willard Van Orman. *From a Logical Point of View. Nine Logico-Philosophical Essays.* 2nd ed. New York, 1963.
—. *Ontological Relativity and Other Essays.* New York, 1969.
—. "The Ways of Paradox," *The Ways of Paradox and Other Essays* (New York, 1966), pp. 3–20.
—. *Word and Object.* Cambridge, Mass., 1960.
Quintilian. *Institutio oratoria*, tr. H. E. Butler. 4 vols. Cambridge, Mass., 1936.
Richards, I. A. *The Philosophy of Rhetoric.* New York, 1965.
Ricoeur, Paul. "Husserl and Wittgenstein on Language," *Phenomenology and Existentialism*, ed. Edward N. Lee and Maurice Mandelbaum (Baltimore, 1967), pp. 207–217.
Robins, R. H. *Ancient and Medieval Grammatical Theory in Europe with Particular Reference to Modern Linguistic Doctrine.* London, 1951.

Robinson, John Mansley. *An Introduction to Early Greek Philosophy*. Boston, 1968.

Rorty, Richard. "Functionalism, Machines, and Incorrigibility," *The Journal of Philosophy*, LXIX (1972), 203–220.

Rorty, Richard, ed. *The Linguistic Turn. Recent Essays in Philosophical Method*. Chicago, 1967.

—. "Metaphilosophical Difficulties of Linguistic Philosophy," *The Linguistic Turn*, ed. Rorty, pp. 1–39.

—. "Pragmatism, Categories, and Language," *Philosophical Review*, LXX (1961), 197–223.

Roos, Heinrich. *Die Modi significandi des Martinus de Dacia. Forschungen zur Geschichte der Sprachlogik im Mittelalter.* Beiträge zur Geschichte der Philosophie und Theologie des Mittelalters, vol. 37, no. 2. Münster, 1952.

Ross, James F. "Analogy as a Rule of Meaning for Religious Language," *International Philosophical Quarterly*, I (1961), 468–502.

Rousseau, Jean-Jaques. *Essay on the Origin of Languages*, tr. John H. Moran. New York, 1966.

Russell, Bertrand. "Descriptions," *Semantics*, ed. Linsky, pp. 93–108.

—. "Mr. Strawson on Referring," *Readings*, ed. Copi and Gould, pp. 127–132.

—. "On Denoting," *Readings*, ed. Copi and Gould, pp. 93–105.

Ryle, Gilbert. *The Concept of Mind*. New York, 1968.

Ryle, Gilbert. "Ordinary Language," in *Philosophy*, ed. Caton, pp. 108–127.

Santoni, Ronald E., ed. *Religious Language and the Problem of Religious Knowledge*. Bloomington, 1968.

Saussure, Ferdinand de. *Cours de linguistique générale*, ed. Charles Bally, Albert Sechehaye, Albert Riedlinger. Paris, 1965.

—. *Course in General Linguistics*, ed. Charles Bally, Albert Sechehaye, Albert Riedlinger, tr. Wade Baskin. New York, 1966.

Sellars, Wilfrid. "Naming and Saying," *Essays*, ed. Copi and Beard, pp. 249–270.

Simon, Josef. *Das Problem der Sprache bei Hegel*. Stuttgart, 1966.

Snell, Bruno. "Die Sprache Heraklits," *Hermes*, LXI (1962), 353–381.

Staiger, Emil. *Grundbegriffe der Poetik*. 3rd ed. Zürich, 1956.

—. *Die Kunst der Interpretation. Studien zur deutschen Literaturgeschichte*. 3rd ed. Zürich, 1961.

—. *Stilwandel. Studien zur Vorgeschichte der Goethezeit*. Zürich, 1963.

—. *Die Zeit als Einbildungskraft des Dichters. Untersuchungen zu Gedichten von Brentano, Goethe und Keller*. Zürich, 1939.

Steinberg, Danny D. and Leon A. Jakobovits, eds. *Semantics. An Interdisciplinary Reader in Philosophy, Linguistics and Psychology*. Cambridge, 1971.

Stenius, Erik. *Wittgenstein's "Tractatus"*. Oxford, 1960.

Strawson, P. F. "Analysis, Science and Metaphysics," *Linguistic Turn*, ed. Rorty, pp. 312–320.

—. *The Bounds of Sense. An Essay on Kant's "Critique of Pure Reason"*. London, 1966.

—. "On Referring," *Readings*, ed. Copi and Gould, pp. 105–127.

Tagliacozzo, Giorgio and Hayden V. White, eds. *Giambattista Vico. An International Symposium*. Baltimore, 1969.

Thomas Aquinas. *Opera Omnia*, ed. Vernon J. Bourke. 25 vols. New York, 1948–1950.

—. *Summa Theologiae*. Vol. 1, tr. Thomas Gilby. New York, 1964.

—. *Summa Theologiae*. Vol. 3, tr. Herbert McCabe. New York, 1964.

—. *Truth*, tr. Robert W. Mulligan, James V. McGlynn, Robert W. Schmidt. 3 vols. Chicago, 1952–1954.

Thomas of Erfurt. *On the Modes of Signifying. A Speculative Grammar*, tr.

Charles Glenn Wallis. Ann Arbor, 1938 (the Latin text under Duns Scotus, Joannes).

Thurot, C., ed. *Extraits de divers manuscrits Latins pour servir à l'histoire des doctrines grammaticales au moyen âge*. Paris 1869.

Tillich, Paul. *Dynamics of Faith*. New York, 1957.

Verdenius, W. J. "Der Logosbegriff bei Heraklit und Parmenides," *Phronesis*, XI (1966), 81–98; XII (1967), 99–117.

Vico, Giambattista. *The Autobiography of Giambattista Vico*, tr. Thomas Goddard Bergin and Max Harold Fisch. Ithaca, 1944.

—. *The New Science of Giambattista Vico*, 3rd ed. of 1744, tr. Thomas Goddard Bergin and Max Harold Fisch. 2nd ed. Ithaca, 1968.

—. *On the Study Methods of Our Time*, tr. Elio Gianturco. Indianapolis, 1965.

Weinreich, Uriel. "Explorations in Semantic Theory," *Semantics*, ed. Steinberg and Jakobovits, pp. 308–328.

Weisgerber, Leo. *Die vier Stufen in der Erforschung der Sprache*. Düsseldorf, 1963.

Weitz, Morris. *Hamlet and the Philosophy of Literary Criticism*. Chicago, 1964.

Wellek, René and Austin Warren. *Theory of Literature*. New York, 1949.

Wells, George A. "Vico and Herder," *Giambattista Vico*, ed. Tagliacozzo and White, pp. 93–102.

Wheelwright, Philip. *Heraclitus*. New York, 1964.

Whitehead, Alfred North and Bertrand Russell. *Principia Mathematica*. 2nd ed., 3 vols. Cambridge, 1925–1927.

Wimsatt, W. K. "Northrop Frye: Criticism as Myth," *Northrop Frye in Modern Criticism*, ed. Murray Krieger (New York, 1966), pp. 75–107.

Wittgenstein, Ludwig. *Philosophical Investigations*, tr. G. E. M. Anscombe. 3rd ed. New York, 1968.

—. *Tractatus Logico-Philosophicus*. German text with English tr. by D. F. Pears and B. F. McGuiness. 3rd ed. London, 1966.

INDEX